A TALE OF TWO HALVES

By

Peter Haworth

DEDICATION

All the previous four volumes of these Premier League Diaries have been dedicated to my long-suffering wife, Julie. It would be remiss of me therefore not to accord the same benefit of this the final episode.

I mentioned in Book 4 that she had been known to complain that she rarely gets a mention in the action. That was remedied by featuring her right at the front of the last volume. On this occasion I have gone one better and included a picture of her! Now we'll see what she has to say about that!

Now that my long hours of tapping away at the keyboard have come to an end, I will be once again, all yours!

ACKNOWLEDGEMENTS

Writing a book like this is never as straightforward as one might think. Self-publishing is exactly what it 'says on the tin' and despite the excellent assistance from Amazon, I always find it somewhat of a challenge.

This is where help from people, some well-known to me, some casual acquaintances and some not known at all, have once again proved invaluable.

First of all, a big thank you to John and Judy Weir for their witty and insightful record of their trip to Athens. For Clarets fans an opportunity such as this is one that probably comes only once in a lifetime. Despite the result I'm sure the couple thoroughly enjoyed their European adventure. John had certainly heeded the lesson 'beware of Greeks bearing gifts' when it came to the proposed scarf exchange!

My old stalwarts Ed Skingsley, now a firmly established writer of books relating to local rivals Preston North End, and Steve Calderbank my émigré amigo in far flung Wragby, Lincolnshire, have once again answered the call.

Ed, this time blighted by ocular problems, has risen to the challenge of proof-reading this mammoth tome with his customary diligence. Any surviving errors are the sole responsibility of the author.

Steve has once again contributed valuable time and expertise in the technical aspects of getting this book to its final printed version. Despite constraints on his time due to newly acquired civic duties, he has still proved a valuable font of knowledge.

Once again, I am indebted to Tony Scholes, editor of the fans website 'Up the Clarets'. His assistance in promoting my previous Premier League Diaries via the website is greatly appreciated. For self-published authors getting their work in front of the target audience is a major headache. Tony through his site is massively supportive of all authors of a Claret & Blue persuasion. Many thanks Tony.

Fellow Clarets author Dave Thomas who continues to produce excellent and informative reading matter for the fans has once more come to my rescue. Desperately searching for suitable pictures for the cover of this volume Dave has used his considerable network of contacts to put me in touch with possible sources.

This brings me to Brian Speak, who after being contacted on Dave's recommendation, has very kindly come up with the goods. Cheers Brian!

My thanks also to James Forsyth, Head of Retail at Burnley FC, for giving me the opportunity to retail previous volumes through the Clarets Store. Hopefully, we will be able to use this facility once more with this book.

Of course, none of these diaries would have been possible without the magnificent efforts of the manager, coaches, players, directors and indeed all concerned with Burnley FC. For a fan approaching 60 years as a 'Claret' the last 10 years have been a sheer delight.

Contents

INTRODUCTION

It's Thursday the 15th June, the first day of the 2018 World Cup Finals in Russia. However, more importantly it's the day the Premier League fixtures for the 2018/19 season are announced.

As I prepare to head off on the regular Thursday Burnley Contingent ramble, on this occasion a relatively easy circular walk starting from East Marton and taking in Bank Newton and Gargrave, I am eagerly anticipating the news. Who will it be first up? Which games will I miss through holidays? Who do we play at Christmas? Will it be a testing start? Will it be a difficult run-in? So many questions!

After a short few weeks break since the end of our last successful season my hunger for football is starting to return. Today feels like the start of a new season, and so is a fitting starting point for this the fifth in the series of Premier League Diaries? Who would have thought back in 2009 when I committed myself to writing volume one, in celebration of that magnificent day in May at Wembley, that nine years down the line I'd still be writing? What's even more unbelievable is that people would still be buying them!

We're already well into the silly season of being fed the usual diet of transfer speculation nonsense. The latest incoming rumours have us bidding £25m for the West Bromwich Albion pair Jay Rodriguez and Craig Dawson. Today's speculation also surrounds Bristol City's Bobby Reid and a reputed £10m offer.

If we are to believe all we read, on the outgoing side will be Ben Mee to Tottenham Hotspur (or Everton), and Nick Pope and James Tarkowski our two latest England internationals, heading to Liverpool.

At least the fixture list will now give we news hungry fans something concrete to get our teeth into, although that doesn't sound such an enticing prospect! So, what did we get when we opened the box?

Well, the opening fixture was a complete contrast to last season's starter at Champions Chelsea. This time we are once again on our travels, and long one's at that, as we head for the south coast and a trip to St Mary's to play Southampton. The Saints had a difficult season last time round and just managed to escape the claws of relegation almost at the death. Following that it's a home game against Watford. I'd like to think there are points to be had from those games.

Strangely the following three away games will all be against the promoted teams from last season's Championship, Fulham, Wolverhampton Wanderers and Cardiff City. I wonder what the odds were against that. Sandwiched between those are home fixtures against Manchester United and Bournemouth.

All-in-all on paper that's a not too difficult start especially compared to 2017/18 when we faced Chelsea, Tottenham Hotspur, Liverpool, Everton and Manchester City in the first five away games. Still, we managed to take a very respectable eight points from those matches which instilled a great amount of confidence and set the tone for an impressive series of results on hostile territory.

Sadly, a much-anticipated home game against Huddersfield Town will be a miss for me as I am due to be soaking up the autumn sunshine in Madeira. Pity that, it's one of my favourite fixtures as it gives me the opportunity to catch up with an old work associate Rob Waterworth, who is a true Town fanatic.

Also posing an initial problem is the December 8th home game with Brighton. This is the date I was looking forward to rekindling my running career with an outing in the Langdale Pudding Run. I'm not giving up on this one yet though as I'm expecting quite a bit of fixture movement owing to Europa League commitments and televised live games.

There's a tasty looking Boxing Day fixture at home to Everton, followed by another Turf Moor outing on the 29th December against West Ham United, so that's some entertaining Christmas fayre in the offing.

Whilst the season's opening fixtures look like they have been kind to us I can't say the same for the closing ones. The last four are Chelsea (away), Manchester City (home), Everton (away), Arsenal (home). Hopefully we will have accumulated sufficient points to achieve our goal before we hit that little lot.

At the end of the day we have to play everybody twice, so I don't suppose it matters too much when they come. Intermingling with these Premier League games will of course be League Cup, FA Cup and Europa League encounters. It could be one hell of a season coming up!

Following the excitement generated by the Premier League fixture announcements, our thoughts turned next to the draw for the Europa

League 2nd Qualifying round. Scheduled for Wednesday 20th June, the tension mounted as we approached the appointed hour.

With the draw being streamed live from Nyon in Switzerland via the official UEFA website, Clarets from around the globe tuned in to see what far off exotic land we would be visiting for the first competitive game in 51 years. As the appointed time approached, 14.00 CET (Central European Time) or 13.00 BST (British Summer Time) all eyes were fixed on the screen. Unfortunately, nothing was happening!

Oh well, time to have a look at the website and get a feel for how the draw would be formatted. A big mistake, the organisers had contrived to make the draw nigh on impossible to fathom.

As time ticked on the screen changed with the announcement of a delay, the draw would now be at 14.20 CET. That time came and went, to be followed by a further delay to 14.30 CET, then 14.45 CET until finally at around 14.50 the action got underway.

There were seeded teams in pots, unseeded teams in pots, mixing bowls on the desk, what appeared to be salt and pepper cellars amongst them all with a gentleman trying to explain the whole procedure - which might as well have been Einstein's Theory of Relativity for all the sense it made. Anyway, it transpired that we were among the seeded teams, Hallelujah!

There seemed to be an awful lot of teams in the draw, and from some pretty exotic locations. I had a fancy for opposition from the Faroe Islands or San Marino. Gibraltar would have been nice or Cyprus. There was the whole of Europe and some places that might be considered beyond to go at. So, who did we get? ABERDEEN!

Seventy-three other teams in the draw besides ourselves and we get ABERDEEN! Now I'm not trying to belittle Aberdeen, on the contrary they may well turn out to be very difficult opponents. However, it would have been nice to have drawn somebody from continental Europe rather than British opposition. The games to be played first leg in Scotland 26th July, with the return at Turf Moor 2nd August, will make for a very busy pre-Premier League warm-up.

Our senior fixtures will start with friendlies at Cork City (13th July), Macclesfield Town (20th July), Preston North End (23rd July), then home fixtures with Montpellier (29th July) and Espanyol (5th August).

That's a grand total of seven fixtures before we kick off the main feature at Southampton on 11th August.

As we stand at Friday 22nd June, we have no new additions to the squad, and we have lost Scott Arfield, Dean Marney, and the returning loanee Georges-Kevin Nkoudou. Furthermore, Nick Pope and Johann Berg Gudmundsson (JBG) are still plying their trade on World Cup duties in Russia. The pair will certainly need a break at the end of that tournament, indeed JBG is currently suffering from a calf muscle tear sustained in Iceland's opening fixture.

On a more positive note last season's long-term injured players, Robbie Brady and Steven Defour are reported as making good progress and are hopeful of making the season's openers. Similarly, James Tarkowski currently recuperating from a hernia operation is said to be 'on schedule'.

Without doubt there will have to be additions to the squad as the quest for honours on four fronts will put heavy demands on what is one of the smallest Premier League squads. As the end of June approaches and with the return to pre-season training imminent, I am confidently expecting new faces, or perhaps some returning old ones, to be appearing soon.

On Monday 2nd July I leave sunny Burnley for a summer vacation in equally sunny Portugal. I am confidently expecting a host of new faces to be in serious pre-season training with the Clarets by the time of my return, 14th July.

In the meantime, I am engaged with watching England's World Cup progress from my Portuguese base. Fortunately, by now the Portuguese are already eliminated so there'll be no gloating from the natives. Similarly, my hotel populated by a significant number of German guests, is falling strangely quiet as the most recent competition's winners fail to make the knock-out stages.

England, as expected survive the group stage, finishing second behind highly fancied Belgium. Suddenly, as a result of some of the more fancied teams taking an early exit, our chances of making the final stages look brighter than for some time. A fractious evening fixture against Colombia is survived by the skin of our teeth, as for once we manage to win a penalty shoot-out. Glory be!

Next up is a highly winnable fixture against a dour Swedish team who look distinctly goal shy. If we can score first against these then we must have a good chance. That is precisely what happens, a goal in each half sees Southgate's young lions incredibly through to the last four. Unfortunately, despite taking an early first half semi-final lead against Croatia, we are ultimately outplayed and exit the competition to an extra-time winner.

Still, all-in-all a good effort from a relatively inexperienced team and a fourth placed finish is more than what most fans would have expected ahead of the competition. I have to say that watching from a more detached position away from the growing hype in England, I felt we were somewhat fortunate to make the semis.

Qualification through the group stage was achieved by beating two unfancied teams in Tunisia and Panama. The third group game against Belgium was lost and showed our deficiencies against the stronger nations. We then got lucky with the draw and struggled to overcome a Colombian outfit not shy at employing 'the darker arts.' Sweden proved to be as toothless as expected, giving us a dream route to our best chance in years of taking the crown. However once again stiffer opposition proved insurmountable. Oh well there's always 2022 to look forward to in the searing heat of Qatar!

Anyway, refreshed from my Portuguese sojourn I return to find the number of new Claret signings at zero. For one reason or another our targets are once again proving exceedingly difficult to land. Whilst the club remain consistently tight-lipped, we are believed to have made a combined bid of £25m for the West Bromwich Albion pair of Craig Dawson and Jay Rodriguez. This appears to be well below the selling club's valuation and as the stand-off develops, time rolls on.

After some weeks of stalking this pair by late July we seem to be giving up on the idea and our attention seems to have switched to Swansea City. Here we are believed to be showing an interest in last season's target Sam Clucas, and highly rated central defender Alfie Mawson.

Pre -season friendlies are now well under way, currently showing mixed results, and by Sunday 22nd July we are only four days away from the first competitive match. This will be the first leg of the Europa League 2nd Qualifying Round tie against Aberdeen at Pittodrie. At this point the squad looks a touch thin in places, and hopefully with now less than three weeks left in the transfer window, some of our targets can soon be 'bagged'.

On Monday 23rd July it is the draw for the 3rd Qualifying Round of the Europa Cup. A bit strange that as we have yet to play the 1st leg of the 2nd round. Anyway, once again the draw throws up an intriguing tie. Should we defeat Aberdeen we will meet İstanbul Başakşehir of Turkey in the next round. Once again, it's not an easy draw as the Istanbul side finished 3rd in the Turkish league last time and has some big name, if ageing players. Having been in Istanbul on European football nights one thing is assured, a hostile reception! Still, we'd better not get ahead of ourselves there is the little matter of Aberdeen to overcome first.

The date of the first leg at Pittodrie is closing fast and on Monday evening we play a friendly at near neighbours Preston North End. Sean Dyche fields a strong line-up for the first half, mostly the 'first team' but with some notable absentees. There's no sign of Nick Pope, still on holiday following his England World Cup duties. Also missing are Steven Defour, Ashley Barnes and Chris Wood.

Shortly after the second half resumes, the starting XI are replaced by the remaining available squad members and a handful of youngsters. A good competitive warm-up game ends 3-2 in our favour, with goals from Dan Agyei and the highly promising Dwight McNeil. After the game Dyche confirms Defour will be unavailable for Thursday's fixture at Aberdeen, but we must wait and see on the others.

A new name linked with the Clarets is French defensive midfielder Abdoulaye Toure. The French Under-20 international, currently at Nantes is rumoured to be the subject of a €10-12m bid. I'll believe it when I see him roll up at Turf Moor on his bike with a string of onions round his neck!

If any of you are familiar with my previous Premier League Diaries, you will be aware of my other passion, which is walking on the high moors and in the valleys of our green and pleasant land. Tuesday's are reserved for outings with a group of like-minded souls from around Lancashire, appropriately named Lancashire Dotcom Walkers. Tuesday 24th July marks the last walk before the summer recess and is a little different to our usual trek.

Nominally annually, but realistically more like bi or tri-annually, we have a little diversion to walk in neighbouring Yorkshire. Our friends in the group from West Lancashire have some sort of affliction that prevents them from saying the word Yorkshire and so these ventures are known as trips to TOP (That Other Place)!

Today is one such day and we are going to enjoy a rare treat... a trip on a steam train! Yes, this morning we will travel to Oxenhope station to board the 11.30 steamer to Keighley. On this occasion we are not going the whole way but will alight at Ingrow West and walk back to Oxenhope via Haworth. It's a sort of celebration of the 1970 classic British film, The Railway Children. It's kind of being re-enacted by a bunch of pensioners entering their second childhood!

Ahead of the trip Group leader Bob Clare asked people who were likely to attend to let him know they were coming. I emailed him with the message:

"Please reserve me a seat on the train, forward facing, not too near the engine, and with a young Jenny Agutter sitting on my knee".

Younger readers should perhaps Google it to grasp the significance. Bob's response was, *"I think Peter you had better keep your fantasies to yourself".*

Anyway, at the duly appointed time a gaggle of pensioners boarded the train much like a bunch of excited schoolkids. Clutching our senior's concessionary fare tickets, £5.50 instead of the full £6 (Wow!), we were ready for the off. I must say the engine, (for you train spotter's No. 41241, built in 1949 at Crewe) and carriages were in immaculate condition. In high glee and with much whooping as we went through the tunnels a highly enjoyable journey was had by all. I'll bet the rest of the passengers were glad to see the back of us, it was akin to the last bus back from Manchester on a Saturday night!

All too soon we had reached our destination, well I say all too soon, it took 15 minutes to cover something like five miles, with stops at Haworth and Oakworth! Alighting at Ingrow West, which Bob Clare quite rightly pointed out didn't seem big enough to have a West, let alone a North, South, and East, it was time to walk.

On an extremely hot and humid day a pleasant meander was thoroughly appreciated, despite the odd wrong turning which led to a climb into Haworth which must have been like the ascent of Everest. Refreshed by a 30-minute lunch stop and an opportunity for the more alcoholic walkers to take a beer break, we resumed our trek to Oxenhope, wiser but in some cases poorer.

What a great day out, thank you very much Bob Clare and my fellow walkers. What a credit the Keighley and Worth Valley Railway is to the volunteers who run it. Magnificently maintained, the stations and rolling stock are a pleasure to behold. Well worth a visit is my opinion, go and do it, take the kids.

That trip just sets me up nicely for the first major challenge of the season, the first leg tie of the Europa League competition at Aberdeen. I must confess as Thursday 26th approaches I am getting excited, if a little nervous at the prospect. Still, let the action roll!

2nd Qualifying Round Europa League, 1st Leg - Thursday 26th July, 19.45 – Aberdeen v Burnley

Well at last what we had all hoped and prayed for during the last incredible Premier League season had finally come around. Lucky fans with sufficient loyalty points had set off on their European Journey, well journey to the far north-east of Scotland that is. Others had coughed up a month's subscription (£5.99) to watch the game live on Aberdeen FC's own channel, Red TV. Yet more were flocking to the Turf Moor Fanzone to watch the game beamed back live on a big screen. For me I had opted to try and find a watchable live stream on my laptop, failing which it would be back to the old faithful, Radio Lancashire.

It has to be said that ahead of the game all had not gone smoothly. Burnley FC had chartered a plane to fly the team et al plus kit to the far-flung northern outpost. Unfortunately, and some supporters would say predictably, there were technical problems with the plane and the flight delayed several hours. Under UEFA Europa League rules both opposing managers must give a press conference at 8.00pm on the evening before the scheduled game. This was now clearly impossible for Sean Dyche and the briefing re-scheduled for 11.00am on match day. Not ideal in terms of preparation and there are rumours of official repercussions for not making the appointed time. How petty!

Furthermore, the squad was hit by the late withdrawal of goalkeeper Tom Heaton, suffering a slight calf injury, leaving a bit of a quandary in the goalkeeping position. Would Dyche risk the untried Adam Legzdins in such an important fixture or would he go for the just returned Nick Pope?

On top of that we will also be without Steven Defour, Robbie Brady and Ashley Barnes, still some way short of fitness. With no new signings in as yet, that leaves the squad looking somewhat stretched and the team almost picking itself. But it's no good worrying about that now, time to concentrate on the job at hand and come away with a result that sees us comfortably in the tie come the second leg next week at Turf Moor.

As it turned out the vacant goalie's shirt went to Pope, and the substitute goalkeeping slot to Anders Lindegaard. Where does this leave Legzdins I ask myself? As mentioned, the rest of the team virtually picked itself, the only slight surprise being the return of Chris Wood who had only featured sparingly in the preceding friendly games.

Settling down for the game after completing taxiing duties to deliver my wife Julie and friend to their rendezvous for a 'girlie' night out, I switched to Radio Lancashire. A nice bit of pre-amble by the local lads then at kick-off time the commentary switched to BBC Five Live's coverage. The commentator was Conor McNamara with ex Blackburn Rover Chris Sutton summarising. It was quickly apparent that these two were going to be the proverbial 'pain in the butt'. McNamara clearly favoured the underdog, Aberdeen, whilst Sutton never a big fan of the Clarets seemed content to back him up.

Time for some drastic action so it was out with the laptop. Bingo! A YouTube stream was available and luckily seemed to be functioning quite well. As I played around getting things set up, I continued with the commentary on Radio Lancashire as the sound from the stream was inaudible, or perhaps in a foreign language...Scottish. By now some minutes of the game had elapsed and without my knowledge Burnley goalkeeper Nick Pope had sustained what appeared to be a serious injury.

I was initially alerted to this by WhatsApp message from my long time Claret supporting pal John W, who had taken the plunge and gone for the £5.99 Red TV option. It was at this point I noticed that my live stream was running approximately one and a half minutes behind the radio commentary. How bloody annoying is that? Poor young Nick was unable to carry on and after 11 minutes left the field for a trip to Aberdeen Hospital with what looked suspiciously like a serious shoulder injury. How ironic following so closely behind Tom Heaton's dislocated shoulder last season which had given Pope his big chance.

Well now it was Anders Lindegaard big chance as he made his first team debut for the Clarets. Despite his vast experience his recent outings at first team level had been extremely restricted. Would he rise to the challenge? It wasn't long before he got his first opportunity as on 19 minutes Aberdeen were awarded a very soft penalty for a challenge in the box by James Tarkowski. Beaten comprehensively from the spot by Gary Mackay-Steven it looked like having the makings of a long hard night.

The Clarets clearly rattled by the loss of Pope and the concession of the soft penalty took some time to settle. A very robust and physical approach from the home side, bayed on by a fanatical home crowd, had us ill at ease for some time. However, as the first half wore on the ship began to settle and we came more into the game without creating any particularly likely openings. Aaron Lennon was certainly posing a threat but too often passes were misplaced and moves broke down. To be fair we were probably relieved to get in at half time just the one goal down, but hopefully we had weathered the storm.

A more confident and determined approach was immediately noticeable at the start of the second period. Only a tremendous reflex, one-handed save by the Dons keeper prevented Jack Cork's flying header from levelling the scores on 51 minutes. As we started to control the game Aberdeen were pushed further and further back, relying on occasional quick counters. Lindegaard made a couple of saves, one notably one-handed parry from a close-range header, which must have done wonders for his (and mine) confidence.

Relentlessly though we were now building the pressure and once again Sean Dyche produced his now customary masterstroke. On 66 minutes Sam Vokes replaced Jeff Hendrick as we opted for more 'beef' up front. Almost immediately Sam's physical presence started to ruffle some feathers in the Dons defence. As time started to run out and it looked like we may be heading for the second leg with a one goal deficit, all changed in the blink of an eye. A high ball was flicked on into the box and Sam surrounded by numerous red shirts waited patiently, coolly turned and rifled his shot home from close range.

In a moment the whole complexion of the tie had changed. Aberdeen looking like coming to Turf Moor with a goal advantage now were pegged back level. The pendulum had swung our way with the home leg to come, and the benefit of an away-goal which of course would count double in the event of a tie, now made us favourites. Ten minutes plus stoppage time to negotiate and then we could reflect on a difficult night that had been ultimately rescued. There were no real concerns as the clock ran down and the 'Battle of Britain' ended in a 1-1 draw.

There's definitely room for improvement on that performance but my feeling was that, barring a disaster, we should prevail in the 2nd leg.

Result – Aberdeen (Mackay-Steven 19 pen) 1 - 1 (Vokes 80) Burnley

Burnley Team

Pope (Lindegaard 13), Lowton, Mee, Tarkowski, Ward, Gudmundsson, Cork, Westwood, Hendrick (Vokes 66), Lennon, Wood

Subs Not Used – Bardsley, Taylor, Long, Wells, Walters

Aberdeen Team

Lewis, Logan, Devlin, McKenna, Hoban, Ball, Shinnie, McGinn (Wright 79), Mackay-Steven, Ferguson (Gleeson 56), Cosgrove (May 77)

Subs Not Used – Cerny, Forrester, Campbell, Anderson

Attendance – 20,313

Where's the sun gone? After a blistering May, June and July all of a sudden torrential rain. Why would that be? Could it be something to do with the return of football to Turf Moor.

Having spent a lovely evening at the King's Head, Kettlewell it's time for a hearty breakfast and a quick return to Burnley for the first home friendly against Montpellier. Saturday in Kettlewell had seen rain, then sunshine, topped off by hail stones as I sipped my pre-dinner pint of Wharfedale Blonde. By Sunday morning the weather had settled to just a heavy downpour.

It's not much better in Burnley and it's ironic that just as United Utilities hosepipe ban is about to come into force (1st August) I am attending Turf Moor in waterproof gear. Oh well, the garden needs it and hopefully Montpellier, from much sunnier climes, won't like it.

Not surprisingly we are forced to field pretty much a second string, the game being sandwiched between the two Europa League ties with Aberdeen. Only Jeff Hendrick from Thursday's starting XI makes the team, and Adam Legzdins takes the goalkeeping jersey with a trialist keeper on the bench. It's a decent enough workout with the Clarets having probably the best chances, but none are taken and the game ends in a 0-0 draw.

It was good to see Ashley Barnes and Robbie Brady returning from injuries get some meaningful game time. Unfortunately, Brady who was originally scheduled for 45 minutes succumbs after 40 to what appears to be a hamstring injury. A big blow that for the Clarets, Brady's creativity and dead-ball expertise are sorely missed in his absence. It looks like we will have to manage without him and Steven Defour for some time yet. The good news is that Barnes seems to have come through unscathed and hopefully will be ready to feature soon. There are promising performances from youngsters Aidan O'Neill, Jimmy Dunne and Dwight McNeil, who if we fail to make new signings may well be pressed into action sooner rather than later.

With the transfer window closure rapidly approaching, the failure to bring in new faces is once again giving rise to major concern among the fans. Judging by comments in the media it's not only the supporters but also the manager who is feeling the pressure. Added to that, the growing list of injuries, the goalkeeping situation being a particular worry with both first-choice keepers currently out, is more than a little problematic as we enter potentially our most challenging season yet in terms of fixtures.

By Monday 30th July only Tottenham Hotspur and ourselves amongst the Premier League clubs are yet to make a signing. Let's hope we can pull some rabbits out of the hat before August 9th.

AUGUST

Setting off for the weekly Thursday Burnley Contingent walk, a classic eight-mile circuit starting from the Turkey Inn at Goose Eye and taking in Keighley Moor reservoir, the discussion quickly turns to tonight's prospects.

I have to say that this morning I am feeling rather apprehensive about the visit of Aberdeen in the second leg of the 2nd Round Europa League qualifier. Last week after the game at Pittodrie I was fairly confident of progressing. We had come away on level terms and with the advantage of an away goal despite not playing well. Surely an improved performance on home soil would prove too much for our Scottish visitors.

However, July had come and gone without any additions to the first team squad, both first choice goalkeepers were currently side-lined, and injuries to outfield players seemed to be mounting. The lack of activity in the transfer market with the window due to close in one week's time, was causing concern amongst the fans and seemingly also with the manager. All in all, there was a gathering air of gloom beginning to envelop the club at a time when we should be looking forward to enjoying the fruits of our finest season since 1974.

On top of that a large contingent of Aberdonians were expected, probably in excess of the 2,400 tickets they had been allocated, and they would certainly be up for the occasion. For them this was a do-or-die battle having firmly declared that Europa League success was uppermost in their thoughts. Hopefully the occasion would be sufficient to raise the Clarets fans spirits to counter the barrage of noise generated by the visiting fans.

An excellent walk in perfect weather ensued after negotiating unexpected road closures in Colne. Of course, the highlight of this trek is the after-walk pint at the superb Turkey Inn, a pub not to be missed (although not easy to find), truly a beer connoisseur's delight. Choice of the day was a foaming pint of Goose Eye Brewery's Bitter, A.B.V. 3.9%, and thoroughly recommended.

Cheered by a splendid day out and the beer, further good news arrived on a quick check of the 'Up the Clarets' 'messageboard'. It would appear we had finally woken up to the fact that the transfer market was passing us by. From a point of apparently zero activity we had suddenly on one day lodged bids for no less than three players. Apparently an £8m bid for midfielder Sam Clucas had been accepted by Swansea, whilst offers for Ben Gibson at Middlesbrough and Jay Rodriguez at West Bromwich Albion had been rejected. Hopefully we will be going back in with revised bids for the pair and pretty sharpish.

Having digested this news, and the beer, I am once again feeling a little more optimistic concerning tonight's chance. Just time for a quick bite for tea, then off to Turf Moor. Let battle commence!

2nd Qualifying Round Europa League, 2nd Leg - Thursday 2nd August, 19.45 – Burnley v Aberdeen

Just before I leave home team news comes through, no real surprises here for the Clarets. Sam Vokes following his excellent cameo role at Pittodrie starts up front with Chris Wood in an attack minded 4-4-2 formation. Jeff Hendrick drops to the bench to accommodate him. Anders Lindegaard continues in goal with Adam Legdzins, the only other fit keeper, on the substitutes bench.

As expected, the large contingent of Aberdeen fans are making their presence felt, their part of the Cricket Field Stand (CFS) is a mass of red, and the volume is being cranked up to full. Similarly, the Burnley section of the CFS is well populated and equally vociferous. As kick-off time approaches the ground is filling up nicely and the attendance looks to be much better than earlier predicted. Already there is a 'buzz' in the air and the atmosphere is building. If anybody thinks this competition doesn't matter, it's certainly not the fans of these two teams. What we want now is an early goal to settle the nerves and put us well in control of the tie.

And lo and behold that's exactly what we get! A quickfire start from the Clarets has the visitors rocking, and the home crowd rolling. With only six minutes gone we have a precious lead. A lovely flighted ball over and between the centre backs sees Wood ghosting in to take the ball ahead of Dons keeper Joe Lewis. With deft control he takes the ball with his back to goal, turns and fires high into the net between the two retreating defenders. Just what the doctor ordered and surely the cue to go on and make the tie safe.

Unfortunately, that's not what happened. Instead the battling Dons driven on by some incredible backing from their red army fought their way back into the game. On 27 minutes, disastrously, it's all square. A cross from winger Craig Mackay-Steven is poorly defended and tamely headed back across the penalty area. Aberdeen youngster Lewis Ferguson, positioned about eight yards out and with his back to goal, contrives a spectacular overhead bicycle kick of which there's no stopping. What a goal for the young man, but what a disaster for the Clarets.

In that brief moment we have surrendered completely our advantage, the lead has gone, and the away goal is now cancelled out. What's more if the visitors should score again, we will need a further two goals to go through. As Aberdeen now growing in confidence start to come at us, and we begin to look increasingly ragged, that would seem highly unlikely. To make matters worse the Italian referee is having a 'shocker' and we are getting nothing from him. As half time approaches and we struggle on I notice goal scorer Chris Wood apparently in some discomfort. Not another injury?

Half time and the general consensus seem to be that although we are enjoying the bulk of the possession, we are running up against a brick wall. In fact, Aberdeen are doing very much what Burnley do, and beating us at our own game. Once again, we seem bereft of ideas when it comes down to unlocking a packed defence. The build-up is too slow and there's nobody who can find a 'killer' ball. Ashley Barnes makes an early exit from the substitutes half-time warm up, is he coming on?

The answer is yes as we restart the second period there's no Wood, who has obviously picked up yet another injury. Straight from the off its apparent that harsh words have been spoken in the dressing room. The Clarets are straight onto attack, and with Barnes movement and tenacity, immediately posing a bigger threat. Lewis makes a sprawling save from Johann Berg Gudmundsson, and shortly after an incredible one from Barnes.

However, after some close shaves the Dons start to once again get a toehold on the game. Lindegaard is forced into a good save at his near post, and some wayward shooting from the visitors keeps the score level.

Then as time runs out the closest yet. Sam Vokes rises to power a header from Matt Lowton's cross. Incredibly the ball hits the underside of the bar bounces down and is hacked clear. That certainly deserved a better fate. There are multiple appeals for handball in the Don's penalty area, but our Italian friend is having none of it. He must be bloody blind, or if not certainly incompetent!

As time runs out the game ends with the teams locked at 1-1 on the night and 2-2 on aggregate. I think it's fair to say our friends from the North are happier with that outcome than we are and fancying their chances in a penalty shoot-out. I am feeling physically and emotionally drained after what has been a long day, and now a tense and exciting evening. I don't know about the players, but I could certainly do without 30 minutes of extra-time.

Thankfully as we hit minute 101 of this epic tie, a bit of magic. Charlie Taylor on at left back for Stephen Ward gets down the flank and curls in a perfect cross which is met in the middle of the six-yard box by the leaping Jack Cork, the net bulges! Thank God! The energy and some of the resilience of our visitors seems to visibly drain from them. It's all over on 114 minutes as a cross from the right hits the flawless Scott Mckenna on the arm, and at last after a full season without one, we have a penalty! Ashley Barnes claims the prize and places his shot just inside the post despite Lewis's despairing dive.

Game over, a 3-1 win on the night and a 4-2 victory on aggregate. There's no time to rest though in just seven days' time we are back in Europa League action in Istanbul. What a fantastic night it's been, a real ding-dong battle. The crowd of 17,404 couldn't have wished for a more enthralling contest which certainly lived up to its billing as the 'Battle of Britain'. A game played in a tremendous atmosphere generated by both sets of fans. This is how football should be played, and full credit to the Aberdeen team and fans for a memorable tie. At the end and on the way out of the stadium there is applause and well-wishes from both teams' supporters to their counterparts. How refreshing is that!

This is what those lucky enough as I have been waited 50 years to experience again, and the magic hasn't diminished. Let's have some more of it!

Result – Burnley (Wood 6, Cork 101, Barnes 114 pen) 3 - 1 **After Extra Time** (Ferguson 27) Aberdeen

Burnley Team

Lindegaard, Lowton, Mee, Tarkowski, Ward (Taylor 90), Gudmundsson, Cork, Westwood (Hendrick 105), Lennon (McNeil 87), Wood (Barnes 45), Vokes

Subs Not Used – Legzdins, Bardsley, Long

Aberdeen Team

Lewis, Logan, Devlin, McKenna, Hoban (Ball 88), Considine, Shinnie, McGinn (Wright 80), Mackay-Steven, Ferguson, Cosgrove (May 100)

<u>Subs Not Used</u> – Cerny, Forrester, Campbell, Gleeson

Attendance – 17,404

On Friday 3rd August transfer activity seems to be finally getting into top gear. Reports from South Wales suggest that Sam Clucas is on his way north for a medical ahead of a signing. In mid-afternoon there are reports that ex England goalkeeper Joe Hart is subject to an accepted bid from the Clarets. By early evening the BBC are claiming he too is having a medical. Almost at the same time news from Sky has it that an improved offer of £15m for Ben Gibson from Middlesbrough is now also accepted. Steady on lads I don't think I can cope with all this at once. I'll believe it when I see them all holding Claret and Blue shirts with their names on.

Finally, on Sunday 5th, and with just five days left of the summer transfer window, Burnley FC confirm their first new arrival. Hallelujah! As we play Espanyol at Turf Moor in the last pre-season friendly, the club officially announce the signing of Middlesbrough centre-back Ben Gibson. The 25-year-old defender signs on a four-year deal for a reputedly transfer record equalling sum of £15m. It's fair to say this is a very popular move for the fans who see the player as equally as good if not better than our reported alternative targets of Craig Dawson and Alf Mawson. Another plus is the fact that he is a naturally left-sided centre back, a rarity in the modern game, and will provide competition for Ben Mee who is yet to commit to a further contract. A one club man, having graduated through the Middlesbrough Academy, Gibson has ten caps at England Under 21 level and has been called up previously to the full England squad without being capped. Welcome aboard Ben let's hope that full cap is just around the corner.

Another deal seemingly as good as done is the signing of Joe Hart from Manchester City for a reputed £4m fee. With our current goalkeeping woes, due to injuries to both first-choice stoppers Nick Pope and Tom Heaton, this to me is an excellent move. A goalkeeper of Hart's vast experience at international and top club level will be just the ticket for the intimidating challenges that are fast approaching. It's fair to say that his last couple of seasons, out on loan at Torino and West Ham

United, have not been his greatest. However, at 31 he is not old for a goalkeeper and has not become a bad player overnight. I think his issues are more down to a loss of confidence. With a new permanent contract, and at a club known for its stability, I'm sure that can be addressed. The player is taking a big drop in wages to join us which demonstrates his desire to get his career back on track. If the deal comes off, we will have three current England goalkeepers on the books!

One move that seems to have hit the buffers is the proposed move of Swansea midfielder Sam Clucas who had been undergoing a medical. Rumours are circulating that he has either failed the medical, or we are unwilling to match his wage demands. Whichever, it seems by Sunday teatime that the deal is off. A shame that, we are still desperately short of bodies in view of the current heavy fixture demands. Hopefully we will have a Plan B, but time is short, and we'll need to move quickly.

There's still no movement on the proposed transfer of ex Claret Jay Rodriguez. The Burnley offer is still some way short of West Bromwich Albion's valuation and the stalemate continues. Jay featured for the Baggies in their Championship opener, a 1-2 home defeat to Bolton Wanderers, and still seems to figure in their season's plans. With not much time left in the window it's maybe time to switch targets in view of the midlander's reticence to play ball. We'll see.

The last friendly, once again played in hot sunny weather, ended in a 0-2 defeat. The Clarets, fielding very much a 'second string', were no match for their Spanish opponents on the day. Espanyol looked like a typical La Liga outfit, technically gifted players moving the ball much quicker than ourselves and fully deserving their comfortable victory. Not that any of the Burnley fans present will mind too much. We have much bigger fish to fry this week, with the Europa League trip to Istanbul on Thursday, followed by the Premier League opener at Southampton on Sunday.

On Monday 6th it's apparent that the proposed move for Sam Clucas is indeed off, and the reason seems to be a failure to meet his personal terms. Oh well, he doesn't seem to have such a great pedigree that would tempt the Clarets to breach their pay structure, so adios Sam. Of more concern is the fact that Joe Hart's signing which was said to be 'done', has as yet not been confirmed. With the team jetting off shortly for the Europa League tie in Turkey this is cutting it a bit fine. The Jay Rodriguez situation seems to be drifting away from us and there are rumours of other Premier League clubs' interest. This may well be the reason a new name has surfaced on the rumour board. Matej Vydra of Derby County and last season's top scorer in the Championship is now being linked on some websites. Having recently turned down the opportunity to join Leeds United, apparently because of a desire to play in the Premier League, there might just be something in this link.

Monday also saw the draw for the Play Off Round of the Europa League, once again the draw coming before the completion, or even commencement, of the 3rd Qualifying Round. This time we were unseeded in the most spectacularly convoluted draw imaginable and the outcome certainly whetted the appetite of some fans. If we are successful in the next round, we will go on to meet either Olympiacos of Greece or Luzern of Switzerland. Now that sounds more like a European tie, after draws against a fellow British side (Aberdeen), and İstanbul Başakşehir bang on the boundary of Europe and Asia. Once again, the first leg will be away on 23rd with the return at Turf Moor on the 30th August. Let's not get too far ahead of ourselves though the Turks have to be overcome first.

Thankfully, on Tuesday 7th the signing of goalkeeper Hart is confirmed. He will be a welcome addition to bolster our injury ravaged goalkeeping department. Hopefully he will recover his best form and go on to earn us some valuable Premier League points in the next few weeks. The fixtures are certainly coming thick and fast, before August is out, we could potentially play six Europa League games as well as three Premier League fixtures. As many fit bodies as we can muster will be required.

It's really hotting up now on the transfer front as Wednesday 8th August sees Matej Vydra sign on the dotted line to become the third signing of the summer window. The deal mooted as a possible player exchange plus cash involving Nahki Wells is completed, but with no confirmation of any Wells involvement...

Suddenly, the gloom and despondency about transfer dealings seems to have been blown away in the matter of a few days. There are further rumours circulating that Everton winger Yannick Bolasie is a target at £15m, and other names including Brentford's Ollie Watkins are being thrown into the ring. However, Wednesday passes without any further activity and it's on to the last day for any late deals. The general consensus seems to be that any more will be unlikely. The manager and team have left for Turkey and the focus now switches to the upcoming Europa League tie.

Great news ahead of this game as it is announced on Thursday morning that central defender Ben Mee has finally put pen to paper on a new contract and will stay with the club until the summer of 2021. This is the news most fans have been hoping and praying for and the defence now looks like a very strong unit with excellent cover in all positions.

As well as the ongoing saga of Jay Rodriguez, other rumours circulate all day including a new name, that of Southampton's James Ward-Prowse, but the deadline passes without further additions. All in all, not a bad bit of business this window with a figure of approximately £30m spent. Earlier the chairman Mike Garlick had said that the transfer window would be about bringing in quality rather than quantity. This would appear to have been the case, although I feel an extra winger and central midfielder wouldn't have gone amiss in view of our current injury problems.

Thirty million pounds is a not inconsiderable amount of money to spend for a small club like ourselves. This of course is only transfer money outlay and with it will go considerable wage expenditure over a lengthy period. The criticism is often levied at the board of directors that they are a bit 'tight' when it comes to parting with the cash. They in turn would counter that they are being prudent with the club's finances. Many fans believe that the club is financially well-off following two previous seasons in the Premier League and income generated from the sale of Michael Keane and Andre Gray.

It's widely held that these monies are held in what is known as our 'dry powder store'. Now I have a theory as to why this dry powder may have suddenly been brought into play. Suddenly one day, late in the transfer window, police cordoned off Harry Potts Way leading to Turf Moor and declared it as a major incident. It subsequently transpired that what had happened was a large water main burst close to the football ground. How ironic when United Utilities had just called off a planned hose pipe ban in the area due to the summer drought! My belief is that water must have found its way into the 'dry powder store' and the board anxious not to see it swilled away, decided to spend the 'readies' that were most at risk. It's just a theory mind.

3rd Qualifying Round Europa League, 1st Leg - Thursday 9th August, 19.00 (BST) – İstanbul Başakşehir v Burnley

It doesn't seem like five minutes since that nerve shredding, energy sapping encounter with Aberdeen but here we go again. This time we are in the fantastic city of Istanbul, or are we? It turns out our hosts are some way out in the suburbs. A bit of a strange set up too are our Turkish friends. Only founded in 1990, they are owned by the Turkish Ministry of Youth and Sports. Their home is the Başakşehir Fatih Terim Stadium opened to the public in 2014, with a capacity of 17,800.

It would appear that capacity is a bit over optimistic as on this night the crowd is only around 6000, with some 600 travel weary Clarets among them. The team news for anybody expecting a full-strength line-up comes as a bit of a shock. Joe Hart takes over in goal with Tom Heaton, Nick Pope and reputedly Anders Lindegaard all injured. Adam Legzdins takes the substitute goalkeeper's jersey. Both regular full backs, Matt Lowton and Stephen Ward are on the bench, their places going to Phil Bardsley and Charlie Taylor respectively. In the middle its Jack Cork, Ashley Westwood and Johann Berg Gudmundsson (JBG), then surprisingly Jonathan Walters in place of Aaron Lennon, also benched. Up front is Ashley Barnes with Jeff Hendrick playing behind him and in front of the midfield. It's a formation we have used away from home in the Premier League on many occasions and though not very attack minded is quite often very effective.

Next poser is how to follow the match, there are no domestic TV channels covering and no big screen at the Turf Moor Fanzone. I'll have to try and find an internet stream and there is one rumoured from a Turkish TV site. As a last resort it's going to be radio coverage, but would you believe it there's none of that either. No Five Live, no Talksport (except updates) and unbelievably no Radio Lancashire!!! A major European tie for the counties only Lancashire Premier League club and they have opted to cover the Roses T20 cricket from Headingley.

After a good deal of 'faffing about' after about 19 minutes I manage to get an acceptable stream of the game. The commentary is in Turkish, but I can pick out some words such as Joe Hart, Ben Mee, and what surprisingly sounds like 'foul'. We are playing in an all white strip without sponsors logo, apparently not allowed in Turkey presumably because they are a betting company. The Turks however are proudly displaying the Turkish Airlines logo as their shirt sponsor. The atmosphere from the ground seems slightly funereal except that is for the noisy 600 who are loudly berating Blackburn Rovers for some strange reason.

We may be playing in all white, but we are certainly not playing like Real Madrid. It's pretty dour stuff to watch and we are clearly playing for a draw at this stage. There's a lot of 'hoofball' in the general direction of Barnes and Hendrick, but neither are unable to make it stick and generally its coming straight back at us. We've little attacking threat apart from one effort from JBG which is high and wide. Our hosts on the other hand look neat and tidy and are coming forward frequently but meeting our customary resolute defence. There are a couple of saves for Joe Hart to make and that should give him confidence.

On 41 minutes as feared I lose the stream but fortunately its back in a couple of minutes and we make it to half-time 0-0. I think the first half statistics probably reflect the game so far. Istanbul stats first, Possession 70%/30%, Shots 8/1, Shots on Target 1/0, Corners 2/0, Fouls 4/2.

The second period starts with a half chance falling to Hendrick which leads to a corner that comes to nought. Then normal service is resumed as we retreat to our defensive shape and look to soak up the pressure. The Turks should take the lead on 61 minutes, but the chance goes begging, at the same time Sam Vokes is introduced at the expense of JBG. It is a warm night and a slow pitch, and it looks pretty energy sapping out there, but we are sticking to the task. It's not pretty to watch but it is effective. For all their possession Joe Hart is well protected and pretty much untroubled. Time runs down and despite four minutes added time there never really looks like being a goal. Then it's all over, for us job done, for the hosts disappointment of having no lead to take into next week's second leg.

The Turkish manager Abdullah Avci bemoans the fact that we play 'long ball, long ball' all the time. What did he expect? Had he not done his homework? It was up to them to break us down, and despite their tidy approach, they rarely threatened to do that. Sean Dyche was pleased with the effort and discipline from a weakened team, the result gives us a real chance of progression now with the home leg to come next week.

For those of you who like statistics here they come. Those of you with a nervous disposition, I suggest you look away. Istanbul stats first, Possession 71%/29%, shots 18/2, Shots on Target 1/0, Corners 10/1, Fouls 10/9. Thrilling!!!

Now it's on to the serious business, the Premier League opener at Southampton on Sunday 12th.

Result – İstanbul Başakşehir 0 - 0 Burnley

Burnley Team

Hart, Bardsley, Mee, Tarkowski, Taylor, Gudmundsson (Vokes 62), Cork, Westwood, Hendrick, Walters, Barnes (Lennon 77)

<u>Subs Not Used</u> – Legzdins, Lowton, Ward, Long, Gibson

İstanbul Başakşehir Team

Gunok, Caicara, Da Costa, Epureanu, Clichy, Emre, Tekdemir, Visca, Kahveci (Jojic 58), Elia (Frei 83), Bajic, (Napoleoni 89)

<u>Subs Not Used</u> – Babakan, Attamah, Ucar, Inler

Attendance – Undisclosed!!!

Game 1 - Sunday 12th August 13.30 – Southampton v Burnley

After all the early season glamour and excitement of our European adventure its back to the bread and butter business of the Premier League. I say that but without a doubt our primary focus must be on this competition above all others. This is the club's major source of income and has to be our number one priority. Last season's opener was away to Champions Chelsea, this time its slightly less daunting but still tricky, an away trip to Southampton. Following the long haul to and from Istanbul in the latter part of last week the fixture list has not been over kind to us with a long trek again to the south coast. The unexpected victory at Chelsea undoubtedly built the confidence and belief which eventually led to that magnificent season. Hopefully a good result today at Southampton can kick-start a similar outcome.

Due to the Thursday night game this fixture is one of many over the coming weeks to be moved to Sunday. An early kick off at 1.30 makes for a very odd feeling Sunday. To work off the effects of a breakfast egg and bacon bap at the Stables cafe in Towneley Park, my wife Julie and myself settle for a short walk from Briercliffe, to burn some calories and settle the nerves.

Back home shortly after kick-off I search initially for Radio Lancashire coverage but can't find it on DAB. So, it's on to the laptop and open up the BBC Sports App, and the Up the Clarets website. A quick look at these gives me the team news. Joe Hart retains his place in goal, whilst fit again Tom Heaton has to settle for a place on the bench. Both regular full backs, Matt Lowton and Stephen Ward return after sitting out the night in Istanbul. On the right side of midfield Aaron Lennon replaces Jonathan Walters, whilst up front fit again Chris Wood comes in for Ashley Barnes. For our hosts, two familiar ex Clarets feature, striker Charlie Austin starts, whilst new signing Danny Ings is on the bench.

Now starts the search for a satisfactory internet stream to see if I can get some visual on the game. After about 20 minutes I've got what appears to be a decent one, although the commentary I believe is Croatian! Still I don't need that I think I can follow the action and the individuals pretty well myself.

Playing in the change strip of black shirts and white shorts and socks we seem to have started the game well. A quick look at the BBC's statistics confirms this and we appear to be dominating the early exchanges. That's very refreshing after Thursday's dour but effective fare. We're unlucky not to go ahead on the stroke of half-time as the Saints keeper saves with his legs at the foot of the post from a Jeff Hendrick header, then repeats his heroics shortly after with a stop from Ward. The first half statistics are very positive; Southampton figures first, Possession 42%/58%, Shots 6/12, Shots on Target 1/4, Corners 2/4, Fouls 6/7. Half time 0-0.

It's more of the same at the start of the second period and we're almost ahead on 49 minutes as Johann Berg Gudmundsson's (JBG) close range shot is blocked. This is followed by another good effort from Ward again saved by Alex McCarthy in the Saints goal. Once again, we are well on top at the start of the second half but just unable to turn our advantage into a goal.

My internet stream goes down on 50 minutes but I'm able to resurrect by 55 minutes just in time to see Ings being introduced at the expense of Stuart Armstrong. A close shave for us on 60 minutes as Ben Mee almost manages what Southampton can't, his header from a corner is destined for the top of his own net before Ashley Westwood calmly heads clear off the line. Joe Hart is being well protected by our usual magnificent defence and is looking confident between the sticks. As the half wears on we are unsurprisingly beginning to look a little tired and the Saints are starting to press. Hart makes a good save at his near post, which is followed shortly after by another from a headed corner.

The substitutions are coming thick and fast now, Austin who has been largely ineffective, is replaced for the hosts, whilst we introduce Sam Vokes at the expense of Wood. Southampton is Sam's hometown and how much would he love a goal here! On 75 minutes its Ashley Barnes time as he replaces Jeff Hendrick who has put in a hard-running stint. Southampton are gaining the upper hand but still the impregnable defence stands firm. Charlie Taylor replaces JBG as the game draws to a close, and despite five minutes added time, we comfortably survive to come away with our first Premier League point of the season.

I'd have settled for that at the start, and it was an encouraging display in many ways. We now need to get some of our more creative players up to full match fitness and then we'll see where it takes us.

Result – Southampton 0 – 0 Burnley

Burnley Team

Hart, Lowton, Mee, Tarkowski, Ward, Gudmundsson (Taylor 87), Hendrick (Barnes 76), Cork, Westwood, Lennon, Wood (Vokes 73)

Subs Not Used – Heaton, Bardsley, Long, Gibson, Walters

Southampton Team

McCarthy, Soares (Elyounoussi 56), Stephens, Vestergaard, Hoedt, Bertrand, Romeu, Lemina, Redmond, Austin (Gabbiadini 72), Armstrong (Ings 56)

Subs Not Used – Gunn, Bednarek, Hojbjerg, Ward-Prowse

Attendance – 30,784

Season To Date – Played 1, Won 0, Drawn 1, Lost 0, Goals For 0, Goals Against 0, Points 1

League Position after Game 1 – 11th

Once again, its Thursday so that means it must be Europa League football night. This continuous stream of Thursday night and Sunday football is threatening the very fabric of my domestic bliss. Not only is it significantly affecting my alcohol intake, it is also beginning to irk she who must be obeyed.

However, before this evening's fare at Turf Moor there's the Burnley Contingent's Thursday walk to fit in. It's an early start this morning as we head for Grassington and a lovely walk to Conistone Dib and back via the Dales Way. It's a bit cooler today and I opt for long trousers for the first time in many weeks. Seventeen eager souls plus 'Button the Wonderdog' assemble on the Car Park and after recovering from the shock of £4.50 to park the car and a further 20p to use the toilet facilities, we're chomping at the bit to get started.

Today we are led by none other than Geoff Ashworth (The Leader from the Back) who has his trusty rucksack full of mysterious belongings and his 100-year-old Ordnance Survey map of the area. We are yet to see him consult the map and are convinced it is more than likely brought along as something to sit on at lunchtime. Those of us with more sophisticated GPS navigational aids synchronise our various gadgets and attempt to remember to reset the trip meters. This is an oft forgotten ritual meaning walks are often recorded at 30+ miles as the damn thing includes the mileage from home to the start. It's at this point that Steve Quinn detects a malfunction in his technology. I have Bluetoothed across to him the intended track, but the detailed map is missing from under the imprint. It's on occasions like this that the 100-year-old paper technology comes into its own. However, after a brief technical discussion we conclude that the SD card in his gadget has probably become displaced. A quick fiddle about and he is up and running.

An idyllic walk in limestone country skirting the top side of Grass Wood eventually leads us into the delightful village of Conistone approximately halfway between Grassington and Kettlewell. This is the traditional lunch stop; the thoughtful villagers having provided the perfect resting spot in the centre with benches and rocks for sitting upon. There's even a rubbish bin provided. What more could a walker ask for? Well, a pub would be nice, and Steve Quinn was rather hoping for a pie shop!

After our alfresco lunch it's time for a quick visit to the delightful St Mary's Church and then the ascent to Conistone Dib. Fuelled by my four-course lunch, Ham butty, Banana, Yorkie biscuit and Apple, I'm more than ready for the challenge. It's a very pleasant climb through the, in some parts, narrow gully to the top. Once there the route back is via the Dales Way with some tremendous views in all directions. Then of course the highlight of the day, beer at the Black Horse in Grassington. Today's choice is Black Horse Grassington Best Bitter, although a good selection of other beers are available. A fitting end to a lovely walk that clocked in at 8.2 miles and just the aperitif for an evening's football.

3rd Qualifying Round Europa League, 2nd Leg - Thursday 16th August, 19.45 – Burnley v İstanbul Başakşehir

It would be easy to think that the hard work had already been done in this tie. An away draw in Turkey would seem to make us favourites on home soil to win and progress to the next round. However, the lack of an away goal from the 1st leg makes the position slightly more perilous than it at first might seem. If our Turkish friends should snatch a goal in this game, it would leave us needing to score twice to overcome the away goal should the scores finish level.

There's a rather strange atmosphere at the Turf tonight as there will be no visiting fans present. For some reason best known to themselves İstanbul Başakşehir have decided not to sell any tickets for the return leg at Turf Moor. How strange! I can't help thinking that can only be a disadvantage to the visiting team as the sight of a few friendly faces in the crowd and a bit of support would surely not have gone amiss. In fact, about a dozen Turkish fans are present in the Cricket Field stand believed to be friends and/or relatives of the team. Or perhaps they are locals from the Turkish Best Kebab House situated at the cross-roads of Harry Potts Way and Belvedere Rd.

On the way to the ground I learn the team news and it's a bit disconcerting. Sean Dyche obviously concerned about fatigue in the currently depleted squad, and conscious of the Premier League game against Watford coming up on Sunday, has decided to ring the changes. Joe Hart remains in goal but the back four is massively changed with only Stephen Ward retaining his place from the last game at Southampton. In come Phil Bardsley, Kevin Long and new signing Ben Gibson for his full debut. Midfield sees Jack Cork and Johann Berg Gudmundsson (JBG) rested, Jeff Hendrick takes a centre midfield berth and surprisingly Charlie Taylor normally operating at left back is deployed as a wide left midfielder. We opt for two up front, on this occasion Ashley Barnes and Sam Vokes. All the 'big guns' are on the bench enjoying hopefully a well-earned rest but available if needed.

As we saw in the first meeting this Turkish side are no mugs, they are technically very competent and are very good at keeping possession. From the start this is clearly evident, and I soon get the impression that this may well be a long night. Gradually the Clarets manage to impose some authority on the game and there's a decent chance as Aaron Lennon works himself an opening, but the keeper makes a good save. Similarly,

Phil Bardsley with a powerful effort brings a fine if somewhat spectacular stop by the keeper. Perhaps the best chance is wasted by Ashley Barnes who having done well to get in the clear hits a shot into the side netting when perhaps a squared pass across goal would have been more beneficial.

As the half draws to a close our visitors wrest control of the game from us and their slick passing and clever inter-play fashions a number of decent chances. Once again Joe Hart, in magnificent form, is our saviour and we are slightly relieved to go in at the break still level.

The second half pretty much mirrors the end of the first as the Turks enjoy plenty of possession but tellingly, they are hitting the same brick wall defence that they encountered in Istanbul. It appears that we are able to change personnel but the discipline and shape of our rearguard is such that we are a very difficult unit to break down. For all their possession they are troubling Hart very little. At the other end we are plugging away but without much success. The best chance falls again to Barnes who unfortunately heads wide from a good position when I expected the net to bulge.

Legs tire and substitutions are made as both sides attempt to avoid the need for the extra energy sapping 30 minutes. A familiar face introduced by the visitors is that of Emmanuel Adebayor, formerly of Arsenal and Manchester City. Getting on a bit now in age he seems to be thoroughly enjoying himself and is having amicable conversations with many Clarets players. On for us come initially JBG, followed by Chris Wood and Jack Cork. Adebayor misses the best chance for Başakşehir and with that gone we're heading for extra time.

For the second time in this competition we are set for a late night. Who will have the stamina to come out on top? Let's please have a winner and avoid the torture of a penalty shoot-out.

It's not long before the question is answered. In the seventh added minute after a nice set-up from the right flank, Jeff Hendrick lays off a lovely ball to the onrushing Cork about 25 yards out and fairly central. Without hesitation 'Corky' dispatches a curling effort with considerable power that nestles in the top of the Turkish net. To me it was a goal highly reminiscent of Wade Elliott's 'wondergoal' in the 2009 Championship Play-Off Final. Once more for the second home Europa League tie Cork has broken the deadlock. Ecstasy engulfs Turf Moor, tinged with more than a shred of relief. There's another 23 minutes to see out but our fitness seems to have the better of our opponents and our defence remains resolute.

At gone 10.20 the referee, who by the way was shocking, brings the game to an end. The European tour continues, and it's on to Athens in a week's time.

Once again not a classic performance but a truly battling one. There were some brilliant contributions from often unsung heroes, none more than a terrific whole-hearted display from Phil Bardsley. If ever one man's determination to win was on display, then it was surely his. His contribution as the game went on grew and grew and his marauding down the right flank was tremendous. Kevin Long was similarly immense and thoroughly deserving of the sponsors 'Man of the Match' award. Joe Hart continues to exude and spread confidence from the back, what an astute signing he is turning out to be. Ben Gibson slotted in seamlessly to maintain our impressive defensive solidity. However, once again the performance was not about individuals but about the team.

A game effort from İstanbul Başakşehir, they demonstrated a very tidy and neat and controlled approach. Unfortunately, a lack of punch up front meant they were unable to breach our defence. Their manager once again bemoaned our 'long ball' tactics and felt it was not for the football purist. He hasn't yet realised that there is more than one way to skin a cat. We play to our strengths, that is how it has to be, and it was proof once again that the art of defending is just as important as that of attacking.

Result –Burnley (Cork 97) 1 – 0 **After Extra Time** İstanbul Başakşehir

Burnley Team

Hart, Bardsley, Long, Gibson, Ward, Lennon (Gudmundsson 58), Westwood (Cork 82), Hendrick, Taylor, Barnes (Tarkowski (120+2), Vokes (Wood 82)

Subs Not Used – Legzdins, Lowton, McNeil

İstanbul Başakşehir Team

Gunok, Caicara, Da Costa, Epureanu, Clichy, Emre, Tekdemir (Inler 92), Visca, Kahveci (Jojic 109), Frei (Napoleoni 102), Bajic (Adebayor 66)

Attendance – 16,583

No sooner has one game ended than the next one is quickly upon us. After a long night on Thursday, I've just time to compose myself before the next challenge, Watford at the Turf on Sunday.

A bit of a different weekend this one as my daughter Stephanie is joining us on Friday afternoon. Now resident in Darlington she is down for a Saturday spent wedding dress shopping in Colne with my wife and mother-in-law. Thankfully, I will be spared this event as I am solely employed on taxi duties. I collect the trio in mid-afternoon and learn that the expedition has been a roaring success and large amounts of money have changed hands! A celebratory evening at The Spice Lounge rounds off a very pleasant day and we all retire to bed happily knackered!

Sunday dawns and there's just time for Stephanie to catch up with her Grandad over Bacon & Egg butties at The Stables, Towneley Park, before I head for Turf Moor and she for Darlington.

Game 2 - Sunday 19th August 13.30 – Burnley v Watford

It's a miserable damp drizzly day in Burnley. What has happened to the glorious summer? The hills are shrouded in mist and there's a stiff breeze blowing up Brunshaw Road.

As expected, the team reverts back to what, bearing in mind the current injury situation, is our strongest line-up. Joe Hart after three consecutive clean sheets retains his place in goal as Tom Heaton has to settle for a place on the bench. Defenders Matt Lowton, James Tarkowski and Ben Mee are back, as is Johann Berg Gudmundsson (JBG) and Jack Cork. Chris Wood leads the attack with Jeff Hendrick playing just behind.

It's an explosive start as the Hornets are quickly out of the traps. There are a couple of narrow escapes before on just three minutes ex Claret Andre Gray puts the visitors ahead from a slick right flank move. That's not the start I wanted to see, but as my mate John W says, at least there's plenty of time to get back in the game. As it happens lots of time isn't needed as James Tarkowski heads in from a JBG corner on just six minutes to level the score.

Now it's evenly matched and both teams are trading punches. I am impressed with Watford's attacking play whilst defensively they don't look quite as effective. Noticeably they are moving the ball much quicker than a rather ponderous looking Clarets attack. Troy Deeney and Gray are proving a real handful, and they are well supported by a strong and mobile midfield.

Nevertheless, we are making some decent chances and Watford keeper Ben Foster keeps them level with a good save from a JBG free kick. He's called into action again just managing to stop a poked effort from Hendrick which is heading goal bound. After the dramatic start the game not surprisingly settles and an even first half ends 1-1.

Buoyed by their half time cuppa the visitors start the second half in determined fashion. In fact, it's almost a carbon copy of the first half as they regain the lead on 48 minutes. Some clever inter-play sees Deeney racing on to a lovely through ball to fire past a helpless Joe Hart. If that wasn't bad enough on 51 minutes, there's a mountain to climb as the Hornets sting us once again. A poor cross field pass from Lowton is intercepted by Will Hughes who advances a few yards before despatching a thunderous left -footer past the diving Hart.

I can't see us coming back from this although once again there is plenty of time. The ineffective Wood is replaced by Ashley Barnes, and shortly after Hendrick is sacrificed for Sam Vokes in an attempt to beef up the attack. In all honesty it didn't really make much difference. Watford now content to soak up the pressure and counterattack were seldom troubled by our slow and predictable build up play. It's crying out for that bit of creativity that perhaps Robbie Brady, Steven Defour and Matej Vydra could bring.

From around the 70-minute mark the game fizzles out and we are, on the day, well beaten by the better team. No complaints from me, sometimes it's just not your day. The last Premier League season started with a defeat in the first home game, against later relegated West Bromwich Albion, and look how that finished. Its early days yet and a sharp reminder that there are no easy games in the Premier League, time to keep calm and learn from this one.

Result – Burnley (Tarkowski 6) 1 – 3 (Gray 3, Deeney 48, Hughes 51) Watford

Burnley Team

Hart, Lowton, Mee, Tarkowski, Ward (Taylor 74), Gudmundsson, Hendrick (Vokes 70), Cork, Westwood, Lennon, Wood (Barnes 65)

Subs Not Used – Heaton, Bardsley, Long, Gibson

Watford Team

Foster, Janmaat, Cathcart, Kabasele, Holebas, Doucoure, Capoue, Hughes (Femenia 83) Pereyra, Deeney (Success 89), Gray (Sema 68)

Subs Not Used – Gomes, Prodl, Mariappa, Masina

Attendance – 18,822

Season To Date – Played 2, Won 0, Drawn 1, Lost 1, Goals For 1, Goals Against 3, Points 1

League Position after Game 2 – 15th

Monday 20th August is a sad day for all connected with Burnley FC as the death is announced of probably our greatest and most famous ex player, Jimmy McIlroy. The term 'legend' is much overused today, but not in the case of Jimmy 'Mac'. A fantastic playing career with the Clarets from 1950 through to 1962, saw the quiet spoken Northern Irishman total 497 appearances and score 131 goals.

What would he have been worth today in this ridiculously hyper inflated market? Without doubt a significant fortune, yet Jimmy played most of his career in the era of the 'maximum wage' when players at all clubs had a wage cap, which made for a much fairer competition all round.

As a boy I well remember reading Jimmy's Biography 'Right Inside Soccer' as I attempted to model myself on his elegant and apparently effortless playing style. I also recall the total disbelief that reverberated around the town when he was made available for transfer in 1962, just two years after he had won an English League Championship medal with the Clarets. Many people in the town vowed from that day never to set foot inside Turf Moor again and were as good as their word.

Fortunately, Jimmy after finishing his playing career with spells at Stoke City and Oldham Athletic, including a brief flirtation with football management at the latter, returned to his adopted town. After a career which saw him win 55 International caps for Northern Ireland, scoring 10 goals in the process and spanning 14 years (1951-1965) he took a job in journalism and wrote for a local newspaper.

Jimmy at the height of his career did have approaches from far bigger clubs than Burnley. One notably being from the Italian club Sampdoria on the morning before the 1962 FA Cup Final between Burnley and Tottenham Hotspur. The Italians promised him a villa looking over the Mediterranean, an international school for his children, and wages way beyond what he was getting in England. On returning to the hotel he told his wife who said to him; *"Sure, but why would we want to leave Burnley?"* and Jimmy agreed!

He was a keen golfer and often seen around the town and the surrounding moors. The genial Irishman had certainly won the hearts of the people of Burnley and beyond, who were eternally grateful for the footballing success that his genius had brought to the town. With a Stand at Turf Moor named after him, Jimmy McIlroy will long be remembered in these parts. A gentleman.

The club featured in an interesting piece by the Daily Mail's Chief Sportswriter, Martin Samuels on Tuesday 21st August. Mr Samuels had clearly picked up on the fact that some dissenting voices amongst Clarets fans were questioning the wisdom of our participation in the Europa League. In response to some fans hoping that the European quest would be over by the end of August he wrote:

"To do what, focus on a mid-table finish at best? Where is the fun in just hanging around unless it leads to somewhere – like the Europa League? Eventually Burnley will go down. Not because they are rubbish, just because they're Burnley. It happened to Stoke, to Middlesbrough, to West Brom, to Aston Villa. There are clubs that move between the divisions, up and down. Some stay longer than others, but the rise and fall is inevitable.

A good manager leaves, players are sold, or some signings fail – there are plenty of reasons why a club gets relegated. And then what is to remember? Not all those years of finishing 17th or even seventh, but those standout campaigns, a final or a rare night in Europe. Burnley, managed by Sean Dyche, play Olympiacos, 44 times champions of Greece on Thursday. Win over two legs and they could face one of the great names of European football: AC Milan, Lazio, Sporting Lisbon, Celtic. Burnley in the San Siro, imagine that? For the majority being in the Premier League is a means to that end, a door to something even better, something more exciting for your club. If you don't want that thrill, what is there? You really have only come to see United".

On this occasion Mr Samuels, I totally agree.

As August rolls on, although the transfer window inwards for us is now firmly shut, there is still the possibility of loaning out players to non-Premier League clubs. The penultimate week in August sees two such deals. Firstly, highly promising young centre back Jimmy Dunne leaves to join Scottish Premier League side Heart of Midlothian on loan until the 7th January. There is more good news for Jimmy before he leaves to go north, he signs a new contract at Turf Moor which potentially could keep him here till the summer of 2021.

Shortly after this move striker Nahki Wells is also on his travels on a season long loan to Championship strugglers Queens Park Rangers. It's not been a happy 12 months for Wells since his signing from Huddersfield Town and hopefully the move will give him the opportunity to regain some form and confidence.

When the Clarets trip to Athens was confirmed, and my old mate of many years, John Weir indicated that he and his wife Jude would be making the trip, I hatched a plan. I would commission the pair to write a blog of their adventure thereby saving myself a bit of work. I'm not sure commissioned is the proper term as that suggests some form of payment which I can assure you there won't be! I instructed him to feel free to tell it as it is, warts and all. I'm taking a bit of a risk there as he can be a bit of a 'loose cannon'.

I must forewarn the reader that John, having been at one time amongst several careers a schoolteacher, has laid out his tale much in the form of a laboratory experiment. There is an object, apparatus, method and conclusion although not exactly headed as such. Furthermore, John is a man who has a song for every occasion, and for anybody who has ever walked the hills with him, this can be pretty irritating (and tuneless!). Suffice it to say he has attempted to work in a song title at every opportunity. See if you can spot them all.

Anyway, many thanks to the 'Wandering Weirs' for their mammoth effort which he described to me as being 'War and Peace' with pictures. John some five years or more ago, had indicated to me that he intended to write a walking book entitled '10 Miles from Burnley'. To the best of my knowledge this project has not yet progressed past Page 1. Hopefully his little excursion here into print will inspire him to fulfil his dream.

Pour yourselves a glass of ouzo, get out the olives and sit back and think of Greece.

A Modern Greek Odyssey – or we know a song about that

Introduction

Peter asked me if I would write a blog about our trip to Athens, I was at first quite keen. Especially as he promised, "there will be a drink in it for you – both!". How could I refuse? I thought, I know I'll make a witty, Bill Bryson like travel log. However, many hours of head scratching, writers block, stumbling over match details, remembering events in sequence, pacing the floor at four in the morning (hey I know a song about that) I began to change my mind.

In the end I have produced a record of events, which I hope shed some light on a European away trip with the Clarets.

Choices

Jude and I have been following the Clarets for a very long time. Our greatest trips have been to see them win at Wembley (twice), winning the Championship at Charlton and returning to the Premier league, defeating Chelsea on their own patch, and Robbie Blake's thunderer against Manure! No wonder some people say we are football mad. Hey, I know a song (you get the idea?)

As Burnley's first European adventure for over fifty years began, we were planning a camping trip to France. Not entirely certain where, just getting "lost in France" (see what I did there?). Burnley's progress through the first round caused us to ask the question. "If we get through and play a big European team, do we go camping or go to the match?"

Nervous watching

It was Thursday the 16th August and approaching 9:45 p.m. After a goalless first leg in Turkey, followed by a goalless second leg in Burnley, Burnley and Basaksehir of Istanbul faced extra time for a place in the play-off round of the Europa League.

We were seven minutes into extra time when the ball dropped on the edge of the Turkish side's penalty box to our midfield leader Jack Cork. He made no mistake with a powerful shot into the top right-hand corner. The team safely navigated the remaining 23 minutes without (much) incident, and we were through to the play-off round of the Europa League.

Following the final whistle, cue mayhem, wild celebrations and much singing of "We're all going on a European tour". (Yellow Submarine) Our next opponents, Olympiacos of Athens, had already been decided earlier that evening, when they defeated Luzern of Switzerland 7 – 1 on aggregate. By the time that the ball hit the back of the net Jude and I had a tacit understanding that, if we defeated the Turkish side that we were off to Greece.

So, Greece rather than France it was to be then!

Planning

Returning home at 10:30, we began searching for flights, hotels and deals to Athens. A flight was identified, it appeared to have a reasonable return price of £550. Yippee! Bedtime, approximately 2:00 am, we decided to reserve the actual booking until Friday morning.

By Friday morning the flights had risen to £750, the only hotels available appeared to be in dodgy parts of Athens. Tensions were rising in the Weir household, best summed up in the following discussion:

ME: Found a hotel, it's £30 a night, looks all right, seems to be near the port area.

JUDE: Have you seen it on Google Earth? Vagrants outside the hotel, graffiti all over the walls, Tripadvisor says very poor area, not safe at night.

ME: Look that's about 10 you've rejected, what do you want? The bloody Hilton? 5-star palace?

JUDE: I want somewhere reasonably priced, secure and close to a decent area of the city.

ME: I give up you find one.

JUDE: I can't find one either. I'm going to give up

You could say Peace, Love and Understanding were being stretched here. (Snook another one in there)

We checked flights to Athens with; Wizz, Ryanair, Cobalt, Aegean and B.A. To name a few. We checked routes to Athens, including, Manchester, Leeds Bradford, Bristol, Glasgow. We checked the possibility of driving overland, camping en-route.

Finally, we settled on a route using British Airways via Glasgow Airport, to Heathrow and on to Athens. This route included on site car parking for a very reasonable price. Hurrah! We are off to Glasgow (I belong to Glasgae, dear old Glasgae toon). Once the bookings were secured, we needed our travel documents. A belt and braces approach seemed to suit us best, that is, we would print the boarding passes, details of the car park and BA flights so we had a physical copy as well an electronic copy held on my phone.

Of course, at this moment, the printer ran out of ink. No problem load the new spare compatible ink cartridge I had purchased at a bargain price. The printer now decided, "Oh no, my lad, this is not original ink, I'm not going to work." Our printer is upstairs, our computer is downstairs, so frantic rushing up and down stairs ensued. Following much language of, let's say, Shakespearean content, emerging from my lips I eventually triumphantly persuaded the printer to allow our boarding passes to emerge from its grasp. Weird isn't it how inanimate objects appear to take on a life force of their own, when they won't work. "Ah, well accidents will happen." Phew!

So, what about tickets for the match? The club in its wisdom had decided to utilise a priority purchasing scheme for tickets for the game in Athens. No problem, I had 8,000 points on my card and purchased my ticket immediately. Jude with 3,000 points on her Claret membership card has to wait, and according to "Up the Clarets" web site, priority purchasing for her will be given on Saturday at 9:15. Saturday morning at 9:30 we logged onto the BFC website and...tickets not available. Tears, near panic and rending of clothes ensues, until an amendment is noticed and tickets for Jude will be available from 12:30 lunch time. Phew, again. Is the trip, and the stress of planning worthwhile? Of course, it is!

Shortly afterwards Jude identifies a hotel close by the place we are to collect our tickets on match day. The hotel has good reviews, it's in a nice area, and close to some ancient Greek monuments. Perfick as Pop Larkin would have said. "It's going to be a lovely day".

Then, on Monday the 20th August, it is announced that arguably the greatest footballer ever to wear our Claret and Blue colours has died. A sad day in the annals of Burnley FC, as we discover that Jimmy McIlroy has died. This event will colour, some of the chants and many of the conversations of the coming days if not weeks, months and years ahead. It will travel with Claret fans to Athens, and his name will be roared out by fans, including many who could never have seen him play.

We're Off

On the Saturday before setting of to Athens Burnley played a league game against Watford. We lost the match, and a returning player, who had had a habit of being caught offside wasn't and scored as Watford defeated the Clarets 3-1. Discussions amongst Claret fans following the game centred on whether the Europa adventure was adversely affecting our league form. Opinion was divided, but a consensus seemed to be, if this was our last game (for now) in Europe then Athens wasn't a bad place to have it.

Tuesday 21st August midnight we arose, packed our car and carefully managing not to slam doors and annoy our neighbours, we depart for Glasgow. My immediate neighbour is a Blackburn Rovers supporter and I was tempted to give a chorus of "we're all going on a European tour". However, an old-fashioned look from Jude, and thoughts that if we got a pasting, I would have to face him on my return, persuaded me that discretion is after all the better part of valour. "Oh, we're off, off, off in a motor car."

On arrival at Glasgow, we caught the bus for the terminal, arriving in good time. However, idiot boy me had left his credit cards, wallet and essential documents in the car. Undaunted we returned to the car park amidst good hearted mild admonishments from Jude (not), and a slightly bemused bus driver who only minutes earlier had deposited us at the terminal door!

As a way of lightening the moment, and deflecting criticism away from myself, I took Jude's photo as she stood behind one of those cardboard cut-outs. This one was a Highlander in full regalia, I thought it looked quite fetching, although his hairy knees were perhaps less *flattering than Jude would have chosen for herself. She reminded me of Andy Stewart singing "There was a sodjeer (soldier), a Scottish Sodjeer."*

The flight from Glasgow was flawless, and after wandering around Gucci, Dior and Cartier stores without making a single purchase in the Heathrow Terminal we settled for breakfast in Wetherspoons. Alcohol free I add. (These two certainly know how to live! – the author).

The flight to Athens was called on time and as we boarded, I took a complimentary copy of the Times. I commenced the four-hour flight tackling the biggest hardest crossword in the world. As we landed, I had just completed my third clue and feeling that perhaps Mastermind entry is not such a ridiculous idea, left the aeroplane. We were, "Leaving on a jet plane," it was time for us to "Go Now."

Figure 1 - Judy in full regalia prepares for battle with the Greeks with a blast on the pipes

Figure 2 - The Greeks respond by wearing their kilts but opt for a more intimidating weapon

We made our way to the bus depot at the Airport and purchased tickets for the X95. It is a 45-minute motorway journey (very similar to the M66 in time and distance from Manchester to Burnley) into Syntagma Square at the heart of Athens. My fare (because I am a pensioner) was three Euros, Judes (because she is not a pensioner) six Euros. Very reasonable and high-speed travel. (I bet he tried to use his bus pass – the author).

We alighted the bus next to the Hilton Hotel, and discovered our Hotel "The Illessia" in its shadow. However, Athens is as we discovered, a city of contrasts, and between our perfectly pleasant hotel and the 5-star Hilton was – a strip club! I made an ill-judged joke about, if we run out of money Jude could supplement our cash by working there. No response was forthcoming.

Athens

Wednesday morning found us undertaking the obligatory site seeing tour of the city. We visited the original Olympic Stadium, Zeus Temple, Acropolis, Syntagma Square, Changing the guard by the Parliament building, Lycabettus Hill, and all points in between.

At lunch we decided to eat in the Praki area, well known for various types of Greek National dishes. The area was strangely quiet as we approached, then we discovered why. There had been a power cut throughout the local area and the only food available was cold! By this stage we were hungry, thirsty and our poor feet were reminiscent of Dorgans barking dogs loudly demanding a rest. We found a small restaurant/taverna and sank enough beer to satisfy both our and our dogs' thirst.

Figure 3 - A relic poses in front of a relic. John W takes in the sights of Athens

As we sat enjoying our beer and meal, congratulating ourselves on having travelled 2,500 miles to watch a football game, Jude and I were humbled by the number of beggars in this part of Athens. Particularly poignant were some children who came to our table and held out their hands asking for our untouched bread. Another poor old chap lay nearby sleeping on a wall (drugs, drink, poverty, or all three), he had horrendous sores on his wasting calf muscles, whilst a group of Chinese people on the next table to us took pictures of their plates of food, presumably to share over social media.

Europa League Qualifying Play-Off Round, 1st Leg - Thursday 23rd August, 19.00 – Olympiakos v Burnley

On the day of the match we wandered to the Devani Caravel Hotel to collect our tickets for the game. Approaching the hotel at about 10:45, we could hear singing. As we drew nearer it became distinguishable as the anthemic, "Sean Dyche's Claret and Blue Army" sung as usual at about 300bpm (beats per minute). A large group of early arrival's had congregated in a platia near the hotel and had commenced the festivities, Mythos abounding aplenty!

We met some friends that we had not seen for some time in the queue, Susan and Ken, and joined up with them for the match day experience. We collected our tickets and agreed to meet them at a nearby restaurant, after we had climbed to the top of Lycabettus hill.

We left at 11:00 and returned some two hours later, had a shower and made our way to meet our friends. We ate lunch at a cheerful roadside restaurant, where the owner wished us luck, as he supported Panathinaikos, it was I suspect, more about bad luck to Olympiacos than good wishes for us. We shared a huge bowl of Tzatziki and drank a preparatory beer or two. Leaving the restaurant with best wishes ringing in our ears and smelling comfortably of Garlic and Humus we set off for Aminta Platia, the designated Claret meeting place.

As we approached the meeting place we heard "SeanDychesClaretnBluearmy" probably now at about 450bpm. Also, a slur in the transition between words was beginning to be noticeable. Our little group decanted into Aminta Platia, and as we turned the corner what a sight greeted us. Hundreds of Clarets, some with flags, bunting around the square, people with shirts with all sorts of good luck slogans, some with memories of Jimmy McIlroy, but all singing, drinking and celebrating all things Claret. The main bar in the square ran out of bottled beers, the bar manager told people he still had draft beer but no glasses. Thrifty Burnley fans shared glasses. Some wandered to the supermarket behind the square and bought cans. I suggested he utilise his large paper coffee cups, and a new trade was born.

We sang, drank and cheered for the next 3 hours (by now at about 600bpm). People I had never met before bumped into me and each other and with incredulous faces like children on their first Christmas morning, smiled and said, "all right my mate, all right", then staggered off into the next Claret. A Greek lady home from work at about 5:30 was taking her dog for its evening constitutional past the square, she stopped and stared at the group with incredulity. Open mouthed she asked another Greek something like – "what the hell are they doing?" I think the reply was along the lines of – "having a good time, now take your dog away before they eat it."

Then suddenly, it was time to leave for the match. The match! Almost forgotten in the euphoria of the moment. We boarded buses outside the old Olympic Stadium and were ready for the off. On arrival at one of Europe's best-known grounds, a team that has played in Champions Leagues, Europa League et al, we surely could be forgiven for thinking that this ground will be magnificent. Wrong! No beer on sale, one kiosk to serve the 1,000 plus hungry and thirsty (greedy guzzling) Clarets. The Men's toilets to put it mildly, were nothing to write home about. To put it in perspective those who know the old Turf Moor, think Bee Hole End toilets around half time! Wading through six inches of urine for your turn to pee in a full to the brim urinal. Which of course added more to the general six inches on the floor. Now, you may wonder why we didn't drown here as more and more fans took their turn at adding to the disgusting mess. I discovered the reason why when, a lady emerged from their toilet and announced it was pouring in from the men's side, and flowing out of their door, and down the steps. Classy!

A minor setback to the mighty Clarets singing then occurred. As we sang "We are the Longside, Burnley" and other classics now at 750bpm from 6:45 until 8:45 the Olympiacos Ultras turned up in their section and began to compete. They sang a sort of choreographed version of the Chuckle brothers "to me, to you" thing, going between the two ends of the ground. One end shouted "Olympi" waved their arms and stamped their feet. The other end responded with "Acos", proceeded to stamp their feet *and wave their arms, and then they repeated it. I must admit at a more leisurely 100bpm. Fond memories of Barry and Paul.*

Figure 4 - Olympiakos Stadium - a decidedly hostile place

As the game gets underway the usual footie fans butterfly stomach takes over; "come on, come onnn, good effort, oh etc". Then after 19 minutes Phil Bardsley makes a rash challenge, is penalised and a well flighted free kick finds the back of Tom Heaton's net. One nil down.

After half an hour Chris Wood who has not looked as sharp this season as he did last, turns away from the Olympiacos goal and is rashly bundled over by a Greek defender. He gets up, and despite what looked like incredibly fierce Olympiacos supporters booing, jeering, making the usual noises and faces, calmly slots away the penalty. Queue many Claret fans saying, "I never doubted the lad, knew he'd put it away," for me, I was not at all sure, so well-done Chris. Just before half-time Johann Berg Gudmundsson is booked for an innocuous challenge. Half time arrives, and many fans are thoroughly enjoying our European adventure. Whilst we are not in complete control, we are playing well, and the Greeks apart from the dangerous pair of Camara and Fortounis are being contained. Optimism is high. Roll on the second half.

At the start of the second half our supporters are rife with comments about the Greek team's players and officials surrounding, hounding and threatening the referee and his assistants on the way off the pitch. This apparently continuing in the tunnel and even in the referees dressing room. Their owner has previous form for this type of unwanted intervention, anyway we will soon know the truth of it. Within ten minutes of the restart, Ben Gibson and Kevin Long (our two Centre Backs) are both booked, a free kick in a dangerous position is awarded and inevitably from the free kick a goal is scored against, we are 2-1 behind. COYC!

On 59 minutes the ball bounces up and hits Ben Gibson on the hand, this is, in the referee's opinion a penalty. To compound the problem, Gibson is sent off and with the penalty scored we are 3-1 behind. That is probably enough to settle the game if indeed not the tie. Was it a penalty? It could have been given, they are often not given, and certainly not in the last 12 months to us. However, a sending off as well. Overkill by the referee, bringing inevitably the thought that he's been got at.

Defiant Clarets continue to the last whistle singing, "We are the Longside, Burnley", "Sean Dyche's Claret and Blue Army" and poignantly "He's one of our own, he's one of our own, Jimmy McIlroy he's one of our own." I think the Olympiacos supporters nearest to us were at first concerned for our sanity as we continued singing long after the final whistle. Then many of them waved, in a friendly way (although not all of them I admit), in an admiring show of understanding fan loyalty to the cause. Eventually, after tearful waving to Sean and the team we made our way back to the coach. It was now nearly midnight, and incredibly the police still hesitated to release the buses onto the streets of Athens. This is usual with Olympiacos Ultras on the prowl and is a protection for the visitor.

Our bus deposited us back in Syntagma Square and we were left to find our own way home to hotels etc. As we prepared to leave, a battered, scruffy little car, screeched to a halt in front of us and a young Ultra jumped out holding an Olympiacos scarf. He asked me if I would like to swap scarves with him. As I did not have a scarf, I shouted to Jude that this chap wanted to swap scarves. She looked incredulously at me and said "No! This is new, I don't want that smelly looking thing". At that I looked at the young man's scarf and realised it probably held something thoroughly unpleasant as an exchange. He didn't hang around for long and soon disappeared back with his mates to try his luck elsewhere. I really am a bit gullible, aren't I! "What kind of fool am I?"

At nearly one a.m. we crawled back to our hotel and were told by the concierge that the bar was closed. There were however, three bars still *open around the corner. Two more weary and hungry Clarets appeared together with whom we visited the bar around the corner. A couple of beers later, the lads told us some tales of derring-do undertaken by Burnley fans on the Athens Metro system. Hooded, balaclava wearing, Ultras hiding on street corners, fans mugged, cut with a box cutter knife and punched in the face. This was not the Athens we visited in the daytime.*

(For those who like to see the teams, here we go – the author)

Result – Olympiakos (Fortounis 19, 60 pen, Bouchalakis 48) 3 – 1 (Wood 33 pen) Burnley

Burnley Team

Heaton, Bardsley, Long, Gibson, Ward (Lennon 66), Gudmundsson (Vokes 76), Cork, Hendrick, Taylor, Barnes, Wood (Tarkowski 62)

Subs Not Used – Hart, Lowton, Westwood, Vydra

Olympiakos Team

Gianniotis, Elabdellouai, Miranda, Vukovic, Tsimikas, Camara, Bouchalakis, Christodolopous (Ansarifard 84), Fortounis (Fetfatzidis 89), Castelo Podence, Guerrero

Subs Not Used – Choutesiotis, Natcho, Vrousai, Torosidis, Cisse

Aftermath

On Friday we were, as you will understand a little tired, and decided a trip to the seaside area of Athens, Glyfada would cheer us up. A lovely place visited via a tram trip through the city. On the journey we saw a darker side of the capital, strip clubs, run down suburbs, graffiti on many walls, and under dressed ladies on street corners. Glyfada however was a really nice seaside area, compare and contrast Blackpool with St. Annes. We walked a good stretch of the sea front area and watched people with too much money sail boats that reflected their egos. Something is amiss, clearly one side of Greece has, and the other has not. Jude originally came from Southend on Sea, and periodically needs a fix of sea air, she, "Always like to be beside the seaside."

Our hotel had overnight been invaded by some 75 Chinese people and a large group of "Young Americans" (we know a song about that).

This made breakfast into a fierce MMA type contest (tuck your elbows in, bring your fists up and keep your jab going).

We completed our site seeing tour of Athens, visiting a few other ruins and lunching, now with power in the Plakia area. We felt at home in the city and quite familiar with finding our way around, we toured the sites, like modern day Athenians. I paid 15 Euros for one ticket that allowed me to enter most of the major sites whilst Jude had to pay 30 for the same privilege.

We watched the Greek changing of the guard outside the Parliament building and thought what "Super Troopers." Jude then heard a passing lady comment on the Soldiers tunic that, "They are just like Scotch-men, with those skirts." Now as my friends know, I was born in Scotland and, although pretty much Anglicised, still support the country of my birth in Internationals (Rugby, Football, Tennis and Bowls), and dislike the term Scotch when referring to the people. Scotch is a drink; Scots are the people. Heroically, I just pulled a face, and commented, "I wouldn't be wearing anything that short" and made our way into the Monastraki area of town.

Together with two other friends we have been going to football for a very long time. It has become a bit of a tradition that when on holiday we seek out, bring home and share lucky charms. This tradition has evolved such that we feel we have to have four strings of Belekra or Kolomboi worry beads made to take home as future lucky tokens. Whenever any of us are away from home it is likely that they will return with a string for each of our little gang. Do they work? Well, look where we are. Even if they don't it gives you something to fiddle with in your trouser pocket on a cold winter's day! (Careful! – the author)

Home again

Sunday sees us back on the X95 to the airport, four-hour flight to Heathrow, onwards to Glasgow and a night drive back to Burnley. Home at 2.00 a.m. Knackered, we open a nice bottle of cheap Greek wine. Well, cheap anyway. We slurp it down and retire to a good night's sleep. "We've all been on a European tour, a European tour, a European tour" and "SeanDychesClaretandBlueArmy" 8000bpm ringing in our ears.

Will we ever qualify again? I don't know but if we do, we'll be there. Michael Jackson's "I'll be there," ringing in my head.

Here's what we could have won!

Europa League Group Stage – Group F – Olympiacos/AC Milan/Real Betis/Dudelange

Well done John and Jude for that informative and highly enlightening tour of Athens. I don't think I'll be going there for a while!

Game 3 - Sunday 26th August 16.00 – Fulham v Burnley

Due to my wife and I's annual August Bank Holiday weekend visit to friends in Lincolnshire, for this game I can only give a retrospective review of the proceedings. Any reader who has read the third volume in the series of diaries will be well acquainted with the perils of trying to follow Radio Lancashire when crossing the Pennines. Suffice it to say that this occasion was no more successful than the last. Anyhow through the wonders of modern technology, i.e. the Internet, and the BBC's Match of The Day 2 programme here follows a brief resume of what transpired.

Last week's home fixture with Watford saw an explosive opening with both sides scoring in the opening minutes. For the second week in succession we had the same scenario. Once again, the opposition raced into an early leaded to be quickly pegged back by a Clarets equaliser.

After a bright opening the hosts are ahead on four minutes with a 25-yard screamer from Jean Michael Seri that the recalled Joe Hart can only wave goodbye to. Not the opening we would have wished for after Thursday's hard night in Athens. Still we are nothing if not battlers and are back on level terms in the tenth minute. A break down the right sees Aaron Lennon lay the ball across the penalty area. Chris Wood and Jeff Hendrick are up in support, and the former leaves it to the latter. Hendrick attempts an unsuccessful audacious right foot shot through the legs of a defender. Fortuitously it rebounds to him and this time he fires left footer into the home goal.

A big blow for an already overstretched squad as Johann Berg Gudmundsson (JBG) lasts no more than 19 minutes before succumbing to what appears to be a hamstring injury. With our current lack of creativity JBG is a player we can ill afford to lose.

The game continues at a cracking pace and there are chances being created by both sides. Inevitably there are going to be more goals and there's a spate of them with three coming in a five-minute spell as half time approaches. The first arrives for the Cottagers courtesy of

Aleksandar Mitrovic who enjoys a free header to score from a well-worked set piece corner. If that wasn't bad enough, he repeats the trick two minutes later with another fine headed goal. 3-1 down and it's looking ominous, but before the break we have a lifeline. James Tarkowski pulls one back firing home from close range following a knock back from a Charlie Taylor corner.

With just the one goal deficit and an open game could we still salvage something from the wreckage? Unfortunately, not. The second half once again sees Fulham's adventurous attacking style creating a number of chances, thwarted on many occasions by Hart's fine goalkeeping. We are somehow still alive in the game as it draws to a close but on 83 minutes all hope is gone. Mitrovic is denied his hat-trick as his shot hits the post, but the rebound falls to Andre Schurrle who takes a touch before despatching it past Hart.

It's the first points of the season for newly promoted Fulham, and a blank day again for the Clarets. What has happened to last season's rock-solid defence. Ten goals have been conceded in the last three games and in truth it could have been many more. When the opposition is allowed 25 attempts on goal, 12 of which were on target, the result is inevitable. We are looking jaded and bereft of creativity and we are not yet through August with still a further Europa League game to come. Hot on the heel of this comes the daunting prospect of a home game with Manchester United, before we reach the respite of an international break.

Fulham have been very active in the summer transfer window bringing in 12 players with an estimated spend of £100m. Contrast that to our three signings, one of whom has been a goalkeeper who would not have been a priority but for the serious injury crisis. The squad is already stretched to breaking point, and now we have the added concern over the potential loss of JBG. There is still no sign of a return to action of Robbie Brady and Steven Defour, and Matej Vydra was not considered ready for the bench at Fulham. At the moment it's fair to say that things don't look too great!

Result – Fulham (Seri 4, Mitrovic 36,38, Schurrle 83) 4 – 2 (Hendrick 10, Tarkowski 41) Burnley

Burnley Team

Hart, Lowton, Mee, Tarkowski, Ward (Barnes 66), Gudmundsson (Taylor 19), Hendrick, Cork, Westwood, Lennon, Wood (Vokes 66)

Subs Not Used – Heaton, Bardsley, Long, Gibson

Fulham Team

Bettinelli, Fosu-Mensah, Odoi, Le Marchand, Bryan (Chambers 72), Seri, McDonald, Cairney (Zambo Anguissa 78), Schurrle (R Sessegnon 89), Mitrovic, Vietto

Subs Not Used – Johansen, Christie, Fabri, Kamara

Attendance – 23,438

Season To Date – Played 3, Won 0, Drawn 1, Lost 2, Goals For 3, Goals Against 7, Points 1

League Position after Game 3 – 18th

It's Thursday 30th and a mammoth month of football for Burnley is drawing to a close, but not before one almighty challenge. Can the Clarets overhaul a two-goal deficit cruelly conceded last week in Athens, or will the European adventure be at an end?

In view of what reportedly happened in Greece, I must confess to feeling somewhat aggrieved and antagonistic towards our visitors. The intervention by the Olympiakos owner in the half time break during which he visited the match officials' room, and a subsequent second half performance by the referee which included a sending off and a penalty against us, have left a sour taste in the mouth. Further allegations of intimidation of the officials by the Olympiakos players and coaching staff in the tunnel have also cast a dark shadow over that first leg tie. I have a feeling that God or somebody owes us for that, and hopefully tonight is the time to set that right.

It's a mountain to climb to overcome a two-goal deficit against experienced and cynical opposition, but defying the odds is the name of the game for Burnley FC. One thing for sure is the need to score first and preferably early to give us a chance. The away goal gleaned from the first game may yet turn out to be invaluable. An away goal for the Greeks means its curtains! As they say it's never over till the fat lady sings, at this point she's getting ready but only warming up. Into battle!

Europa League Qualifying Play-Off Round, 2nd Leg - Thursday 30th August, 19.45 – Burnley v Olympiakos

Buoyed by a lovely day walking in the Yorkshire Dales, a 7.2-mile circuit from Hetton rounded off with a welcome, if somewhat expensive pint of Hetton Pale Ale at the Angel Inn, Hetton, has set me up for this mighty challenge.

Whilst appreciating that the squad has had a bit of a battering of a late with two matches per week and long-distance travelling, my preference would have been to 'go for it' in this game and name a full-strength line-up. Although we have a testing home fixture looming on Sunday versus Manchester United there is an international break following and a chance to rest some weary limbs. Well you might think so but Stephen Ward, Kevin Long and Jeff Hendrick are called into the Irish squad, Sam Vokes for Wales and James Tarkowski for England. Jonathan Walters would have been the fourth Irishman called up but was transferred out on the last day of the EFL transfer window on a loan till January to Championship club Ipswich Town.

Clearly Sean Dyche didn't share my thoughts and once again went for what has generally been regarded as the Europa League side. Tom Heaton was back in goal, the only surviving defender from Fulham was Ben Mee and that probably only because Ben Gibson was suspended following his sending off in the 1st leg. In midfield Jack Cork was rested and the central pairing were Jeff Hendrick and Ashley Westwood. Aaron Lennon took the right flank, and a rarity for the Clarets a youngster propelled into first team action on the left. Dwight McNeil at just 18 years of age gets his chance due to injury to Johann Berg Gudmundsson. Two strikers tonight in Ashley Barnes and Sam Vokes as we look to claw back the deficit. All the 'big guns' are on the bench ready to take up the challenge if there's a sniff of saving the tie.

A rather disappointing attendance with only a few hundred excitable and noisily aggressive Greek fans making the trip. There are some big gaps in the home stands also, perhaps not surprising as the match is being televised live on BT Sport. It's a lovely evening and the crowd are certainly up for it.

It's a rather nervy start from the Clarets with a number of seriously misplaced passes. In contrast our visitors have started brightly and are clearly looking for an early goal to kill off the tie. However, we weather the storm and as the half rolls on start to find some rhythm and create some chances. Debutant McNeil after almost calamitously losing the ball recovers his calm and is beginning to significantly affect the game.

He's a tall lad with a silky style, deceptively fast and with a good left foot. It's not long before he finds an exquisite cross to pick out Sam Vokes whose header from close range should find the net but goes wide. Another headed chance from a McNeil right wing corner this time is over the top from Big Sam.

There's another great chance as a fine ball down the left sees Vokes clear, his low pull back to Barnes has our man at full stretch poking the ball agonisingly wide of the post. We are dominating now and with decent finishing would have overturned the deficit. It's a tremendous team effort and the desire is clear for all to see.

Then as a timely reminder a couple of chances for the visitors just ahead of the break as Daniel Podence fires firstly into the side netting and shortly after over the top. It's half time and all square, but it could have been so different.

The second half commences in similar fashion with the Clarets banging on the door. On 47 minutes a lovely move sees Barnes tee up Vokes to the left of goal and outside the box. It's definitely not Big Sam's day as he curls a superb effort with his right foot that leaves the keeper helpless and rebounds from the post. How cruel! A well worked free kick then sees Hendrick set up Barnes but his shot is blocked and scuffed away. After 65 minutes 'Basher' who has given everything makes way for debutant summer signing Matej Vydra. Entering the last 15 minutes it's time to gamble everything and with a last throw of the dice on come Jack Cork, and Chris Wood for Lennon and young McNeil. A standing ovation for a budding talent of whom I'm sure we will be seeing a lot more.

It's gung-ho attacking now and predictably we are leaving huge gaps at the back, giving opportunities to the Greeks on the quick counter. From one such foray Cork is dispossessed and suddenly we are outnumbered. The ball finds its way to Podence to the left of goal who smartly turns his marker Kevin Long and smashes right footed into the roof of the net. That's it, the game is up. How bravely we have fought and how undeserved would be a defeat. Thankfully that's not to be as within three minutes we level from an almighty goalmouth scramble following a corner. I always think it is important for any new striker at a club to quickly get his name on the scoresheet. Fortunately for Vydra that is just what he has done as he bundles the ball in from almost on the goal line. Perhaps not the prettiest goal but not a bad opener for his account coming in a European tie.

Sadly, there's no time for us to come up with the miracle and our European adventure is at an end. There's been no intimidating of referees at Burnley, that's not the way we do things. Every team member has given his all in a thrilling full-blooded display that deserved better than what it got. The team and manager leave the field to a standing ovation, and thoroughly deserved it was.

Our form so far this season has been rather lacklustre, but this was more like our old selves. Hopefully we can take from this game some self-belief and confidence that will get our Premier League season up and running. Watching from the stands was under fire Jose Mourinho, manager of our next opponents Manchester United. That performance should have given him something to think about over the next couple of days

Result –Burnley (Vydra 86) 1 – 1 (Podence 83) Olympiakos

Burnley Team

Hart, Bardsley, Long, Mee, Taylor, Lennon (Cork 75), Westwood, Hendrick, McNeil (Wood 75), Barnes (Vydra 65), Vokes

Subs Not Used – Hart, Lowton, Ward, Tarkowski

Olympiakos Team

Gianniotis, Elabdellouai, Miranda, Vukovic, Tsimikas, Camara, Bouchalakis, Christodolopous, Fortounis (Torosidis 88), Castelo Podence (Cisse 90+4), Guerrero (Hassan Mahgoub 72)

Subs Not Used – Choutesiotis, Natcho, Fetfatzidis, Ansarifard

Attendance – 15,234

A new month and literally a new chapter. August had proved to be a mammoth task for not only Burnley FC but also for myself. The review of the month had run to a staggering 11,000+ words, and that was without counting the additional contribution of the Athens blog by the 'Wandering Weirs'. It's fair to say that August on the playing front had not proved to be particularly successful, particularly with respect to Premier League form. Could the improved performance witnessed against Olympiakos be carried through to produce a morale lifting result against Manchester United?

Game 4 - Sunday 2nd September 16.00 – Burnley v Manchester United

It's been a poor start to the season for last season's Premier League runners-up. One win in the first fixture followed by successive defeats in the following two has put some early season pressure on Jose Mourinho, who is becoming progressively more irritable. There is without doubt some unease between manager, players and directors at Old Trafford, which is leaving 'The Special One' looking decidedly vulnerable. Some suggestions are that a loss at Burnley may well signal the end for him. I can't say I feel any sympathy for the man, particularly after his harsh treatment of Ashley Barnes during his tenure at Chelsea.

Would we be able to inflict that defeat on the stuttering 'Red Devils'? The answer was I'm afraid, definitely not. It was once again a classic example of a Premier League mismatch. The 'haves' proving once again to be the masters of the 'have-nots'. It's days like these that make you question if it's worth a place in the top league when quite clearly, we are unable if the 'elite' teams play to anything like their potential, to compete with them.

On a lovely warm September day, manager Sean Dyche once again rotated the squad. Joe Hart returned in goal, and James Tarkowski in central defence. In midfield Jack Cork was recalled and youngster Dwight McNeil retained his place, a big leap forward for the young man. Both strikers Ashley Barnes and Sam Vokes dropped to the bench with Chris Wood playing as lone striker with Jeff Hendrick in his customary role just behind.

United with an abundance of riches were able to field Romelu Lukaku up front flanked by Alexis Sanchez and Jesse Lingard. In midfield were the likes of Paul Pogba, Mario Fellaini, Nemanja Matic. Such is there strength in depth that they could afford to leave on the bench, Marcus Rashford, Anthony Martial and new signing the Brazilian, Fred.

From the off it was apparent that rumours of the Reds demise were somewhat premature as they quickly took the game by the scruff of the neck. As they stroked the ball around effortlessly, we were left to, on the rare occasions that we had it, punt it forward hopefully in the direction of Wood. Now this I have to say is a rather meaningless exercise, 'Woody' has neither the ability to win it in the air, or the strength to hold the ball till help arrives. This inevitably results in wave after wave attacks coming at us with predictable consequences.

The first of these consequences duly arrived on 27 minutes as a chipped cross in from the left by Sanchez is easily headed home by 'Raging Bull' Lukaku. Big questions here about the central defenders and goalkeeper. My personal feeling was that Joe Hart could have claimed the ball or done more to obstruct a free header from close range. Still perhaps that's a bit over critical as he was keeping us in the game as the Reds attacked at will. The one-way action continued towards our goal and just as I was hoping to reach the sanctuary of half time, the next killer blow.

On 44 minutes goal number two arrives – what a bad time to concede (is there ever a good one?). Not only that but a rather fortunate strike this time from our friend Mr Lukaku who by now is thoroughly enjoying himself. With the sort of luck that consistently seems to defy us he found the ball at his feet following a series of deflections and from close range fired home.

Half time 0-2 down and to be honest, little hope of a comeback so overwhelmingly were we being outplayed. My main concern now was whether we would be able to keep the score down and avoid a confidence draining drubbing.

The second half showed a slight improvement in that we did force David De Gea in the United goal into one or two saves, after a first period in which he could probably have slung a hammock between the posts. However, the more likely team to score always seemed to be the visitors. Lukaku should have had a hat-trick as he gave Ben Mee a terrible second half runaround. Hart continued to perform heroics in goal, even saving a penalty from the arrogant clown Pogba.

The penalty, an extremely soft one in my opinion had been won by substitute Marcus Rashford. What an interesting ten minutes he had! Coming on in the 61st minute and departing again on the 71st minute, red-carded for a head butt on Phil Bardsley. Silly boy!

At this point Vokes had already replaced Hendrick and with a man advantage we decided to throw on Barnes for McNeil who had once again been a shining light for the Clarets. Without doubt there is a player in there. On 84 minutes, again in my opinion far too late, we introduced Matej Vydra, but all to no avail. To be fair the one-man advantage didn't appear to be an advantage at all, and we never seriously looked like getting anything from this game.

That's four Premier League games gone and only the one point to show for them. A return that sees us second bottom sitting just above a pointless West Ham United. Thankfully there's now a two-week break for international fixtures. Hopefully this will give us time to reflect and evaluate what are the problems whilst additionally giving time to get some key players near to match fitness. At the moment the only way is up, almost!

Result – Burnley 0 – 2 (Lukaku 27,44) Manchester United

Burnley Team

Hart, Bardsley, Mee, Tarkowski, Taylor, McNeil (Barnes 80), Hendrick (Vokes 58), Cork, Westwood, Lennon, Wood (Vydra 84)

Subs Not Used – Heaton, Lowton, Ward, Long

Manchester United Team

De Gea, Valencia, Smalling, Lindelof, Shaw, Fellaini, Matic, Pogba (Bailly 90+2), Lingard (Herrera 76), Lukaku, Sanchez (Rashford 61)

Subs Not Used – Grant, Young, Fred, Martial

Attendance – 21,525

Season To Date – Played 4, Won 0, Drawn 1, Lost 3, Goals For 3, Goals Against 9, Points 1

League Position after Game 4 – 19th

Tuesday 4th September and a chance to expunge Sunday's disappointing performance from the memory banks as Tuesday Dotcom walks re-start. This week's walk is from Clough Head Information Centre, Grane Road, Haslingden and is a new route for me taking in Hoddlesden.

If I thought it was going to be a chance to forget the United game, I was quickly proved wrong. First job on the agenda before leaving the car park was the settlement of the wager from last season between Preston North End fan, Jim (Skipper of the Yard) and myself. This is an ongoing annual event whereby I back Burnley and PNE to be in different divisions come the end of the season, whilst Jim favours them to be in the same. It's a tad optimistic of him to think that PNE will make the Premier League so invariably he is reckoning on a Burnley relegation.

Anyway, the score currently stands at 2-1 in my favour and the recipient of this year's winnings will be Pendleside Hospice. Needless to say, after our stuttering start to the current campaign he is fancying his chances of levelling the scores. Although it was pointed out to him that PNE have hardly set the world alight in the Championship so far and are nearer the bottom than the top! This quietened him for a short period before he came up with a further suggestion. He advised me to invest the money on a treble with the bookmakers, taking Cardiff City, Huddersfield Town and Burnley to make the drop! Cheeky Bugger!

The weekend, blank of any meaningful football action, gives me the opportunity to reflect on a disappointing start to the 2018/19 campaign. The phrase 'missed opportunity' is one that comes readily to mine and other fans minds. I have a niggling feeling that the failure to add additional bodies and strengthen during the summer transfer window may ultimately prove costly.

Coming off the back of two successful Premier League seasons one would assume there must have been cash in the bank to fund some serious transfer action. If we add in the potential of playing European football, we were probably as attractive a proposition as we were ever going to be to attract potential signings. However, for whatever reasons it didn't happen.

The consequences are that now we have to get through to January with the squad that we have. Injuries already to Steven Defour, Robbie Brady, and Johann Berg Gudmundsson are seriously impacting on our creativity. The addition of a further winger and centre midfielder would undoubtedly have gone some way to addressing this problem.

The fact is that whilst we didn't like the prices being quoted in the summer, they are highly likely to be more expensive come the January window. Selling clubs who are reluctant to part with players will realise that they have us 'over a barrel'. Factor into the equation the fact that we can no longer offer European football, are possibly in a relegation dogfight with significant wage drops if this happens, and we don't then appear to have the same allure.

Hopefully, the injury situation will ease over the coming weeks and with it an upturn in fortunes on the pitch. Coming up soon are what would be classed as 'easier' games with trips to Wolverhampton Wanderers and Cardiff City, and home games with Bournemouth and Huddersfield Town. It is imperative that we get a decent return from these fixtures before the stiffer challenges that lie ahead.

On Monday 10th September I had the pleasure of a conducted tour of Burnley FC's Barnfield Training Centre (Gawthorpe to us old-timers). The visit, arranged by Burnley Civic Society, was a rare opportunity to get a glimpse behind the scenes of our new state of the art training facility. The whole set up is a massive improvement on the rather run-down facilities previously on offer and the club can be rightfully proud of it's now Premier League training complex.

Meticulous planning has gone into the academy, medical, catering and gymnasium amenities. No expense has been spared to provide a modern comfortable environment that is a major feature in a modern-day player's preparation. Clearly the management, coaching staff and players spend much more time here than at Turf Moor which is only a one day a week venue. Clearly evident throughout the main complex are the motivational message boards. These are designed to extract that extra bit of effort that may just give that little advantage when it is needed.

Many thanks to 'Sherpa' Ed Walton for his kind invitation, and to Burnley FC for allowing a very illuminating visit.

Ahead of the recommencement of Premier League action comes the news of the departure of a loyal servant of many years in the recent era. Michael Duff former player and more recently Under 18's and currently Under 23's coach, has left to take up the vacant manager's role at his former club Cheltenham Town. 'Duffer' has been at Burnley FC since his signing for a bargain £30,000 in July 2004, and in his time with the Clarets notched up over 300 first team appearances. Playing either at right back or centre back he also amassed 24 International caps for Northern Ireland. An extremely popular character with both his colleagues and the fans he will be missed, but we all wish him well in his new post. Who knows, we may one day see him back at Turf Moor in some capacity.

Also, ahead of the Wolverhampton Wanderers fixture, the club announced that Belgian midfielder Steven Defour had extended his contract. This will now take him through till the summer of 2020. Another very popular player with the fans, the highly talented playmaker has had more than his share of injury problems with us and we hope that these are now coming to an end.

Game 5 - Sunday 16th September 13.30 – Wolverhampton Wanderers v Burnley

Oh dear! If we thought the International break was going to be the catalyst for our revival, how wrong we were proved in this game. In fact, if anything we exit this fixture in a more forlorn state than that in which we entered it.

The wings appear to have sheared off and we seem to be into some sort of disastrous tailspin. From front to back, with one or two notable exceptions, the team is misfiring on all cylinders. We are being majorly overrun in games and appear lifeless and bereft of attacking ideas. We are changing personnel but the system, that was once infallible, is now looking hopelessly ineffective.

I've no intention of dwelling on this fixture as from a Burnley perspective there is precious little positive to say about it. Once again, we are saved from a heavy defeat by some superb goalkeeping from Joe Hart and some inept finishing by the Wanderers. Yet again we have allowed the opposition a mammoth 30 attempts at goal. How can we possibly hope to survive against that? Fortunately, our hosts were somewhat wayward in their finishing and only managed to get seven of those on target. Unfortunately, one of those efforts managed to find the back of the net.

Conversely, we could only muster seven attempts of which only two required the goalkeeper's attention. It's becoming increasingly obvious that the opposition only needs to score, and the game is lost. So woeful is our attacking threat that after five games we have managed only three goals, and two of them have come from centre back James Tarkowski!

Before the season started the general consensus was that we had a fairly comfortable opening fixture programme. Only one game in the first five was against a serious title contender (Manchester United), with two against teams thought likely to struggle (Southampton and Watford). The other two were against newly promoted teams (Fulham and Wolverhampton Wanderers). The feeling was that there were points to be had in most of these fixtures, and that would get the season up and running. Sadly, after this run, we have but a solitary point gleaned in the first game at Southampton.

Personally, I'm not so sure that early season is the best time to meet newly promoted teams. Invariably they are buoyed by the feelgood factor generated by their promotion and still have some momentum from a successful season. That has certainly been the case in our games with Fulham and now Wolverhampton Wanderers. However, on current form it is impossible to select opposition against whom we would come out on top.

Sean Dyche in his after-match comments believes that a 'fog' has descended on the squad. If that is so it feels like a real pea-souper! Something has to change and quickly if we are not to be cast adrift. The next three games are vital, and we must get some results to boost confidence.

The final kick in the teeth on a bleak Sunday came with West Ham United's 3-1 away victory at Everton. That lifted the previously pointless Hammers above us and dropped us to rock bottom. Enough said, I think.

Result – Wolverhampton Wanderers (Jimenez 61) 1 – 0 Burnley

Burnley Team

Hart, Bardsley, Mee, Tarkowski, Taylor, Gudmundsson, Hendrick (Westwood 79), Cork, Lennon, Barnes (Vydra 56), Vokes (Wood 70)

Subs Not Used – Heaton, Lowton, Ward, Long

Wolverhampton Wanderers Team

Patricio, Doherty, Bennett, Coady, Boly, Otto, Neves, Moutinho, Costa (Traore 66), Jota (Gibbs-White 88), Jimenez (Bonatini 76)

Subs Not Used – Ruddy, Hause, Saiss, Vinagre

Attendance – 30,406

At last after the gloom and doom of yesterday Monday 17th September brings a glimmer of hope. The Under-23's have a fixture against Bolton Wanderers and whose name is in the starting line-up? None other than our Belgian maestro Steven Defour! Praise the Lord and keep him from further harm. Expected to play 45 minutes he actually notches up 59 before being pulled. Hopefully, that is step one of his return completed and we will soon be seeing him gracing the Premier League again. Hallelujah!

On Tuesday 18th September we are featured in a lead article by Martin Samuels, the Daily Mail's Chief Sportswriter. With the rather risqué title 'Small clubs in the big league can't keep it up, just ask Burnley', he accurately assesses our current predicament.

Echoing one of Sean Dyche's favourite topics he goes on to explain the importance of 'margins', pointing out that last season 12 out of 14 Burnley victories were by a single goal. He quite rightly concludes; *"That's tight. No Manager, nor fan for that matter, is ever happy with a one-goal lead. "One goal isn't so much a cushion as a very itchy eiderdown. No-one is getting any rest."*

He goes on to point out that outside the top six 'elite' clubs, the tiniest alteration in fortune can be the difference between a season of relative glory and doom:

"Last year Burnley became used to victory in tight matches. By October 1 they had already recorded three league wins by single-goal margins and had drawn away at Tottenham and Liverpool against the odds. On day one of this season they drew 0-0 at Southampton.

A reasonable result it seems, but the type of game they would have found a way to win a year ago – as they did with an 81st minute winner from Sam Vokes.

Matches are often tighter than the scoreline looks. Going into the 83rd minute at Fulham this season, Burnley were 3-2 down, a goal away from equalising. Then Andre Schurrle scored for Fulham to make it seem as if Dyche's team had been slaughtered. Even Sunday's defeat at Wolves is a fixture that might have panned out differently 12 months ago. Wolves were different class and had a mighty 30 attempts at goal, but Burnley defended magnificently, Joe Hart was outstanding – without doubt he is in the top three English goalkeepers again – and, in similar circumstances we have seen them hang on.

A match at Manchester United in 2016 was certainly little different and Burnley got away with 0-0. Yet their X-factor is missing now.

The results are not coming, the pressure is growing. They are no longer confounders of expectation; they are plain old Burnley. And it's very hard to be Burnley, or any small club in the Premier League. The Championship is full of teams – from Swansea to Middlesbrough – that were bitten by reality.

Before the season began, Dyche surprised people by referring to his club as 'the minnow of the Premier League'. How could he say that when Burnley were seventh and in Europe? Yet Dyche knew.

With the spending power of others – and not just those inside the top six – Burnley cannot outrun their circumstances forever. This does not mean their current predicament is permanent, or that they will be relegated – there are worse teams in the league than Burnley – more that this early crisis is no great shock.

Bournemouth visit Turf Moor on Saturday on a high.

They were behind at West Ham, behind against Everton, but came back to take four points from those games. And now they have momentum, which Burnley must steal, even by the smallest margin.

That is how it is, at the bottom. Nothing is guaranteed for six months, let alone permanent."

How very true! Let's hope he's right in his statement that there are worse teams than us in the league.

For those of you who like to keep abreast of the walking adventures, we managed to get in a couple in the week leading up to the Bournemouth fixture. The first a Dotcom walk on Tuesday 18th was a 7.4 miler from Chipping. Dotcom leader Bob Clare was absent for this one being otherwise engaged on a cruise in the Mediterranean. How the other half live!

Leadership duties for this one fell to a relative newcomer Tom Rice, which I have to say left me a little apprehensive. Tom's only previous foray into leadership had gone down in the annals of Dotcom walking history as he led the troops on a bog ridden, slurry mounded trek in the Trough of Bowland.

As we left Burnley at 9.15 for the rendezvous at Chipping, I have to say the omens didn't look good. There was heavy and persistent drizzle, the kind that soaks you to the skin. Nevertheless, an optimistic Mike McDevitt turned up in his shorts vowing that it was about to clear shortly. On arrival at the meeting point, somewhat early due to the lack of traffic, conditions had seriously worsened, to the point where we refused to leave the vehicle.

Undaunted, the Preston Mob decided the best solution to don waterproofs was to head for the nearby toilet facilities, which they promptly did en-masse. It's to be hoped nobody needed to use the now makeshift changing rooms for their original purpose as there was now no room!

At the appointed time a party of 21 clad against anything the elements could throw at them set off. Incredibly before we'd even left the village the monsoon ceased and despite a strong wind a very pleasant temperature led to a mass dis-robing. Despite the odd small shower, a very pleasant and scenic round of the Bowland countryside ensued. Lunch was taken on a sheltered hillside in warm sun with magnificent views.

On arrival back in Chipping a straw poll quickly established a pub call was necessary. (After all this is the primary objective of the walk) A select band consisting of the full Burnley contingent and some Prestonian beer connoisseurs decamped to the Tillotsons Arms. A pleasant surprise for the landlady who suddenly found her lounge previously seriously under occupied, now full of tired but happy quaffers. Pints of Moorhouse's White Witch were the order of the day (we like to support a local business), and splendid they were too. Another good pub recommendation from the gang.

Leader for the day Tom could relax in the knowledge that today's outing had passed without incident and there would be no tales to tell our sea faring commander on his return.

Thursday's Burnley Contingent walk was scheduled for a Dales trip. The plan was to start at Ribblehead viaduct and take an approximate seven-mile circuit via Chapel-le-Dale. However, the weather forecast was decidedly unpromising and by 6.00pm Wednesday the decision was taken to abandon the idea and go for a more local alternative.

Ed 'Sherpa' Walton as usual came up with the goods and in surprisingly warm and pleasant weather 11 hardy souls departed Towneley Rotunda car park. The route took us up through Cliviger Laithe and Hurstwood then across rough terrain towards Causeway House. The rain scheduled for 2.00pm. duly arrived at 1.00pm so lunch was taken hastily in the shelter of some trees before donning full waterproof gear.

After lunch we crossed the Long Causeway and headed down towards Cliviger in steadily worsening weather. The main road was crossed at Bridge End and the track followed up to just below the 'Fireman's Helmet' hill before coming back to meet the main road at Walk Mill. The final stretch back through the fields to the car park was taken at a brisk pace as the heavens now opened. All made it back safe and soaked, especially the Wandering Weirs (WWs)who foolishly had opted for shorts! Still, undeterred the gang headed for the usual haunt, the Rifle Volunteer. Mine was a pint of Reedley Hallows, Filly Close Blonde whilst the WWs, currently on day 18 of an alcohol-free stint, enjoyed an orange J20 and soda! What a way to round off the day, wet through outside and a non-alcoholic sugar overload inside. Rather them than me!

Game 6 - Saturday 22nd September 15.00 – Burnley v Bournemouth

Hooray! It's back to Saturday football and at a sensible time. The first opportunity for pre-match pints at the Talbot this season and the feeling that things are returning to normal. Hopefully that will be reflected on the pitch as well as at the pub.

Today's opposition Bournemouth are enjoying a good start to their season and come to Turf Moor lying in fifth position. Their opening five fixtures have yielded 10 points from 3 wins, a draw and a solitary defeat. They are in good form but a feature of Eddie Howe's team, their Achilles heel, is their tendency to leak goals against. Whilst not as bad as we are so far, they have conceded up to press, seven times. Perhaps some hope for us there.

This week there have been more positive noises coming from Turf Moor. Sean Dyche feels we have lost our DNA! That sounds a bit drastic but is really a rallying cry to get back to doing the things which we normally do. What with being in a fog, not being able to see through the noise and now losing our DNA things have certainly conspired against us so far. Will today be the day the tide turns?

The answer to that come almost five o'clock was an emphatic yes. The fog has been blown away and we can see clearly now (Apologies for that – I slipped into one of John W's song title insertions)

The team news sees Matt Lowton recalled at right back, and a full debut for summer signing Matej Vydra. Sam Vokes leads the line presumably for Vydra to benefit from Sam's ability to win balls that are knocked up to him.

On a fine pleasant autumnal day, we are quickly out of the blocks and its apparent that we have been instructed to start the game at a high tempo. We have been guilty of some sluggish starts this season and the concession of early goals can quickly put us on the back foot. The game settles after about 10 minutes into a fairly even contest with both sides probing the respective defences. With Johann Berg Gudmundsson (JBG) looking much more like his old self, and Aaron Lennon also looking more positive we are certainly posing a bit more threat than has been the case.

With half time approaching and the score deadlocked we suddenly grab the lead. The plan of feeding off Vokes' aerial ability works fine as a cross into the box is headed back to find Ashley Westwood. He goes for goal, but it's blocked, a second attempt suffers the same fate but rebounds into the path of Vydra who needs no second invitation. Last year's Championship top scorer certainly knows where the net is, and we have the precious lead.

Better still just two minutes later JBG repeats the performance this time with a perfect cross that sails over two defenders to land at the feet of Lennon at the back post. Our diminutive winger wastes no time in sliding it delicately home and we have a two-goal cushion.

I remark to John W that we now need to negotiate the next few minutes and get in at half time two goals up. Without too much concern this is duly achieved, and we can head for a comfort break with some comfort!

Clearly our high-flying visitors are going to be rattled by that two-goal burst and we can expect them to come out for the second half in determined fashion. That's exactly what happens as the visitors begin to dominate possession and push forward. However, on this occasion we are looking much more like our old defensive selves and the shape is excellent. The Cherries are being held at distance and forced into some long-range shooting.

Looking decidedly pacier on the break than previously this season, we pose sufficient threat to prevent them over committing men forward. Sean Dyche strengthens his hand in this respect with the judicious use of fresh legs up front. On 60 minutes Vydra gives way to Chris Wood and shortly after Vokes is replaced by Ashley Barnes.

A good save by Joe Hart from the impressive David Brooks keeps the two-goal lead intact. That should serve as a timely reminder to watching England manager Gareth Southgate that perhaps Hart's international days are not yet over.

As we enter the last 10 minutes a third goal for the Clarets and the feeling of relief is palpable. Good work down the left by Lennon and Charlie Taylor sees the winger get to the by-line and cross. As the ball drops it is volleyed goal bound by JBG only to see it rebound off the post. However, there to pick up the pieces is Barnes who simply taps home.

Four minutes later the icing is on the cake as we quickly break from defence. Westwood starts the break and finds Lennon this time moving at pace down the right. Spotting Barnes' arrival on the edge of the box his perfect pass is neatly despatched into the corner of the net.

Thank God! The first win of the season and a climb out of the relegation spots. Let's hope that is the catalyst to spark our misfiring season! It was without doubt a much-improved performance and the score line, if somewhat flattering, is just what we needed.

Result – Burnley (Vydra 39, Lennon 41, Barnes 84,88) 4 – 0 Bournemouth

Burnley Team

Hart, Lowton, Mee, Tarkowski, Taylor, Gudmundsson, Westwood, Cork, Lennon, Vydra (Wood 60), Vokes (Barnes 68)

Subs Not Used – Heaton, Bardsley, Long, Hendrick, McNeil

Bournemouth Team

Begovic, Smith (Defoe 78), S.Cook, Ake, Rico (Francis 46), Brooks, Lerma, Surman, Fraser, Wilson (Stanislas 68), King

Attendance – 18,636

Season To Date – Played 6, Won 1, Drawn 1, Lost 4, Goals For 7, Goals Against 10, Points 4

League Position after Game 6 – 16th

Tuesday's Dotcom walk was an uneventful stroll from Ribchester in very pleasant and often sunny weather conditions. A bit of a novelty is an uneventful walk when it is led by Nigel 'the hex' who usually manages to contrive a walk abandonment or broken bones. However, on this occasion no such traumas and all topped off with a pint of Robinson's Dizzy Blonde at the Ribchester Arms. The Preston North End contingent were in sombre mood as two successive league defeats had sunk them to the bottom of the Championship table. Tonight, both ourselves and North End are in EFL Caraboa Cup action, we at League 1 Burton Albion whilst they host Middlesbrough.

EFL Caraboa Cup 3rd Round - Tuesday 25th September 19.45 – Burton Albion v Burnley

A later than usual entry into the competition this time for the Clarets owing to our involvement in the Europa League. I think it's fair to say that of late we have had a pretty abysmal run in the cup competitions, so a chance here to put that right and make some progress on the road to Wembley.

The team shows six changes from Saturday's starting eleven against Bournemouth. Out go Joe Hart, James Tarkowski, Charlie Taylor, Jack Cork, Aaron Lennon and Sam Vokes. There is a long-awaited return for Steven Defour, and also coming in are Tom Heaton, Kevin Long, Stephen Ward, Dwight McNeil and Chris Wood. That still looks a pretty strong line-up and should be enough to see off a mid-table League 1 outfit.

It's a good start by the Clarets as we look to seize the early initiative. However, no quick goal is forthcoming and after a while the game starts to even up. By all accounts Defour is playing well on his comeback, and we are unfortunate as he threads in Chris Wood whose effort is chalked off as he is ruled offside.

It's not long before Kevin Long joins the party also having his 'goal' disallowed for offside. However, he's not going to be denied for long as on 40 minutes he powers home a towering header from a Johann Berg Gudmundsson corner. That's more like it and we leave the field at half-time a goal to the good. At this point I'm feeling pretty confident that we are going to go on and win this one comfortably.

I should by now know better than that! We start the second half as the first, well on top. But on 62 minutes we are rocked back by an equaliser as Liam Boyce's shot squirms through Heaton's grasp. That was a bad time to concede as we had taken control of the game which means we now have to regain some momentum.

To be fair that is just what we do. Ashley Barnes replaces Matej Vydra, and within minutes has beaten the keeper but hit the post. Defour, who for 73 minutes has not lost the ball once, makes way for Jeff Hendrick as we continue our pursuit of a winner. Barnes sets up Ashley Westwood with a good opportunity, but he fires over the bar.

Then on 83 minutes the 'sucker punch' as Boyce plays a perfectly weighted ball for Joe Allen to poke home. From then on, it's the hosts who look the more likely scorers as our challenge fizzles out.

How disappointing, what a catastrophe. At the start of August, we were chasing success in four competitions but by the end of September we are down to two, one of which looks at this early stage as being something of a relegation battle. It's another opportunity against lower league opposition missed. A game we could and should have won comfortably has once more drifted away. We have now lost to Burton Albion, Accrington Stanley, Lincoln City and Port Vale in the past four seasons in the League and FA Cups. That really is not good enough.

Once more I am hearing fans saying that they are not bothered that we are out of this competition and that we can put all our efforts into the primary objective, Premier League survival. I'm not so sure about that, wins breed confidence and a good cup run can lift the team. Sean Dyche seems to think that the poor cup form is down to the player's mindset. Well if that's the case it shouldn't be! They are supposed to be professionals and are being well paid to do a job. I think it's not so much a lack of effort but rather on too many occasions we are just not good enough!

Once again, we are dumped into the recycle bin at an early stage. Some small consolation is that Manchester United suffer the same fate losing a penalty shoot-out at home to Championship Derby County at Old Trafford. Our old friends at North End fail in similar fashion as they too lose on penalties to Middlesbrough.

Game 7 - Sunday 30th September 16.00 – Cardiff City v Burnley

Yet again it's a strange kick off time, 4.00pm on a Sunday, to accommodate our lords and masters, Sky TV. The team news reveals a reversion from midweek back to last Saturday's successful starting line-up. Steven Defour continues his rehabilitation with a place on the bench, this game likely to be a bit too physical for his liking.

Cardiff have had a difficult start to their Premier League campaign following last season's promotion. Currently they sit second bottom of the table, winless and three points behind us. We can today expect a highly physical encounter as backed by a vociferous crowd they will surely throw the kitchen sink at us. We have to be able to withstand the battering and counter with superior guile. One thing's for sure we will be the first game on Match of the Day 2 tonight. However, by the same token we will also be the last. It's the only Premier League game being played today!

As anticipated as I tune into Radio Lancashire's commentary it appears, we are having a rocky start as we are pushed back in the early exchanges. Twenty minutes have passed, and the commentators are reporting we haven't got going yet. This is echoed by BBC Sports App pundit Kevin Kilbane who is singularly unimpressed. There's bad news on 27 minutes as James Tarkowski is forced off with what they are indicating is a shoulder injury (later reports on the BBC suggest a groin injury) and is replaced by Kevin Long.

Cardiff City as expected are playing a very direct style launching high balls into our box at every opportunity including many prodigious long throw-ins from Sean Morrison. We are trying to play but clearly without much success.

Thirty minutes have passed and neither side have registered a shot on target, although the Bluebirds Josh Murphy has struck the outside of the post. The general consensus is that the game is dire in the extreme. Cardiff are pressing but poor whilst we are offering nothing. The BBC commentators reckon that Joe Hart has seen more of the ball than our two forwards Sam Vokes and Matej Vydra.

As half time approaches, we are hanging on, and there's a let off as Vydra heads one off his own goal line and over the bar. It's a dreadful first half performance and it has to be said not for the first time this season. Once again, we have contrived to allow very average opposition no less than 10 shots at goal whilst managing only one in reply. Fortunately for us only two of the 10 have been on target. Disaster is lurking!

With this in mind, and also because my tea is nearly ready, I decide to ditch the Radio Lancashire commentary. My phone is set for goal alerts and it's not long into the second period before it pings. Fearing the worst, I am forced to look but am mightily relieved to see we have the lead thanks to one of the rarest of rare things, a headed goal by Johann Berg Gudmundsson (JBG).

Foolishly I re-don the radio headphones only to hear on 59 minutes that the lead is short lived as the dangerous Murphy restores parity. That's it for the radio it is clearly a bloody jinx, and I will rely on the phone. As I tackle my slow roasted Gammon shank (and very nice it was too) a number of pings emanate from the device. One is from old pal John G with a very succinct WhatsApp message which reads; *Sam.* From this I can only assume that Sam Vokes has once again given us the lead. This is rapidly confirmed by the BBC as they report a clever header by Vokes from a JBG assist.

There's no way I'm going to put that radio back on for the final 20 minutes so it's a case of hoping not to hear any more alerts for at least 25 minutes (allowing for added time). As I finish the washing up and conclude that time must be up, another ping. A look at the phone and an almighty outpouring of relief as it confirms a final score of Cardiff City 1-2 Burnley.

It was never going to be pretty. Pretty awful it certainly was but at the end of the day the result was what mattered. The three points lift us temporarily up the table to 12th Whilst we await the result of Monday's Bournemouth v Crystal Palace fixture. More importantly it opens up a five-point gap between ourselves and the bottom three, Huddersfield Town, Cardiff City and Newcastle United. With Huddersfield to come to Turf Moor next week hopefully a chance of three more points to repair the damage inflicted by the four defeats early in the season. Onwards and upwards!

Result – Cardiff City (Murphy 60) 1 – 2 (Berg Gudmundsson 51, Vokes 70) Burnley

Burnley Team

Hart, Lowton, Mee, Tarkowski (Long 27), Taylor, Gudmundsson, Westwood, Cork, Lennon, Vydra (Wood 72), Vokes

Subs Not Used – Heaton, Bardsley, Hendrick, Barnes, Defour

Cardiff City Team

Etheridge, Manga, Samba, Morrison, Cunningham, Camarasa, Arter, Ralls (Madine 79), Murphy, Paterson, Zohore (Ward 71)

Subs Not Used – Bennett, Richards, Reid, K Harris, Murphy

Attendance – 30,411

Season To Date – Played 7, Won 2, Drawn 1, Lost 4, Goals For 9, Goals Against 11, Points 7

League Position after Game 7 – 12th

Game 8 - Saturday 6th October 15.00 – Burnley v Huddersfield Town

This game unfortunately coincides with my annual pre-winter break in Madeira. I'm consequently only able to follow the action by website links and smartphone messages from friends back home. It's not a game I would have chosen to miss but the holiday had been booked for many months prior to the fixture list announcements for 2018/19.

As it transpires it was probably not too much of a miss as by all accounts the Clarets turned in once again a pretty dire performance. The points, or should it be point, are (is) shared as the Terriers come back with a second half equaliser to cancel out Sam Vokes' first half header. I suppose it's another point gained towards survival, but some would argue it's a precious two points dropped against a team likely to be in the relegation mix. Still it's seven points garnered from the last possible nine and in this league that's an achievement not to be sniffed at. The worrying aspect is the manner of performance and the fact that the next sequence of games coming up look decidedly tricky. In our current form the preferred opposition would not be Champions Manchester City away followed by Chelsea at home, but that's what we face.

The team showed just one change from last week's victory at Cardiff City. James Tarkowski injured in the game in Wales was sufficiently recovered to be selected but the surprise change was the inclusion of Ashley Barnes to partner Vokes up front in place of Matej Vydra. I suppose it shouldn't have come as a surprise really being as I had just selected Vydra in my Fantasy Football team and that's what usually happens when I bring in a player!

In the first half it was a good thing that Tarkowski had made the team as he rescued the side with crucial blocks on a couple of occasions after a very much 'out of sorts' Ben Mee had given the ball away. Vokes had a chance from an Ashley Westwood cross but could do no better than head straight at Town keeper Jonas Lossl. Still that miss was soon forgotten as on 20 minutes Big Sam gave us the lead heading home Johann Berg Gudmundsson's right wing cross.

That should have given us the impetus to go on and clinch a victory against a side coming into the game sitting bottom of the table and without a Premier League win so far this season. However, as on many occasions this time round it didn't, and once again we allowed the opposition to dominate possession. Thankfully the toothless Terriers certainly lacked bite and rarely troubled Joe Hart in the Burnley goal.

If the first half could be described as lacklustre then the second was for us even worse. Not once did we seriously threaten to add to our tally. Huddersfield continued to plug away, and it came as no real surprise when on 66 minutes they had a headed equaliser from the German defender Chris Schindler. From then on, the visitors continued to dominate play but without the quality to break down our stubborn defence. Eight minutes of added time were played following an injury to Schindler but predictably nobody could break the deadlock.

So, a point each from what from our perspective was a hugely disappointing performance. These two sides do seem to have an uncanny knack of bringing out the worst in each other. Last season's fixtures produced two goal less draws so I suppose at least this time there was a little more excitement.

For me in sunny Madeira it was time for wife Julie and myself to hit the bar for Happy Hour. It could have been made so much happier if we had gone on to win, but as they say, that's life!

Result – Burnley (Vokes 20) 1 – 1 (Schindler 66) Huddersfield Town

Burnley Team

Hart, Lowton, Mee, Tarkowski, Taylor, Gudmundsson, Westwood (Hendrick 73), Cork, Lennon, Barnes (Wood 61), Vokes (Vydra 90)

Subs Not Used – Heaton, Bardsley, Long, McNeil

Huddersfield Town Team

Lossl, Lowe (Hadergjonaj 86) Schindler, Zanka, Durm, van La Parra (Mounie 59), Billing, Hogg, Mooy, Pritchard, Depoitre (Mbenza 59)

Subs Not Used – Hamer, Stankovic, Kachunga, Diakhaby

Attendance – 20,533

Season To Date – Played 8, Won 2, Drawn 2, Lost 4, Goals For 10, Goals Against 12, Points 8

League Position after Game 8 – 12th

I can't quite put my finger on it but after only eight Premier League games, and of course the six European ties, this season has for me a rather uneasy feel about it. Something just doesn't seem right; the form is poor and the whole atmosphere seems flat. Usually what is a tightly knit and happy squad seems this time to be lacking the usual enthusiasm for a fight.

There are already rumours of not so much discontent but certainly unhappiness by one or two players. In newspaper articles both Tom Heaton and Jeff Hendrick have expressed concerns about losing their first team places. Of course, this is perfectly understandable but at the same time these guys must realise that Premier League football is about the squad not just the starting eleven. They will just have to be patient and bide their time whilst their opportunity comes.

Even manager Sean Dyche has expressed his disappointment that more players were not signed in the summer transfer window. He feels consequently that we are players short, and I don't think he meant just in stature. Going into the season and participating in four major competitions demanded a 'beefing up' of the squad to cope with the increased demand. However, for whatever reasons this did not materialise. I believe the club, albeit a little late, has recognised this failing and moves are afoot to rectify this situation by the creation of a new role of 'Director of Football'. To this end the recruitment process is already underway and hopefully somebody will be in position in good time for the opening of the next transfer window.

The injury situation has not helped the cause, Steven Defour and Robbie Brady who were both long term casualties from last season, were reported to be raring to go in July. By mid-October neither has played a single minute of Premier League football. This is a serious problem when both of our most creative players are side-lined for a significant period of the season. Surely knowing the seriousness of their injuries, attempts should have been made to cover their likely absence with a player of similar creativity.

On Tuesday 16th October there is some good news on both the above-mentioned players as the club reveal that both have successfully negotiated a full 90-minute work-out in a behind closed doors friendly against AFC Fylde. Hopefully this signals a return to first team action for both, although Defour would appear to be further down that road than Brady.

This good news is tempered by the revelation that left back Stephen Ward, a notable absentee on many occasions already this season, is to undergo knee surgery ruling him out for a number of weeks. A big miss is Ward not least for his attacking qualities and we hope that he can make a speedy recovery in time to play a major part in the battle.

I have recently been reading an illuminating and thought-provoking book by the historian Yuval Noah Harari. The book entitled 'Sapiens' is subtitled; 'A Brief History of Humankind'. In Chapter 12 headed The Law of Religion he goes on to outline the main religions and their impact on humanity throughout history.

Out of all these words, and I can tell you there are a bloody lot of them, I suddenly experience a moment of revelation. I am introduced to the principles of Buddhism and at once can see the sense of some of it.

The central figure of Buddhism is not a God but a human being, Siddhartha Gautama. Apparently, he was the heir to a small Himalayan Kingdom around 500 BC. He was deeply affected by the suffering evident all around him, and that people constantly suffered from anxiety, frustration and discontent. Now, being a Burnley fan, this certainly struck a chord!

He embarked on a six-year investigation of the cause of all this suffering travelling as a vagabond and listening to all sorts of gurus. At the end of it all he concluded that man's suffering was all down to cravings. The poor man craved to be rich, the rich man craved to be richer still, and so nobody could ever be truly content. His philosophy then became to banish from the mind all cravings. This was done by developing a set of meditation techniques that train the mind to experience reality as it is, without craving. Focus the mind on 'What am I experiencing now?' rather than on 'What would I rather be experiencing?'.

Without getting too deeply into it, when craving is replaced by a state of perfect contentment and serenity, you have reached Nirvana.

Inspired by this passage in the book I decided to share with my wife my new-found knowledge. However, I get the impression that after a few attempts to convince her, she is not as far down the road to spiritual enlightenment as I. In fact, she told me to "Bugger off and be a Buddhist then"!

I have to confess that a similar reaction ensued when I explained my findings to our group of Dotcom walkers as we took lunch at Scorton War Memorial. I have to say that my teachings were largely met with ridicule, and suggestions that Buddhists don't drink or have sex, neither of which I can confirm nor deny. Anyway, they'll be sorry when I turn up for a walk in my orange tunic and sandals and a look of perfect contentment on my face!

After last week's break for international games its back to the important stuff, Premier League action. I hope we are well and truly rested as I feel Saturday will see us chasing shadows and looking longingly at the ball. Yes, it's no lesser task than an away fixture at current Champions and unbeaten league leaders Manchester City. They have even rushed back into action following injury none other than their outstanding Belgian midfielder Kevin de Bruyne. They must be worried!

I think Saturday afternoon is going to be spent hiding behind the sofa and praying for five o'clock. I have laid in a supply of super strength Gin in order to numb the pain if events turn out as I fear they may.

Game 9 - Saturday 20th October 15.00 – Manchester City v Burnley

Well my pre-match forebodings were certainly well founded on this occasion. Another lovely autumnal day had me donning shorts and heading for the lawn mower ahead of kick-off. Hopefully that will be the last grass cutting this year but in the current spell of pleasant October weather I'm by no means certain of that.

Grass cut, and garden tidied it's time to catch up with the early team news, and as expected Steven Defour makes his long-awaited return to Premier League action. Unsurprisingly, we revert to a cautious 4-5-1 formation with Sam Vokes getting the lone striker role. Thankfully there's only a place on the bench for Kevin De Bruyne, but one look at the City line-up confirms that he is unlikely to be required. Included in their star studded XI are no lesser names than Sergio Aguero, David Silva, Benjamin Mendy, Leroy Sane and Riyad Mahrez to name but a few. Even Raheem Sterling, England's hero in the midweek victory in Spain has to settle for a watching brief from the bench.

It's certainly a lively start and there are good chances for both sides in the opening minutes. Our's coming from a Sam Vokes header guided over the top following a free kick resulting from a brutal studs up lunge by Vincent Kompany on Aaron Lennon. An offence deemed by many viewers to be a straight red card earns the City man only a yellow, and the unjust refereeing tone is once again set for the afternoon. The assault coming as early as the 35th second, could and should have handed the Clarets a handy advantage, but as is so often the case was not to be.

Vokes's miss is quickly followed at the other end by the usually lethal Aguero heading over with the goal beckoning. Jack Cork promptly follows Kompany into the referee's notebook as City pick up the pace.

On 15 minutes there's a fantastic save by Joe Hart, returning to his old stomping ground of many years to deny Aguero. However, he's not going to be thwarted for long and on 17 minutes he converts a David Silva cross from close range. Our difficult task suddenly got a good bit harder.

Our defence and midfield are so hard worked and starved of the ball that I note after 25 minutes that I've not heard a single mention of Defour. Is he actually playing? Just after the half hour Jeff Hendrick follows Cork into the referee's notebook and it's fair to say we are well and truly under the cosh! The movement and fluidity of the Champions attacking play is awesome and we are attempting to repel wave after wave of attacks.

We are battling doggedly and as they say, 'giving it a go'. There is a massive chance for Hendrick on 35 minutes, but his effort is blocked by John Stones. We are as usual in these games getting nothing from the referee. It's incredible that whenever a 'small club' comes up against one of the 'elite' every contentious decision favours the bigger club. Sean Dyche patrolling his technical area is livid!

On the stroke of half-time another great save by Hart denies David Silva's header and Aguero misses on the follow up. So, we are in at the break trailing but only by the single goal and the game is theoretically still alive.

Unfortunately, it's not for long as within two crazy minutes early in the second period, it is game over! And what a catastrophe of poor refereeing it is that kills off any remote chance we had.

As Sane enters the box slightly to the left of centre he theatrically hits the deck. Penalty claim the City players, dive claim the Clarets. The referee puts his whistle to his mouth to give one or the other. The Burnley players have all stopped awaiting the decision, meanwhile the ball trundles unattended towards the goal line and out of play. However, David Silva who had been off the pitch behind the goal line returns to the action putting himself in an offside position. Undeterred he crosses the ball which is now apparently over the line to his namesake Bernardo Silva who dispatches it into the net. Was it a penalty? Should Sane have been booked for a dive? We will never know now, but what is clear is that even if the ball was not out of play David Silva should have been given offside! Once again, we are the victims of injustice from the officials. Some criticism could be levelled at the defence and goalkeeper for not playing to the whistle, but it all seems horribly unfair.

Clearly upset by this non-decision we are at sixes-and-sevens and within two minutes Fernandinho has put the game massively out of reach firing home impressively from a partially cleared corner. It's now a case of trying to keep the score down and avoid a drubbing. City with the game won take the opportunity to give De Bruyne a half hour run out, which fortunately he is unable to mark with a goal.

However, further goals do arrive and very good one's at that as Mahrez on 83 and Sane on 90 minutes add the gloss to the victory.

A very good team are Manchester City and already looking probable Champions again. I'm sure that without the poor refereeing decisions they would have proved to have far too much for us. Having said that our task was difficult enough from the outset without the officials handing our illustrious opponents a helping hand. There's a saying in the game that the luck evens itself out over a season. In that case we are owed a very big slice of it. Can we have it next Sunday against Chelsea please!

Result – Manchester City (Aguero 17, B Silva 54, Fernandinho 56, Mahrez 83, Sane 90) 5 – 0 Burnley

Burnley Team

Hart, Lowton, Mee, Tarkowski, Taylor, Gudmundsson, Defour (Barnes 75), Cork, Hendrick, Lennon (Westwood 69), Vokes (Wood 69)

Subs Not Used – Heaton, Bardsley, Long, Vydra

Manchester City Team

Ederson, Stones, Laporte, Kompany, Mendy, Mahrez, Fernadhinho, B Silva (De Bruyne 58), D Silva (Foden 75), Sane, Aguerro (Jesus 66)

Subs Not Used – Muric, Zinchenko, Otamendi, Sterling

Attendance – 54,094

Season To Date – Played 9, Won 2, Drawn 2, Lost 5, Goals For 10, Goals Against 17, Points 8

League Position after Game 9 – 13th

For those who like to keep up with the walking programme the week following my Madeira vacation provided two corkers. First up was the Tuesday Dotcom walk from Grizedale Bridge, taking in Nicky Nook with a lunch stop at Scorton before returning via Grize Dale. A cold start quickly warming up to give a lovely warm pleasant day, and as previously mentioned a chance to inform my fellow walkers of my new-found Buddhist teachings. A great day out except for the lack of a pub stop. One was available in Scorton, The Priory, But I'm not sure that's a good name for a public house. However, this opportunity occurred at the mid-point of the walk and we are not great lovers of mid walk drinkies, preferring the reward at the end.

No such problem for the Thursday Burnley Contingent walk led by the 'Wandering Weirs'. This week was a hilly favourite starting at Todmorden Leisure Centre. Once again it was a cold start, for me woolly hat and mittens, for the sun worshipping Ian McKay – shorts! The steep climb out of the valley and on to Keelham Heights soon had clothing being shed as the sun shone through a cloudless sky. On for lunch at the Bride Stone Rocks and I can honestly say it's the first time I've been there when its not been either blowing a gale, or raining, or both.

Not today though, 17 intrepid walkers and three dogs enjoyed a scenic 7.5-mile walk enjoying the countryside of the North at its glorious best. After some confusion as to which pub to debrief at we headed for The Ram at Cliviger. The Rifle Volunteer and the Kettledrum in Burnley running the Ram a close second. A chance to sit in the beer garden and quaff a well-earned pint of Worsthorne Brewery's, Palomino, a fine ending to another great day. What's more an opportunity to sell a few copies of the recently released Premier League Diary Volume 4, 'From Pies to Paella', to my adoring readership. Perfect, a walk, good company, good beer, and money in the bank!

Tuesday 23rd October is the day of the annual Dotcom Preedy's Pendle challenge. Following co-leader Teresa Preedy's death last year this will be a particularly poignant walk. Husband Dave is taking the opportunity to scatter Teresa's ashes in all of her beloved places and Pendle Hill certainly features highly on that list. Let's hope the weather is kind and we have a bumper turn-out in honour of Teresa.

Well! That was the week that was! What started badly just got worse and worse. After a perfectly normal weekend getting over the trauma of the Manchester City defeat, I took to my bed at a perfectly respectable time on Sunday evening. Even more laudable in view of the fact that I was alcohol free for the day.

It didn't take long before I developed a nagging ache in the big toe area. From previous occurrences it didn't take long for me to self-diagnose a bout of oncoming gout. Now any of you who have ever suffered with this condition, and I'm sure there will be many, know that it can be very painful and persistent. A very disturbed night's sleep led to a difficult Monday and any thoughts of a gentle jog to stretch the legs went straight on the back burner. As the day progressed so did the condition to the point that I had to admit defeat on the proposed Preedy Pendle trial walk scheduled for Tuesday.

By this time, it was getting extremely painful to put on a shoe and almost impossible to walk. Time for some action, particularly as a weekend at my daughter's in Darlington was planned and this would inevitably mean some walking in Swaledale. A number of years ago I had been prescribed some very effective medication for this problem, so time for a hunt in the drawer for the magic pills. Alas to no avail, I can only conclude that the surplus dosage had gone over the expiry date and been jettisoned as no longer needed. Oh well, back to the Ibuprofen and hope that would do the trick.

There was indeed some improvement but by Wednesday evening insufficient to permit me to join the Thursday Burnley Contingent annual walk from Settle to Feizor and Stainforth Force. More worrying was the approach of my trip to the North East which was scheduled for Friday. On waking Thursday morning, I opted for a decisive course of action. I would ring the doctor's surgery and hope for an appointment. I informed my fellow walkers that once again I was unavailable for walking but if all went well, I would join them at Feizor tearooms for the traditional bacon bap.

I didn't get an appointment with the doctor but did manage the next best thing a phone call with the Triage nurse. After explaining my predicament that the condition was easing but not quickly enough, she suggested that the previously prescribed meditation would 'give it a bit of a kick'. I assured her that a kick was the last thing I wanted to give it! Anyway, prescription duly collected I was on my way to Yorkshire and the aforementioned porcine delicacy.

After consuming this little treat, I decided to take a tablet of the prescribed medication. This done I then made my way by car, as the walkers continued on theirs to the next stop, Stainforth Force and lunch. The lunch was excellent but the lack of salmon leaping rather disappointing. I only saw the one, I think they were hiding.

At the end of the walk the group debriefed at the Hart's Head, Giggleswick and another lucrative session for myself as seven more copies of 'From Pies to Paella' were gobbled up (see what I did there) by eager readers.

It was from this point that things started to go badly wrong. Leaving for home and taking a diverted route due to road closure back via Wigglesworth and Paythorne I was nevertheless making good progress. On leaving Gisburn and starting to climb towards the Todber caravan park I suddenly started to feel a bit 'whoozy'. Being not far from home I thought no more of it until…. After passing the Moorcock Inn I momentarily 'drifted off', next thing I know I have hit the wall and flipped the car onto its roof. All hell has let loose as the horn is blaring the hazard warning lights are flashing and I am hanging upside down fastened in by my seat belt! My first thought was a need to get out fast as I could, presumably petrol would be leaking, and a fire was the last thing I wanted. After a brief struggle with the belt I managed to free myself and miraculously extricate myself through the driver's door window which had smashed.

I could feel blood dripping but fortunately it just seemed to be coming from my nose, which I presumed had been caused by the airbags deploying. By this time other road users were on the scene and I have to say looking after me expertly. One young lady who I only know as Lucy put me in her car, rang the emergency services and informed my wife. Lucy then had to depart to pick up children and the local farmer who's wall I had recently become acquainted with took over the responsibility until the emergency services arrived.

Fortunately, quickly on the scene was an off-duty emergency medic who proceeded to check me out prior to the ambulance's arrival. Miraculously the only injury was the minor one to my nose which was subsequently confirmed by the ambulance paramedics. After all the trauma, the car now in a horrendous state was recovered to Macadam's Garage at Colne and I was taken home by the attendant police officer who I have nothing but the highest praise for. Indeed, I can honestly say that everybody involved in the whole traumatic experience acted not only extremely professionally but with great consideration. I cannot thank all of them enough.

Without wanting to bore everybody with more gory detail suffice it to say that I was still able to make it up to Darlington for the weekend. My wife was magnificent about it and it's at times like this that you realise what are the important things in life. I was a very lucky boy and certainly won't be taking any of the medication again before driving. The car was not so lucky and is about to be despatched to the scrap heap. That's a real shame as I had got quite fond of it.

The trip to Darlo was just what I needed, and it certainly helped to take my mind off what could have been. It was great to see my daughter and her partner and old friends Steve and Noreen. Oh! And the gout was much improved. I even thought that after a traumatic week that things were on the up, and then came the football…

Game 10 - Sunday 28th October 13.30 – Burnley v Chelsea

87

After last week's mauling at the hands of Manchester City who would we not want to meet next. Well, an in-form and high riding Chelsea would be well up the list, along with Liverpool and Tottenham Hotspur.

For myself it's a second consecutive home game missed, and I'm struggling to recall a time when that has been the case for me. A lovely autumnal morning was spent walking in Richmond, North Yorkshire, along the River Swale and taking in the magnificent ruins of Easby Abbey. Henry VIII has a lot to answer for! As we approached the town centre there was just time for a quick peak at my phone to get the early team news.

Encouragingly for us both Robbie Brady and Steven Defour, two players who have been sorely missed, both make the starting eleven. Further good news as the mercurial Belgian Eden Hazard succumbs to a back injury and fails to make the visitors team. It's going to be a hard game to follow for me as the strange kick-off time and the necessity to drive back to Burnley conspire to make life difficult.

As we eat lunch in Penley's café in Richmond before starting the two-hour journey south east, another sneaky peek at the phone reveals we are once again in this difficult season, trailing. Its only midway through the first half, plenty of time for an equaliser but deep down I just know that's not going to happen. Am I getting cynical or being realistic?

By the time we have 'legged' it back up the hill to the car, parked at the side of the old Richmond Racecourse, its half-time. Thankfully, there have been no more goals against but by the same token, none for. One down at the halfway point is not a disaster, we are still in the game and if we can keep it tight who knows we might snatch an equaliser from a set-play or God forbid even a penalty.

Now we are on the road and no chance of any radio commentary in the wilds of North Yorkshire, so I decide its best to just wait till home and either be highly surprised or majorly disappointed. Well, I don't suppose I need to tell most of you which it was. As soon as I enter the front door the Wi-Fi kicks in and the goal alerts come through like machine gun bullets. We have once again failed miserably to keep it tight and conceded a further three goals to lose the game 0-4.

That gives us zero points from the last two games with no goals scored and nine conceded! I suppose considering the quality of the opposition, Manchester City and Chelsea, that should come as little surprise. At home Sunday night I decide in view of the week that I've just had that I haven't the stomach to watch it on Match of the Day. As I write this review its now Thursday and I still haven't got sufficient enthusiasm to put myself through it.

Everybody with whom I have spoken seem totally despondent not only with the results but also the manner of performance. Where has the fight gone? It appears that once we concede we are beaten. I am informed that we have stood off our opponents allowing them to run at the defence. This is suicidal against players of the quality that the likes of Chelsea can muster. Once again, the number of shots conceded tops the twenty mark. With the best will in the world teams getting so many attempts at goal are sure to score with some. Apparently, Joe Hart with some unbelievable stops has once again kept the score down, but still we have conceded four. At the other end we have managed one shot on target in the whole 90 minutes.

The fans are feeling it badly and there is an air not so much of disappointment but more of resignation. What had the makings of a glorious season with a European adventure has turned sour after only three months. The performances not so much against the 'elite' sides but against teams likely to be relegation strugglers are totally unconvincing. We are being dominated by the poorer outfits and can count ourselves fortunate to have collected points against both Cardiff City and Huddersfield Town.

The fans are grimly shaking their heads and looking for an answer. Some feel that the January transfer window may be our saviour. I'm not so certain, by then we will probably be well embroiled in the relegation scrap. Players are unlikely to join us in that situation if they know they will be taking a big pay-cut should the axe fall. Certainly, selling teams will see our predicament and demand unrealistic fees for our targets. In short it all looks a bit of a mess from here. In Dyche we trust, but he'd better start finding some answers soon. Two difficult away fixtures coming up next at West Ham United and Leicester City. Anybody confident?

And so endeth my 'septimana horribilis'. As they say in the song, 'things can only get better'.

Result – Burnley 0 – 4 (Morata 22, Barkley 57, Willian 62, Loftus-Cheek 90+2) Chelsea

Burnley Team

Hart, Lowton, Mee, Tarkowski, Taylor, Gudmundsson, Defour, Cork (Westwood 73), Hendrick (Barnes 65), Brady, Vokes (Wood 59)

Subs Not Used – Heaton, Bardsley, Long, Vydra

Chelsea Team

Arrizabalaga, Azpilicueta, Rudiger, Luiz, Alonso, Kante, Jorginho (Fabregas 78), Barkley, Pedro (Loftus-Cheek 30), Morata (Giroud 74), Willian

Subs Not Used – Caballero, Kovacic, Zappacosta, Cahill

Attendance – 21,430

Season To Date – Played 10, Won 2, Drawn 2, Lost 6, Goals For 10, Goals Against 21, Points 8

League Position after Game 10 – 15th

After that God-awful week culminating in the defeat by Chelsea, things at least away from football began to return to something approaching normal. My sore big toe joint subsided to the point where I could resume walking and managed two outings on Tuesday and Thursday totalling 16.7 miles. Thankfully this improved my mood sufficiently to give me the courage to finally watch the Chelsea game highlights on Thursday evening via the BBC iPlayer. It didn't take me long to get the drift of what all those present had been telling me. A performance almost devoid of hope.

Still I'm feeling much better now and tomorrow (Saturday) is a fresh start. It's a trip to the capital for the Clarets and a date with West Ham United at the London Stadium. Whilst we don't usually fare too well at the home of the Hammers, last season was certainly different. For once we thoroughly enjoyed our trip to 'the smoke' and came away with a thumping 3-0 victory. The Hammers fans enjoyed it so much they decided to join in by encroaching the pitch on several occasions and threatening their owners with violence. Let's hope that tomorrows trip can end in the same fashion, we could certainly do with a confidence booster!

Game 11 - Saturday 3rd November 15.00 – West Ham United v Burnley

Team changes for this one as injury and the need to try and find a winning combination take priority. In comes Ashley Westwood for the injured Jack Cork, on the wing Aaron Lennon gets the nod over Robbie Brady and up front Matej Vydra gets a rare start partnering Sam Vokes.

However, if we thought this was going to be the start of a revival all those hopes disappeared as early as the 10th minute. Inexplicably James Tarkowski with time to either clear the ball or get it back to Joe Hart, did neither. Instead he allowed Marko Arnautovic, with whom he had become involved in a running battle, to nip in and dispossess him before slipping the ball past Joe Hart for the opener. Life is difficult enough for the Clarets at the moment without shooting ourselves in the foot.

Buoyed by their early success the Hammers proceeded to dominate the first half. A stroke of luck for once as Steven Defour tripped youngster Grady Diangana in the box, but the penalty not awarded. Sean Dyche admitted the incident deserved a spot kick and praised the young man's honesty. Dyche a vocal critic of divers said, *'Credit to him for just falling normally, I've seen it back, they should get a penalty".*

Relentlessly the home team pressed but incredibly we make it level terms on the stroke of half-time. A poor defensive header by Issa Diop falling to Ashley Westwood who threads a lovely pass through for Johann Berg Gudmundsson to touch home. In the words of the radio commentators, we have offered nothing in the first half but gone in level.

As is becoming increasingly common this season that state of parity didn't last long. On 68 minutes the Brazilian Felipe Anderson, a £40m summer buy from Lazio restored the home team's lead, firing through Hart's legs.

Time for the substitutions as we attempt to salvage something from the wreckage. Ashley Barnes and Chris Wood replace our 'V' force, Vydra and Vokes. Then with 15 minutes to go Brady comes on for Lennon. Within two minutes we have once again levelled as a thumping Wood header from a Brady corner gives us renewed hope.

Alas not for long as Anderson regains the lead with his second of the game via the aid of a deflection. Six minutes to go now and we are not quite done as Wood heads on to the bar, but to no avail. It's all wrapped up in the second minute of added time as substitute Javier Hernandez puts the icing on the cake with goal number four.

So, another disastrous day on the pitch. In the last three games we have been comprehensively beaten, conceding 13 goals whilst scoring only two in the process. Its relegation form for sure and only the poor form of a number of fellow strugglers is, for the moment, keeping us out of the bottom three. Something is sadly amiss. Once again, we have allowed 21 shots at our goal, ten of which were on target! We cannot hope to get anything from games with those sorts of statistics. The defence is all at sea, the midfield non-existent and the strikers starved of any sort of meaningful service.

Oh, for a Joey Barton right now, a midfield enforcer with leadership qualities. I don't know if there is one out there but even if there is, we are stuck with what we have till January. At our current rate of decline we will be certainly in the 'mire' by then. Another extremely tricky fixture coming up next at Leicester City. I'm not relishing that one!

Result – West Ham United (Arnautovic 10, Anderson 68,84, Hernandez 90+2) 4 – 2 (Gudmundsson 45, Wood 77) Burnley

Burnley Team

Hart, Lowton, Mee, Tarkowski, Taylor, Gudmundsson, Defour, Westwood, Lennon (Brady 75), Vydra (Barnes 72), Vokes (Wood 72)

Subs Not Used – Heaton, Long, Hendrick, McNeil

West Ham United Team

Fabianski, Zabaleta, Balbuena, Diop, Cresswell, Rice, Diangana (Antonio 86), Obiang (Hernandez 61), Snodgrass, Anderson, Arnautovic (Ogbonna 90+1)

Subs Not Used – Adrian, Fredericks, Masuaku, Perez

Attendance – 56,862

Season To Date – Played 11, Won 2, Drawn 2, Lost 7, Goals For 12, Goals Against 25, Points 8

League Position after Game 11 – 15th

I have to say that I'm not looking forward to the game at Leicester City. Our poor form for almost the whole of the season to date, and the fact that our opponents are as they say 'no mugs', means the odds are very much stacked against us.

On top of this we are visiting a club and city that are currently riding a wave of emotion following the death of their chairman and benefactor, killed in a helicopter crash after their last home fixture.

The media will be in full attendance as the city and footballing world pay homage to Vichai Srivaddhanaprabha and our opponents will be in determined mood to commemorate the occasion. Once again we are set up as the 'fall guys' as the tide of sympathy envelops the afternoon's proceedings.

I am sure that off the pitch we will play our part in showing all due respect. However, I am hoping that once on the pitch we will be fully focused and determined more than ever to get a result and halt our slide.

Game 12 - Saturday 10th November 15.00 – Leicester City v Burnley

Quite rightly, and as we knew it would, this day was not really about us. We were the supporting cast in what was to be a day of remembrance and thanksgiving for the people of Leicester. In true Burnley fashion the club and fans responded with the utmost respect for the solemnity of the occasion and can be proud of the part they played on this sombre day.

The Clarets showed no less than three changes for the fixture, missing through injury was James Tarkowski, his place being taken by 'Mr Reliable', Kevin Long. Returning from injury was Jack Cork who resumed a central midfield pairing with Steven Defour, Ashley Westwood dropping to the bench. Also, back to the bench went Matej Vydra as the striking pack was shuffled to try yet another combination, Chris Wood partnering Sam Vokes.

After an immaculately observed two-minute silence, from the off our hosts were quick out of the traps. A torrid first thirty minutes ensued requiring good saves by Joe Hart and a goal-line clearance by Matt Lowton to keep the scores level. The game was following an all too familiar pattern of heavy pressure from our opponents and a backs-to-the-wall defensive blockade.

Having said that after the half hour mark, we started to claw our way back into the game having weathered the early storm. The sanctuary of the dressing room was reached with the scores still level at the break.

With the defence showing much more solidity than of late the second half saw a much-improved performance by the Clarets. As the Foxes began to run out of steam following their wearying and traumatic week, some optimists amongst us started to dream of a snatched victory. Indeed, had Chris Wood not lifted our best chance over the top, the unlikely may just have been possible. However, injuries to Defour, worryingly another knee problem, and Johann Berg Gudmundsson, did little to help the cause.

Leicester's efforts to achieve a poignant victory foundered on the now much more familiar solid defence and at the end a hard-earned point was ours. On what was always going to be a difficult day it wasn't the Clarets back to their best, but it was a big improvement on recent weeks. Hopefully, with yet another international break coming up next weekend, we can get back to winning ways on our return to Turf Moor on Monday 26th.

Result – Leicester City 0 – 0 Burnley

Burnley Team

Hart, Lowton, Mee, Long, Taylor, Gudmundsson (Brady 65), Defour (Hendrick 55), Cork, Lennon, Wood, Vokes (Barnes 73)

Subs Not Used – Heaton, Bardsley, Westwood, Vydra

Leicester City Team

Schmeichel, Pereira, Morgan, Evans (Soyuncu 90), Chilwell, Mendy, Ndidi, Albrighton (Iheanacho 60), Gray (Okazaki 84), Ghezzal, Vardy

Subs Not Used – Ward, Simpson, Fuchs, Iborra

Attendance – 32,184

Season To Date – Played 12, Won 2, Drawn 3, Lost 7, Goals For 12, Goals Against 25, Points 9

League Position after Game 12 – 15th

Well we are in for a dearth of meaningful football again, no Premier League action for Burnley till Monday 26th of November. So, for you word hungry readers I'll just have to keep you abreast of what's been happening in my other world.

Tuesday 13th marked a big day in the Lancashire Dotcom Walkers calendar. Yes, once again it was time for the eagerly anticipated and bitterly contested annual quiz!

An added attraction this year was the prospect of a 'free lunch' courtesy of the Clog and Billycock pub at Pleasington. I suppose it really should be courtesy of the generosity of group leader Bob Clare and his sidekick Dave Johnstone (Satnav Dave). These two fine upstanding gentlemen had during the year devised and led some walks on behalf of Ribble Valley Inns. Instead of receiving payment for their services, the duo requested that the company provided a lunch for the Tuesday walking group at no cost. During the course of the year Ribble Valley Inns sold their pubs to another group who very generously offered to honour the arrangement previously agreed.

The quiz was to be preceded by a short walk from the pub. Unfortunately, on this occasion I was unable to participate due to a medical appointment. However, not being a man to let his team down there was no way I wasn't going to make the quiz. Some unkind individuals have suggested that the motivating factor was the offer of the 'free lunch' rather than the team's need. I'll leave you to decide on that one.

Anyway, at the duly appointed time I arrived at the venue in time to see the walkers straggling in towards the pub. Equipping myself with a pint of orange and soda, so as not to numb the brain cells, I promptly took up position awaiting the arrival of my other four teammates. At this point I was joined by two more Burnley Contingent members, old pal Geoff Ashworth and his better half Dianne. Now these two were not assigned to our team but clearly were also not going to miss out on the aforementioned 'free lunch'.

At the group leader's discretion, the pair were allowed to join the team, thereby boosting the Burnley team's pool of knowledge (hopefully). So hard fought has this annual joust been in previous years that accusations of foul play and 'sharp practice' have previously been levelled. I well remember the occasion when the Quizmaster, one Chris McCann (of the Preston brethren), emptied a pint of ale into his laptop computer destroying any prospect of a music section to the quiz. This was clearly done to nullify the Burnley Contingent's advantage of superior musical knowledge.

This time there was no laptop. Instead we had the pleasure of Chris playing the music on his mobile phone and relaying it via Bluetooth connectivity through a hand-held speaker, whilst he wandered from table to table. No expense spared on this one, who says the old codgers don't embrace modern technology!

A big mistake for the opposition though re-instating the music round. Led by the unstoppable Mike McDevitt the boys in Claret and Blue recorded a maximum points round. Take that you North Enders! You're not singing anymore!

After an extremely mentally tasking hour, lightened only by the superb Lancashire Hotpot and Spiced Red Cabbage, followed by Chocolate sponge with Chocolate sauce and Ice cream, it was time for the count. Heavily outnumbered by four opposition teams, the 'Vintage Clarets' reclaimed their crown as Quiz Champions, pipping the 'Fulwood Barrackers' (a semi-professional outfit) by one point.

The day was rounded off by group leader Bob Clare selling copies of the 2019 Dotcom Calendar (£7). Then there was a whip round for the Clog and Billycock staff (£2) a pint of foaming ale (£3.70) and the orange and soda (£1.70). So much for a 'FREE LUNCH', and that doesn't include the cost of the petrol for the 35-mile round trip. A suggested collection on behalf of Dave Johnstone's favoured Charity, the Air Ambulance, was deferred, allegedly so as not to get the various monies mixed. I think more likely because nobody had any money left. Still, a great day was enjoyed by all and the accolade of Brainiest Borough in Lancashire once again rests with the Clarets!

It's been a slow start to the season for Premier League manager sackings but Wednesday 14th November finally gets the ball rolling. Last season the first casualty went after only four league fixtures, that being Frank de Boer following Crystal Palace's early season loss at Turf Moor. This time the axe has fallen after 12 games and the unfortunate recipient is Stefan Jokanovic at Fulham. After guiding Fulham to promotion from the Championship last time round he unfortunately couldn't continue his success at the higher level. Despite a summer outlay of £100m the Cottagers lie bottom of the league following seven consecutive defeats. Ironically their only victory coming at home to the Clarets back in August. He is replaced by none other than 'The Tinkerman' Claudio Ranieri who will be hard pushed to emulate his feat of guiding Leicester City to become Champions of the Premier League.

On the same day news breaks of an obscene plan to pay retiring Premier League supremo Richard Scudamore a £5m 'golden handshake'. This will be funded by a donation of £250,000 each from the 20 current Premier League clubs. The scheme was concocted by his pal the Chelsea Chairman, Bruce Buck, and despite strong opposition from fans was given the go-ahead. Now, whilst it could be argued that the guy has done a very good job in increasing Premier League revenues, he has at the same time received a handsome reward, rumoured to be £2.5m per annum (including bonuses). Not bad that, I could live off that! Its yet another example of the lunacy of football finance.

Thursday 15th Burnley Contingent walk turns out to be a classic. Starting at the lay-by at Clough Foot on the Widdop Road between Burnley and Hebden Bridge, the route continued along Graining Water to Blake Dean. The path then crossed the road and entered the woods of Hardcastle Crags. Having started from Clough Foot well layered up and complete with woolly hats and gloves we were amazed to find that in no time at all we had stripped down to T-shirts. T-Shirts? In Burnley? In November??? Has the world gone mad?

Ambling along on our merry way, lunch was taken in a field at Lady Royd Farm overlooking the crags and the magnificent scenery to the west. Here we were joined by an inquisitive sheep who seemed to take an unhealthy interest in our lunch. Shortly after several of its mates joined the party and formed up in rank facing us. At this point the rest of the flock probably 100 strong decided to make an appearance. As the sheep stared, and we ate, there was a growing sense of menace as the woolly beasts, emboldened by their weight of numbers encroached nearer and nearer. Some of our more cowardly members were by this time contemplating making a run for it, however the day was saved by some judicious stick waving by Judy Weir who drove the beasts off down the field. It almost went down in history as the first known sheep attack.

Fortified by lunch, and I suspect anxious to escape the sheep, we pressed on completing a loop via Shackleton and the Calder/Aire Link to Walshaw. However, our animal encounters were not over for the day as at Abel Cross word had undoubtedly got around among our four-legged brethren. Once again, we were encircled by the woolly grass munchers, these were then followed by a couple of rather attractive donkeys, and then to round off our wildlife adventure, a herd of goats! Undeterred we headed back via New Laithe Farm, Black Dean and alongside Alcomden Water to the vehicles at Clough Foot.

What a fantastic day, 9.4 miles in glorious unbroken sunshine and with views as good as you'll see anywhere. All that was needed now was a restorative pint of foaming ale. This time it fell to the Craven Heifer at Harle Syke to come up with the goods and they didn't disappoint. A lovely pint of Reedley Hallows Brewery, Pendleside went down a treat and helped erase the memories of the 'devil sheep'. A good pub is the Craven Heifer with the patrons trying very hard to build a successful business. If you are in the area give it a go, you'll be made most welcome.

Still no football to report on but Tuesday 20th Dotcom walk could be said to have a football theme. This week's amble was on home territory for Group leader Bob Clare being almost from his front door in Penwortham. Now I know you might think that Penwortham is not a particularly nice place to stage a scenic stroll, and you would be right! However, our leader had an ulterior motive in selecting this particular suburban location. Bob, an author in his own right, had previously at some literary festival encountered a chap called Michael Barrett. Mike, it transpired had penned a graphic history of the birth of Preston North End FC and their unbeaten double-winning team of 1888-89!

The author was to hold a book signing in the most appropriate location, the Sir Tom Finney pub in Penwortham. Bob had therefore arranged a walk conveniently starting and ending with lunch at the pub. Good idea Bob and a good opportunity for Mike to sell a few books after a riveting 5.8-mile peramble of the scenic delights of Penwortham. These including the by-pass (under Construction), the bridge over the River Ribble and the flood defence pumping station. Thankfully on this occasion the electricity sub-station was deemed not worth a visit, as we headed back for the main event, the pub!

An excellent effort by the pub staff ensured 29 walkers, plus several non-walking guests, were all served a cooked lunch of their choice without serious delay. Bob Clare having introduced the main attraction of the day Mike Barrett, kindly arranged a photo opportunity for both Mike and I to pose holding copies of our respective volumes. I then had the chance to have a long and meaningful discussion with a fellow writer about the problems of publishing, promoting and marketing.

It's an interesting concept is Mike's book entitled 'Preston North End – The Rise of the Invincibles'. The 152 full-colour pages and 11 chapters chart North End's journey from humble cricket club in the 1860's through to their historic campaign of 1888-89 – the season they finished undefeated to claim the first ever Football League and FA Cup double.

The book is a graphic novel beautifully illustrated by *Roy of the Rovers* artist David Sque. If any of you are closet North Enders, or just enjoy an interesting and different football read, give it a try. It is available from www.invinciblebooks.co.uk and all good bookshops!

So, a pleasant enough stroll, a two-course lunch for £8.95, a decent pint and a good chat with a fellow football enthusiast. A good day out once again!

Thursday's Burnley Contingent walk should have been altogether a more scenic affair in beautiful East Lancashire. However, mist and freezing drizzle meant our circular walk from Salterforth, taking in Foulridge and Kelbrook, had only limited visibility. A nice end to the day though at the Anchor Inn, Salterforth, another pub to add to the recommended list.

Figure 5 - The author gives PNE's fellow author Mike Barrett some sound advice.
"Next time choose better subject matter"

At long last by Friday 23rd my long-awaited return of Premier League action is getting tantalisingly close, albeit we must wait till Monday to be the last fixture of games week 13 as we host Newcastle United. Over the last few weeks I've chatted to many Clarets fans, and to a man or indeed woman, none have exuded any positivity. How have we come to this? Only a few months ago we were looking forward to our European adventure and now many are contemplating a serious relegation battle. Without a doubt Monday is a big, big game for us. It may be a bit early to describe it as a six-pointer but for sure with tough games looming we need to keep the points tally ticking over.

Ahead of this game the results of the weekend fixtures had left us in an increasingly perilous position. My interpretation of the situation before these games was that you could perm any three from six for the drop. Those teams were Huddersfield Town, Cardiff City, Fulham, Southampton, Newcastle United and us. Over the weekend Cardiff not unsurprisingly lost at Everton, whilst Southampton lost out by a single goal margin at Fulham. Huddersfield then pulled off a very creditable 2-0 victory at Wolverhampton Wanderers and that shot them up from 20th to 14th. Those results left Fulham, Cardiff and Southampton in the drop zone all level on eight points. We dropped to 17th place just above the bottom three on nine points, the same as opponents Newcastle United and Crystal Palace. That's too close for comfort!

Game 13 - Monday 26th November 20.00 – Burnley v Newcastle United

Not a good start to the night! A game already scheduled to start later than the normal evening kick-off time of 7.45 is further delayed by another 30 minutes. There's a good crowd of over 20,000 for a Monday evening televised game, and my first suspicion is that the club have spotted the opportunity to sell more ale and pies. How cynical of me! It later transpires that the delay is due to a medical emergency in the player's tunnel where Referee's Assessor Eddie Wolstenholme has collapsed with a suspected heart attack. Fortunately, after treatment Eddie seems to be OK, it may have been seeing the price of the ale and pies that brought it on. Anyhow it's now an 8.30 pm kick -off on a freezing cold night and an anticipated arrival home not much before 11.00 pm. Good job there is no extra time and penalties!

When we finally get to the action, we see the Clarets lining up with just one change from last time out, Robbie Brady replacing the injured Johann Berg Gudmundsson. If ever there was a game where we needed a good start this was it. Did we get one? Did we Hell! A disastrous opening as we trail inside four minutes. A speculative shot from outside the box is deflected by Ben Mee wrong footing Joe Hart and looping into the net. When your luck is out, it's out.

Now with their tails up the visitors proceed to look more like championship challengers than relegation strugglers. It's no surprise when on 23 minutes they extend their lead to two goals. A sloppily defended right-wing corner gives an unmarked Ciaran Clark the opportunity to glance a header across goal and in at the far post.

Thankfully from this point the rampant Magpies backed by the usual Geordie hordes decide its game over and go back into their shell. That's the cue for us to take over and have a real go at them. However, what we got was a lot of sideways and backwards movement with absolutely no penetration. It's what has become the usual fare, too slow and predictable in the build-up, one dimensional football. Big Sam Vokes is doing what he does and winning more than his fair share of headers, but no one is getting to the by-line and cutting the ball back.

Then on 40 minutes a goal out of the blue. A long ball from just over the halfway line is met by a thumping Vokes header. He must be almost on the edge of the penalty area but with the keeper slightly off his line it's over him and in the net. He's as good a header as anybody in the league, if only we had somebody that could provide decent ammunition.

Suddenly its game on and we get five minutes of goal inspired attacking action. Martin Dubravka in the 'Toon' goal is called into action thwarting Chris Wood on a couple of occasions. So, we go in at half-time with a glimmer of hope.

The second half after a sluggish start continues in similar vein. We have lots of possession but little guile and creativity. A number of half chances are created from long balls into the box, all falling to Wood who unfortunately fails to convert any. On another night he may have scored three or four but tonight he's firing blanks.

I can't recollect Hart making a single save in the Burnley goal, yet ironically Newcastle go closest to scoring. A calamitous mix up between Robbie Brady and Charlie Taylor hands a golden chance to Matt Ritchie. From no more than two yards out he contrives to put a 'cert' wide of the gaping net. He'll have nightmares about that for ever more. Then after more 'thud and blunder' from the Clarets, the Magpies substitute Joselu cracks a fierce drive against the foot of the post only to see it come bouncing back from whence it came.

Once again, we fail to make any substitutions until too late in the game. Around the 82-minute mark Brady and Steven Defour depart to be replaced by Ashley Barnes and Jeff Hendrick. What chance have they of influencing the game at this late stage?

The board goes up showing four minutes of added time and we are then treated to the bizarre sight of Joe Hart leaving his goal and joining the outfield players. Now call me old fashioned if you like but I prefer my goalkeeper to save shots rather than embark on futile forward forays. I think our Joe has been reading too much 'Roy of the Rovers' stuff. It's the sort of thing 'Tubby' Morton might have got up to. If only we had a 'Blackie' Gray!

Needless to say, we almost paid the price as yet another long-ball attack broke down, but thankfully the defence managed to scramble clear. I don't think we would have been seeing this sort of desperation last season, and that may be a pointer to what has gone astray this time. One last chance to salvage a point disappears as Vokes header from a free kick goes over the bar, and our late night finally comes to an unhappy end.

Once again, it's been a poor performance, not through lack of effort but through a serious lack of quality. We are overrun in centre midfield and have ineffective wingers who are reluctant to try and beat a man. Consequently, the strikers are devoid of any sort of decent service and are feeding off knockdowns and scraps.

That's now 13 games gone and only nine points on the board. In previous relegation seasons at this stage we had 17 and 11 respectively, so we are already behind the tallies that sent us down. I pray I am wrong but to me the writing is clearly on the wall. Its Crystal Palace away next who on their day have the potential to inflict some serious damage. Then back at the Turf the following Wednesday for none other than the visit of high-flying Liverpool who score goals for fun. A magic wand anybody?

Result – Burnley (Vokes 40) 1 – 2 (Mee o.g. 4, Clark 23) Newcastle United

Burnley Team

Hart, Lowton, Mee, Long, Taylor, Lennon, Defour (Hendrick 82), Cork, Brady (Barnes 83), Wood, Vokes

Subs Not Used – Heaton, Gibson, Westwood, Vydra

Newcastle United Team

Dubravka, Yedlin, Schar, Fernandez, Clark, Ritchie, Kenedy (Hayden 90), Diame, Ki Sung-yueng, Perez, Rondon (Joselu 71)

Subs Not Used – Woodman, Manquillo, Shelvey, Atsu, Murphy

Attendance – 20,682

Season To Date – Played 13, Won 2, Drawn 3, Lost 8, Goals For 13, Goals Against 27, Points 9

League Position after Game 13 – 17th

Game 14 - Saturday 1st December 15.00 – Crystal Palace v Burnley

Once again there are two team changes ahead of the fixture at Selhurst Park. Johann Berg Gudmundsson comes straight back in after illness, replacing Robbie Brady. More surprisingly Sam Vokes, Tuesday's goal scorer, loses his place in the starting line-up and is replaced by Jeff Hendrick in what is without doubt a tactical move. Strangely Ben Gibson who made the bench on Tuesday has once again disappeared and is joined in his absence by Matej Vydra. James Tarkowski returning from hernia surgery and Phil Bardsley fill the remaining substitute positions.

It looks like we are setting up for a return to a 4-4-1-1 formation in an attempt to bolster the midfield, but we look awfully weak up front. There's 20 minutes to kick-off and I have to say I'm not feeling too hopeful. That's a bit sad really as our opponents are so far winless at home, having scored only twice there this season, both of which were penalties. But that's a measure of how much my confidence has drained in this so far disastrous campaign. I only hope the players are not feeling the same.

I'm tuned in for an afternoon's listening to Scott Read and Chris Boden doing the commentary on Radio Lancashire. That is until a poster on the 'Up the Clarets' 'messageboard' suggests a good live stream for the game and I decide to give it a go. Bingo! Success, I have a perfect ring-side view of the action.

After a few minutes I'm beginning to wonder if perhaps I haven't made a mistake in watching the stream. It's fair to say the action all seems to be going one-way, and that is towards Joe Hart's goal. Palace may lack a natural goal scorer, but they have two very quick and skilful forward players in Wilfried Zaha and Andros Townsend. Zaha in particular is soon proving a major threat and giving Matt Lowton a torrid time.

There's a good stop by Hart on eight minutes from Max Meyer but almost inevitably we are once again trailing after only 16 minutes. An innocuous looking low cross from James McArthur somehow manages to elude everybody and bobble in at the far post. What a soft goal to concede and typical of what has happened so frequently in this ill-fated season. The rest of the first half is best described as much of the same, repeated attacks punctuated by desperate defending and good stops by

Hart. At the other end of the pitch, nothing! The Palace keeper Wayne Hennessey could probably have nipped off for a fag and a Bovril for all the action he was seeing. It's painful to watch.

Off at half-time miraculously still just the one goal down surely we are going to come out fighting after the break. Well I'd like to think so but no it's the same old rubbish and I'm fearing a rout. In an effort to create some forward momentum Steven Defour is replaced on 60 minutes by Vokes. A damning statistic shows that in the first hour we managed the grand total of ZERO shots at goal.

It's just a case of waiting for the next goal to hit the net, and that moment almost arrives on 66 minutes as Zaha rattles the crossbar with an effort that deserved a better fate. Still it's all over shortly after as Townsend cutting in off the right flank unleashes a left foot howitzer that rockets into the top corner. I think the expression is a 'worldy'!

I can barely bring myself to watch the closing minutes as we go agonisingly through the motions. The game ends 2-0, it could have been 10. We have been comprehensively outplayed to the point of embarrassment. The match statistics are truly shocking, and the number of shots rained in on our goal totalled a staggering 29 of which nine were on target. In retaliation we fired a paltry four, none of which troubled the keeper! At the risk of repeating myself, how do we expect to get anything from games when we are allowing the opposition to fire at will!

I don't know how Sean Dyche is going to explain away that performance, but the fans can see that things are seriously wrong on the playing side. The problem is that none of us can see any light at the end of the tunnel. Twenty-four games to go in this campaign and at the moment that looks like a lot more grief! Once again Saturday night ruined! Down to next to bottom of the table, doomed!

Result – Crystal Palace (McArthur16, Townsend 77) 2 – 0 Burnley

Burnley Team

Hart, Lowton, Mee, Long, Taylor, Lennon (Brady 45), Defour (Vokes 60), Cork, Gudmundsson, Hendrick, Wood (Barnes 80)

Subs Not Used – Heaton, Bardsley, Tarkowski, Westwood

Crystal Palace Team

Hennessey, Wan-Bissaka, Tomkins, Sakho, van Aanholt, McArthur (Schlupp78), Milivojevic, Kouyate, Meyer (Puncheon 90+2), Townsend (Sorloth 88), Zaha

<u>Subs Not Used</u> – Ward, Kelly, Guaita, J Ayew

Attendance – 25,098

Season To Date – Played 14, Won 2, Drawn 3, Lost 9, Goals For 13, Goals Against 29, Points 9

League Position after Game 14 – 19th

After a troubled few days of reflection following the Palace game, I must confess to feeling a little disappointed with myself regarding my negativity, which you can't fail to have picked up on. This is unlike me and normally I am the type of person who preaches the value of positive thinking. Just imagine the atmosphere at training sessions and in the player's dressing room if Sean Dyche was similarly afflicted. So, as of Wednesday 5th December I am wiping the slate clean and attempting to look much more positively at our prospects. Starting with tonight's game, which I suppose can be viewed as a 'free hit' being as nobody realistically expects us to get anything from the game. I'll try and take the positives.

Game 15 - Wednesday 5th December 19.45 – Burnley v Liverpool

As mentioned above pre-match expectations for this one are zero. The Clarets sit next to bottom in the league having won only twice all season, whilst our visitors sit second top chasing leaders Manchester City hard. There's an array of attacking talent at the disposal of manager Jurgen Klopp, and with players such as Sadio Mane, Mohammed Salah, and Roberto Firmino they can inflict serious damage to any team.

However, Mr Klopp clearly fancies his chances at Turf Moor as he makes no less than seven changes to his team that won Sunday's Merseyside derby with a late Divock Origi goal. Out are the entire 'terrible trio' mentioned above and striking duties are handed to Daniel Sturridge and Origi.

Sean Dyche also rings the changes, out go Matt Lowton, Kevin Long, Steven Defour, Aaron Lennon, and Sam Vokes. Their places are taken by Phil Bardsley, James Tarkowski, Ashley Westwood, Robbie Brady and Ashley Barnes. Of those missing, Long and Vokes can both count themselves very unfortunate to be left out as their recent contributions have been excellent. However, Sean Dyche goes for the more experienced Tarkowski, and the more aggressive and mobile Barnes as he searches to find a winning formula.

It's been an absolutely foul day for weather in Burnley with persistent heavy rain, but the pitch is still in immaculate condition, a far cry from the mudheaps of the 60's and 70's. There's a good crowd swelled by a large and vociferous Scouse contingent. The home fans seem to be adopting my new philosophy of positivity and are giving the team some great early encouragement.

It's a decent start by the Clarets and on 10 minutes an opening created by Barnes gives Chris Wood an opportunity. Unfortunately, 'Woody's' confidence is so low at the moment that instead of going for goal straight off he opts for a couple of further touches. You don't get that luxury at this level and a good chance goes begging.

It's a much-improved performance from these battling Clarets and we go close again as Phil Bardsley fires in a 'thunderbolt' from distance which flies narrowly wide of the post. As the half wears on with little from the Liverpool strike force to trouble Joe Hart, we are preciously close to an opener. A fine Brady free kick from the left wing is met by a crashing Barnes volley that Allison in the Reds goal can only wave goodbye to as it scorches past him into the net. Unfortunately, the assistant referee has spotted our Ashley in an offside position and the 'goal' is chalked off.

All square at half-time and a very encouraging first 45 minutes from a very determined looking Burnley side. Jurgen Klopp can't have been too happy with what he saw from his title contenders in that first period and I can only assume it won't be long before he summons his 'big guns' from the bench.

The second period is not long underway before suddenly, and probably just about deservedly, we have an unlikely lead! A right-wing corner is headed goalward by Tarkowski, the keeper deals with it unconvincingly, Wood takes a swipe at it and misses and the ball breaks to Jack Cork for a simple tap-in. Phew! The home crowd are ecstatic although as the young chap behind me correctly points out, there's over 30 minutes still to go.

Jurgen Klopp has seen enough, clearly his second string are not good enough to see off the Clarets and straight into a touchline warm up go the 'big guns'. Unfortunately, as so often seems to happen, we are unable to hold the lead for long. On 62 minutes, following some nice set-up play, James Milner's precise shot from the edge of the box beats Hart at his left-hand post.

That's the cue for the visitors to 'go for it' and promptly on come Salah and Firmino, and on 69 minutes the Reds take the lead. A free kick outside the box is punted through by Trent Alexander-Arnold, Virgil Van Dijk is first to reach it to the left of goal and lays it back across the face for Firmino to tap in with his first touch of the game.

To our credit the lad's heads don't go down and the fans backing is unwavering. The game is opening up now and Liverpool are finding it easier to find the gaps. The danger is apparent but thanks to some fine saves from Hart and some brilliant last ditch defending the score remains close.

As we enter time added on at the end of the game we are pressing hard for an equaliser. There's a close shave as goalkeeper Alisson pulls off a terrific one handed save to claw out a header bound for the top corner. A bit of a scramble ensues which the defence manages to just about clear. As the keeper retrieves the ball before it goes out for a corner, he makes a quick throw out to Sturridge in space on the right flank. His early ball is into the path of Salah who deftly plays it with the outside of his left boot to the unmarked Xherdan Shaqiri who makes no mistake from inside the penalty area.

We didn't deserve that, but it's typical of the way things are going for us at the moment. At one end of the pitch almost an equaliser and at the other undone by a quick counterattack. However, this was a performance more akin to last season's Burnley. A real battling performance where everybody fought like tigers. Is this the turning point? We'll soon get a chance to find out as on Saturday we host Brighton. If we play with the same fire as tonight surely, we will get something from this one.

Result – Burnley (Cork 54) 1 – 3 (Milner 62, Firmino 69, Shaqiri 90+1) Liverpool

Burnley Team

Hart, Bardsley, Mee, Tarkowski, Taylor, Brady (Lennon 71), Westwood, Cork, Gudmundsson, Wood (Vokes 71), Barnes (Vydra 83)

Subs Not Used – Heaton, Lowton, Long, Hendrick

Liverpool Team

Alisson, Gomez (Alexander- Arnold 23), Matip, van Dijk, Moreno (Salah 65), Shaqiri, Keita, Henderson, Milner, Origi (Firmino 66), Sturridge

<u>Subs Not Used</u> – Mignolet, Camacho, Fabinho, Lallana

Attendance – 21,741

Season To Date – Played 15, Won 2, Drawn 3, Lost 10, Goals For 14, Goals Against 32, Points 9

League Position after Game 15 – 19th

As previously mentioned Wednesday 5th had seen rainfall in Burnley approaching monsoon proportions. It was with some trepidation therefore that seven hardy, or should that be foolhardy, souls of the Burnley Contingent set out for the Thursday stroll. This week it was a proposed eight-mile circuit starting at the White House pub on the A58 Halifax road just out of Littleborough.

We've done this walk on several occasions and it starts with some lovely moorland walking on good tracks taking in several reservoirs including Blackstone Edge, Light Hazzles and Warland, before dropping down for a stretch on the Rochdale canal. On arrival at the White House it was apparent our fears were well founded, as we were met with thick mist, strong winds and intermittent heavy rain. The splendid views afforded by this walk were today just a distant memory as it became increasingly difficult to see further than your fellow walkers. Still it did make the occasional 'comfort break' easier as there was little chance of being espied. Well zero chance actually as there was nobody else daft enough to be up there.

Anyway, after about four miles we reached the lowlands and relative sanctuary of the canal. Here a soggy picnic lunch was enjoyed and the opportunity to wring out sodden gloves before the ascent back to the pub. Strangely the White House decides to close at 3.00pm before re-opening later so there was nothing for it but to head back for a debrief at the Kettledrum, Red Lees. Here fortified by a welcome pint of Moorhouses White Witch the talk soon turned to thoughts on last night's Liverpool game. All who attended agreed that it was a much-improved performance and were heartened by the display.

The general consensus was that we should all 'get a grip', cut out the moaning and enjoy what the rest of the season had to give. After all we have been in much worse scrapes than this. When you consider that back in the dark days of the 1980's we were trounced 0-6 at home by Hereford it certainly puts yesterday's close encounter with Liverpool into perspective. Come on you Clarets, all is not lost!

It transpires that following the game there was a bit of a 'spat' between Jurgen Klopp and Sean Dyche. Klopp took exception to our strong tackling particularly a challenge by Ben Mee which was perfectly legitimate but resulted in a fractured ankle for Joe Gomez. By his own admission Mr Klopp agreed there was no foul, thereby somewhat weakening his point.

Mr Dyche retaliated by branding Liverpool's Daniel Sturridge a cheat and accusing him of diving. So, a bit of aggro after that game and I don't think the managers will be exchanging Christmas cards this year!

Game 16 - Saturday 8th December 15.00 – Burnley v Brighton & Hove Albion

Hooray! A rare occurrence, a proper Saturday kick-off time which is becoming in this age of televised football something of a rarity. This is what I like, the opportunity to grab a couple of pints in the pub and talk football related nonsense with like-minded people ahead of the game. And what an important game it is today. On the back of Wednesday's encouraging performance can the Clarets go on and record a desperately needed third victory of the season.

Once again, it's a miserable cold wet afternoon in Burnley, but then again what would you expect in the north west of England in December. Sean Dyche impressed with the midweek passion and commitment unsurprisingly names the same starting XI, and the same substitutes. The crowd is a couple of thousand down on Wednesday's but the travelling support from the south coast is nowhere near that provided by nearer neighbours Liverpool.

We start the game attacking the Cricket Field end as is our want and it's a steady enough opening. Our visitors don't carry anything like the attacking punch of the Scousers and are causing little anxiety from the start. As the first half wears on we are enjoying lots of possession and controlling the game without creating too much threat. However, the latter stages of the first period see us step up the pressure. Visiting keeper

Mat Ryan being forced into two good saves, smothering a close-range effort from Chris Wood, and also denying Robbie Brady.

Then on 40 minutes our increased momentum pays off as the Seagulls fail to deal with a free kick from the right-wing despite having several chances to clear their lines. The ball eventually falls to Jack Cork who drives it goalwards where it gets the faintest of touches from James Tarkowski's chest before hitting the net. Ahead at half-time and probably just about deservedly so.

Despite the lead being only a single goal, I'm pretty much relaxed at the interval and hopeful that we can retain or even increase our advantage in the second period. Joe Hart has been untested in the opening half and the visitors it has to be said look pretty toothless.

It's similar fare for most of the second half as Brady creates an opening that just eludes Wood at the back post. Lewis Dunk then prevents a second and possibly killer goal with a terrific sliding block to stop Ashley Barnes shot from another Brady set-up. There are loud appeals for a penalty as Yves Bissouma catches a rampaging Phil Bardsley in the head with a high boot. However, the referee is clearly aware that Burnley don't get penalty awards and maintains the consistency of that jurisdiction.

Entering the final stages nerves, fatigue and an increased urgency from Brighton contrive to make the closing stages a bit of a 'nailbiter'. As the visitors build up a head of steam the familiar resilience of the old Burnley defence comes back to the fore. Tarkowski and Ben Mee stand resolute, ably aided by both full backs Bardsley and Charlie Taylor. It's edge of the seat stuff for the last few minutes as we concede multiple corners and Brighton throw the kitchen sink at us. However, it's all to no avail and we stand to applaud the first victory since the end of September. Boy, how we needed that!

The result takes us out of the bottom three and sets me up for an extremely pleasant evening with my wife, daughter and future son-in-law. No silent teas tonight, its curry and beers at the Spice Lounge to celebrate, and what's more I don't mind paying!

Result – Burnley (Tarkowski 40) 1 – 0 Brighton & Hove Albion

Burnley Team

Hart, Bardsley, Mee, Tarkowski, Taylor, Brady, Westwood, Cork, Gudmundsson (Lennon 72), Wood, Barnes (Hendrick 85)

Brighton & Hove Albion Team

Ryan, Bruno, Dunk, Balogun, Bernardo, Knockaert (Locadia 63), Propper, Bissouma, March, Gross (Stephens 79) Andone (Murray 63)

Attendance – 18,497

Season To Date – Played 16, Won 3, Drawn 3, Lost 10, Goals For 15, Goals Against 32, Points 12

League Position after Game 16 – 17th

Two interesting walks this week, first up being a rather unusual stroll and venue. Tuesday's Dotcom outing involved bizarrely a train ride on the East Lancashire line! The start point for the day was Rishton railway station where it was intended to board the 10.29 'rattler' to Hapton. The plan being then to walk it back to Rishton via the Leeds-Liverpool canal taking in the historic buildings and idyllic scenery.

On arrival at Rishton station it came as no surprise that the intended Northern Rail service to Colne was running approximately eight minutes late. Still, that allowed time for the purchase of 20+ tickets for the journey. Techno-geek Tom Rice decided he would take responsibility in cajoling the fairly recently installed ticket-machine (Rishton being an unmanned station) to part with its wares. All went well in the early stages but clearly the demand for so many tickets, all bound for Hapton, was too much for the machine to cope with. It promptly shut itself down and refused to play ball leaving a number of walkers to purchase their permits from the conductor/guard on the train. Interestingly the plan is to get rid of conductor/guards on these trains, and this is the cause of considerable disruption due to industrial action by the operatives. What will happen when they are gone, presumably all those without tickets will travel for free!

Having boarded the train and alighted three stops later at our destination, the walk commenced. I can honestly say that this was the flattest 7.7-mile walk I have ever undertaken. I can also say without fear of contradiction that it is very short on interesting historic buildings and idyllic scenery. The one memorable feature of the walk was crossing the canal's meridian at Church. Photographs were taken as we crossed the mid-point of the route, 63.6-miles from both Leeds and Liverpool. No change in time-zones here though. This was truly one of the highlights of the day!

Figure 6 - The Author poses astride the Church 'meridian' on the Leeds/Liverpool canal. The half-way point!

The other highlight, and probably more memorable, was the distribution by Bob Clare, group leader, of the new Lancashire Dotcom Walkers T-shirts, commemorating the 10-year anniversary (2009-2019) of the group. Whether intentionally to cause mayhem, or accidentally by oversight, I am not sure, however quite a stir ensued. To the joy of a rather depleted Burnley Contingent the shirts turned out to be a beautiful claret with light blue lettering, almost good enough to be considered by Burnley FC as their next kit. Needless to say, this didn't meet with the approval of the Preston mob, who could be heard murmuring their discontent. To be fair the leader did offer to make the 20th Anniversary shirt in PNE colours. However, some 'wags' did point out that by that time the group would probably have to meet by way of a 'seance'.

Nearing the end of the walk we had a very lucky chance encounter with a missing member of the Burnley Contingent. Well known ex Burnley schoolteacher Dave Preedy had, shall we say, overslept a little. On waking in good time at 7.50 he had decided he could afford another half hour's kip. Availing himself of this luxury he then proceeded to overindulge not awakening till 10.00. At this point he decided that it was too late to catch the train, but he would proceed to Rishton then walk along the canal in the direction of Hapton to meet the returning group. Fortunately, we just managed to espy Dave as we left the canal almost back at Rishton and he joined us for the last mile. I pointed out to him that he must have had a pretty short walk. "Not so" said Dave. "How's that"? I asked "I got on the canal and started walking the wrong way" said Dave, only noticing when he saw a sign that said Blackburn! Honestly, you couldn't make it up!

In contrast this week's Burnley Contingent walk was an altogether more scenic affair. Starting from Roddlesworth Moors, Crookfield Rd car park, just off the A675 Belmont road. It took in Roddlesworth Woods, Sunnyhurst Woods, Darwen Tower and a return via the Witton Weavers Way. A 9.3-mile walk in extremely cold, but mostly sunny conditions with great visibility particularly from the top of the tower, was thoroughly enjoyed by all. A pint of Filly Close Blonde at the Rifle Volunteer on return to Burnley capped a fine day's outing.

Game 17 - Saturday 15th December 15.00 – Tottenham Hotspur v Burnley

Today marked the first of two very demanding trips to the capital on successive weeks. First up are Spurs at Wembley Stadium, their home ground still being in a state of construction. Next week it's the equally daunting task of a trip to the Emirates Stadium to face Arsenal.

There's an early surprise in Sean Dyche's starting XI as he unusually opts for three centre-backs, Kevin Long recalled joining Ben Mee and James Tarkowski. The radio commentator's suggestions are that we will play three at the back but looking at the line-up I feel it's more likely five at the back. Ashley Barnes will play as a lone striker in front of a midfield four.

Tottenham also show a number of changes from the team which earned a very creditable Champions League away draw with Barcelona at the Nou Camp. There are some notable omissions from their line-up notably Christian Eriksen and Son Heung-Min, but they still field a formidable eleven.

It's a cold, wet, miserable day in London and I'm hoping that our recent improved form can add to the host's discomfort. With our new formation in place it's obvious that we are not going to be seen much as an attacking force. Indeed, the first half soon settles into a familiar pattern of continuous waves of attack by the opposition. However, we seem to have recovered some of our old defensive resilience and I'm pleased to see we are holding them fairly comfortably.

We are defending deep and taking the opportunity to waste time as much as possible without incurring the referee's wrath. Inevitably with the amount of possession Spurs are enjoying they are making the occasional half chance, but Joe Hart is relatively untroubled. Then on half time an opportunity for Ashley Barnes as he gets his head to a Phil Bardsley cross, but his effort goes high and wide.

Half time 0-0. It wasn't pretty to watch but the shape and effort were highly effective in limiting the opposition. The second half almost opens even more promisingly as a Barnes volley is blocked by none other than Harry Kane.

The game soon settles back into the pattern of the first period with Spurs making the running but continually being frustrated by a magnificent defensive performance. On the rare occasions that the rearguard is breached Hart is again in impressive form to save the day. The custodian excels on 75 minutes with an outstanding save from Erik Lamela that has the match commentator drooling. The referee has by this time had enough of the 'game management' tactics and is flourishing yellow cards first at Robbie Brady, and then Bardsley.

Time is edging painfully slowly on and I'm beginning to wonder when we might start to see some theatrical dives in our penalty area. Spurs in Dele Alli have an ace protagonist in that particular 'dark art' and as their desperation grows it's a distinct possibility. Eriksen and Son Heung-Min are both now on as substitutes and the latter goes close on 85 minutes but thankfully misses the target.

The 90 minutes are up and we almost there, an extremely unlikely away point is almost within our grasp. Well almost! In the first of four minutes of added time we are finally undone as an attack down the Spurs left sees Kane feed in Eriksen who makes no mistake with a fierce shot past Hart.

Not for the first time, how bloody cruel was that! In the words of BBC Sport match reporter Saj Chowdury:

"The result was cruel for Burnley.

This was the sort of resolute performance against one of the 'Big Six' we got used to seeing from Sean Dyche's side last season. They defended from the front and restricted the space for attacking players Kane, Dele Alli and Lamela by hunting them down in pairs"

Once again, a great effort ends with nothing to show for it. Fortunately, on the same day two of the sides below us lose, Huddersfield Town at home to Newcastle United and likewise Fulham to West Ham United. However, on Sunday Southampton defy the odds to overcome Arsenal at St Mary's. Ironically all the Saints goals came from ex Burnley players, two for Danny Ings and one for Charlie Austin. That result put us back in the drop-zone courtesy of an inferior goal difference. Ain't life a bitch!

Result – Tottenham Hotspur (Eriksen 90+1) 1 – 0 Burnley

Burnley Team

Hart, Bardsley, Mee, Tarkowski, Long, Taylor, Brady (Hendrick (90+2), Westwood, Cork, Lennon (Vokes 90+3), Barnes (Wood 80)

Subs Not Used – Heaton, Lowton, Gibson, Vydra

Tottenham Hotspur Team

Lloris, Trippier, Alderweireld, Davies, Rose, Sissoko, Skipp (Son Heung-Min 75), Lamela (Llorente 82), Alli, Lucas Moura (Eriksen 65), Kane

<u>Subs Not Used</u> – Gazzaniga, Winks, Walker-Peters, Eyoma

Attendance – 41,645

Season To Date – Played 17, Won 3, Drawn 3, Lost 11, Goals For 15, Goals Against 33, Points 12

League Position after Game 17 – 18th

It's almost Christmas and for poor beleaguered writers of topical books like myself that's make or break time. Despite the best efforts of the Clarets Store and Burnley Memorabilia in Burnley Market Hall, sales are disappointingly down on last year's effort. Sales on Amazon of Volume 4, 'From Pies to Paella' are a fraction of what would normally be expected. I note that the High St stores are taking a bashing, and even Internet retailers are already heavily discounting, so perhaps it's no surprise that little old me is also feeling the pinch. It must be Brexit effect as we lurch ever closer to D-Day, or should that be B-Day, with no satisfactory conclusion in sight.

In an effort to boost the flagging sales I decide to attempt to spread the net a little and find other potential outlets. I know from previous experience that this can sometimes be a rather soul-destroying experience. Often retailers whom one would expect to be interested in retailing books with a local flavour fail even to respond to a request. However, on this occasion two new outlets have generously offered to assist, these being Clitheroe Books, and the Gift Shop at Towneley Hall. A big thank you therefore to these two enterprising booksellers for giving the little guy a chance.

Anyway, enough of that for now and back to more pressing matters, i.e. the need to get some more points on the board. Tomorrow sees us on yet another London jaunt, last week at third placed Tottenham Hotspur, this time at fifth placed Arsenal. With a paltry 12 points under our belts from the first 17 league matches a visit to the Emirates Stadium would not have been a first-choice venue for a chance of success. Still we have to play all the teams at some point so it's no good moaning about it. We must go out and demonstrate the same determination as that shown in the last three matches and hope that for once Lady Luck decides to smile benignly down on us.

One player definitely not making the trip to face the Gunners is Aaron Lennon who this week has undergone cartilage surgery on his knee. Hopefully Johann Berg Gudmundsson will have recovered from injury to reclaim the vacant slot, or alternatively Sean Dyche may once again turn to rapidly developing youngster Dwight McNeil. Once again, the kick-off is moved, this time to 12.30 for the benefit of TV viewers.

Oh! By the way, in all the pre-Christmas excitement I forgot to mention that on Tuesday 18th Manchester United parted company with manager Jose Mourinho. Yes, the 'Special One', or 'Moaninho' as he has become more commonly known, has finally been shown the door. It has seemed only a matter of time before his brooding presence got too much for the United board. At almost halfway through the season and 19 points behind leaders Liverpool its 'Bye Bye Jose'! There won't be too many tears shed here in Burnley after the way he cynically character assassinated Ashley Barnes over an incident with a Chelsea player during his reign at the Bridge. Ironically there probably won't be many shed by Jose himself as he collects his severance pay and waits for the next stop on the managerial merry-go-round.

Game 18 - Saturday 22nd December 12.30 – Arsenal v Burnley

Premier League games against Arsenal have of late often left a bitter taste in the mouth. We have had a multitude of goals in added time, offside goals, hand-ball goals and penalties, without fail all going against us. For some reason the match officials seem incapable of spotting the blatantly obvious when we come up against these southern media darlings. Would today be another such case?

The team news is again interesting and somewhat experimental. Sean Dyche has decided to stick with the three central defenders and two full backs that worked so effectively at Tottenham. However, in an effort to introduce a bit more firepower he has opted for two strikers, Chris Wood coming in to partner Ashley Barnes. Also recalled is Jeff Hendrick as we move to a central midfield three, in what looks like a 5-3-2 formation. Going out are both wide men, the injured Aaron Lennon and Robbie Brady who somewhat worryingly doesn't even make the squad. We are set to be almost like Sir Alf Ramsey's 1966 'wingless wonders', well almost!

It's a formidable looking Arsenal XI captained on the day by the enigmatic German Mesut Ozil. On his day he is the supreme artist with the ball, not on his day he is a disappearing non-entity. Which Ozil are we going to get today?

I'm following the opening period via the BBC Sports App and they are reporting a cracking start to the game. There are early chances at both ends and after only three minutes it could be 1-1 with efforts from Pierre-Emerick Aubameyang and Ashley Westwood going close. After 10 minutes there have been four shots on target and Saj Chowdhury prophetically claims that this one seems unlikely to be goalless.

How right he is as on 14 minutes the Gunners take the lead. A tremendous pass by Ozil, curled behind the Clarets defence, finds Sead Kolasinac who sets up Aubameyang and he finishes nonchalantly. A quality goal from a quality side and I'm already fearing the worst. However, the worst doesn't arrive, and the battling Clarets pick themselves up and set about the task. Frailties in the Arsenal defence give us some hope of rescuing something from this. The game is getting feisty and there's a booking for Barnes as he tangles with the Greek centre back Sokratis Papastathopolous who escapes any punishment. Surprise, surprise! Not for long however as after another tussle with our Ashley he is yellow-carded. Ironically if he had received the deserved penalty from the first offence that would have been red!

Half time arrives with no further damage and we are still alive in this game. What we don't need after the break is another Arsenal goal, but that's exactly what we get. On 48 minutes we are undone again as Aubameyang nets his second from a quick counterattack. The Clarets once again rally and on 63 minutes a lifeline as Barnes converts following some poor defending by the hosts. The 'diving' and 'playacting' is ratcheting up a gear and the Gunners have players who are highly adept at this tactic. Referee Kevin Friend, who is certainly not our friend, is falling for it all and he's dishing out bookings like confetti at a wedding. That is to us of course!

We have the bit between our teeth now and the goal has given us a real sense of belief. As we push for the equaliser the home fans become increasingly nervous. A good shout for a penalty as Kevin Long is pushed in the back two-handed by Kolasinac, but once again its dismissed! That's now 61 Premier League games since we won a penalty award. Another chance for Barnes who looked certain to score from six yards before Mr Friend pulled the game back for a free kick. Then a chance for Jack Cork who sent his shot spinning wide from a tight angle.

The final irony arrives as it so often does against Arsenal in added time. With men committed forward seeking the leveller we are caught on the counter. Substitute Alex Iwobi finishes the move from a marginally offside position, but you guessed it, it still counts! Game over and another defeat, this time by a somewhat undeserved 3-1 scoreline.

After the game Sean Dyche is decidedly unhappy at what he perceives as 'cheating' by some of the Arsenal players, and inconsistent refereeing decisions. In the after-match press statement he said:

"So many went against us. Ashley Barnes got an elbow in the face from an unnatural movement, yet he comes out with a booking. Two dives again, but nobody got booked.

The biggest one for me. I think it's now 60 games without a penalty, there was a two-handed push on Kevin Long, but the penalty wasn't given because he went down naturally.

Apart from that I was quite happy with the referee's performance."

A nice little touch of sarcasm there Sean!

The result leaves us in 18th position, still in the drop zone. Below us Fulham manage a rare clean sheet in a 0-0 draw at Newcastle, whilst Huddersfield Town go down heavily at home to fellow strugglers Southampton. Just above us Cardiff City are battered 5-1 at home by resurgent 'Mourinho less' Manchester United. At this point, one game shy of the halfway point in the season I feel the relegated three will come from four clubs, ourselves, Fulham, Huddersfield Town and Cardiff City. With two home games coming up over the Christmas period, Everton and West Ham United, points are vital. A run of three defeats from our last four games has done us no favours at all. However, the manner of performance in those games which have included three games against 'elite' teams, have restored some hope.

Result – Arsenal (Aubameyang 14,48, Iwobi 90+1) 3 – 1 (Barnes 63) Burnley

Burnley Team

Hart, Bardsley (Lowton 83), Mee, Tarkowski, Long, Taylor, Hendrick, Westwood, Cork, Wood (Vydra 77), Barnes (Vokes 77)

<u>Subs Not Used</u> – Heaton, Koiki, Gibson, McNeil

Arsenal Team

Leno, Maitland-Niles, Papastathopolous, Monreal (Lichtsteiner 37) Kolasinac, Elneny (Torreira 59), Xhaka, Guendouzi, Ozil, Aubameyang, Lacazette (Iwobi 78)

<u>Subs Not Used</u> – Cech, Ramsey, Nketiah, Saka

Attendance – 59,493

Season To Date – Played 18, Won 3, Drawn 3, Lost 12, Goals For 16, Goals Against 36, Points 12

League Position after Game 18 – 18th

Game 19 - Wednesday 26th December 15.00 – Burnley v Everton

Boxing Day always used to be one of my favourite days for football viewing. It's nice to get out after being cooped up all day on Christmas Day and today's 3.00pm kick-off gives me the rare opportunity of a couple of pints at the pub pre-match. Its unusually mild for late December and there's no need for the customary thermals on this occasion as we enjoy alfresco beer at The Talbot.

For somebody who rarely made team changes Sean Dyche has suddenly become a 'tinkerman'. Today its three again with surprising changes to the defence which has recently shown improved form. In come Matt Lowton and Ben Gibson who is making his Premier League debut. The rather unfortunate players who lose their shirts are Phil Bardsley and Kevin Long. Up front the badly out of form Chris Wood gives way to Sam Vokes as we stick with the new 5-3-2 formation.

Presumably Lowton is preferred over Bardsley for his greater potential attacking threat. However, on this day we are unfortunately not about to witness much of that. Yes, calamitously we are behind after only two minutes. I've barely had time to take my seat before I'm watching Charlie Taylor needlessly concede a corner when he could easily have cleared for a throw-in. From the resulting flag-kick the ball is only partially cleared and the recycled cross from the opposite flank is headed home from inside the six-yard box by an unmarked Yerry Mina. It's not as if they couldn't have seen him coming, the man is a bloody giant! What has happened to our once magnificently resolute rearguard, it's now as porous as a London brick.

If I thought that didn't augur well, worse was to come on 13 minutes as Lowton body checks a marauding 'Toffee'. The resultant free kick from outside the box is well-struck by Lucas Digne, and despite Joe Hart getting a hand on it he can only paw it into the net. Everton, now thoroughly enjoying themselves after their weekend mauling by Spurs, must have thought all their collective birthdays had come together. We were at this stage in a word, hopeless! By 21 minutes we were completely blown away.

James Tarkowski dallied with the ball and was dispossessed by the Brazilian, Bernard. As he bore down on goal 'Tarka' made a miraculous recovering challenge in the penalty area to get the ball out for a corner. Across came the kick and straight through the customary ruck of players and out the other side, to be surely cleared. But no, the referee is blowing and pointing to that thing much underused by the Clarets, the penalty spot. It looked like nothing to me but to Michael Oliver it was a handball by Ben Mee. Inevitably up stepped the Icelander Gylfi Sigurdsson to send Hart the wrong way with his powerful shot and that made three.

Any festive spirit that had been present among the Clarets fans had by this point clearly disappeared. Mumblings of discontent rather than 'glad tidings of great joy' were now very much the order of the day. We could very much have done with a visitation from the 'Angel of the Lord' at this point to ease our troubled minds but Burnley is a long way from Bethlehem these days.

Then when you hoped things couldn't get much worse, suddenly a flicker of hope. A free kick from the left flank brought a fine flicked header from Ashley Barnes that Jordan Pickford in the Everton goal manged to save at the expense of a corner. The resulting flag kick found Tarkowski at the far post whose header seemed to have crossed the line but not according to referee Oliver. Not to worry the ball fell to Ben Gibson who turned to fire home and complete the job.

Half-time and maybe that goal was enough to give us a toe hold in the game. An early second half goal for the Clarets could make things very interesting despite having been outplayed for long periods. And lo and behold it almost came. From a free kick on the left the ball eventually fell to Jeff Hendrick on the right. His cross was perfection to land at the feet of the onrushing Tarkowski who from about the same spot as Mina in the first half contrived to put his shot way over the bar. One of those that looked easier to score than miss went begging and with it our hopes of salvation.

One more decent effort that flashed across the face of goal with nobody able to apply the finishing touch was about as near as we came again. The visitors now confident that they had weathered the storm decided to re-establish their control. On 71 minutes Digne repeated his first half feat, this time firing a 25-yarder low and accurately into the left-hand corner of the net. That was the cue for many long-suffering Clarets to head for the turnstiles. However, the Toffees weren't finished yet and went nap with yet another added time goal. This time a fine through ball was taken under control with one touch of substitute Richarlison's right boot then instantly poked home with his left. That looked simple enough, why can't we do that?

So, yet again we are left to tramp home heads down and not looking forward to the wise cracks from the know-alls who can't wait to tell you 'I could have told you so'! Very knowledgeable sorts are these people, they incredibly know when we are going to win (usually when we have done), and when disaster is looming (currently all the time).

It was never going to be easy against an Everton side smarting from a 6-2 home defeat to Tottenham Hotspur last time out. They look to me to be very much a top 10 team and possess many players of outstanding ability. In Kurt Zouma, Gylfi Sigurdsson, Andre Gomes, Theo Walcott and Bernard they have players capable of gracing the best Premier League teams.

Therein lies the difference between them and us. Last season we finished in 7th position just ahead of Everton in 8th. They and most other Premier League teams have since moved on, improving their squads with quality buys. Unfortunately, we have not. The disastrous summer transfer window bringing in only two outfield players, neither of which have featured prominently, left us standing still. In this league if you stand still you fall backwards and that is the reason for our current predicament.

Result – Burnley (Gibson 36) 1 – 5 (Mina 2, Digne 13,71, Sigurdsson 22 pen, Richarlison 90+3) Everton

Burnley Team

Hart, Lowton, Mee, Tarkowski, Gibson (McNeil 63), Taylor, Hendrick (Gudmundsson 63), Westwood, Cork, Vokes (Wood 73), Barnes

Everton Team

Pickford, Mina, Zouma, Keane, Coleman, Digne, Sigurdsson, Gomes (Gueye 75), Walcott, Calvert-Lewin (Richarlison 67), Bernard (Davies 80)

Subs Not Used – Stekelenburg, Jagielka, Baines, Niasse

Attendance – 21,493

Season To Date – Played 19, Won 3, Drawn 3, Lost 13, Goals For 17, Goals Against 41, Points 12

League Position after Game 19 – 18th

What a way to bring up the mid-point in the season! Still I suppose it just about summed up what has been a disastrous first half of the campaign. In only six games from 19 have we taken any points, and a defence once the envy of most sides is now becoming something of an embarrassment. More goals have been conceded at this point than in the whole of last season. Interestingly we have actually scored one more than at the same point last time, so the reason for our demise is obvious.

It's probably unfair to level all the blame at the defence, it has been said many times that we defend from the front. All sections of the team therefore have a responsibility when we are not in possession to harry and regroup to protect our goal. A major problem as I see it is the lack of 'physicality' in our midfield. Jack Cork who is nothing like the player of last season, Ashley Westwood and Steven Defour (when fit!), have neither the physique and/or creativity to impose themselves on the game. Oh, for a ball winning midfielder, a Joey Barton or a Dean Marney!

Our most creative players, those that can make things happen are without doubt Robbie Brady, Johann Berg Gudmundsson and Steven Defour. However, they have missed so many games with or recovering from injury, that their contribution has been minimal. Consequently, the strikers starved of any meaningful service are feeding off scraps.

The inability to keep hold of the ball inevitably means that the defence is constantly being put under pressure. We can see the result of that clearly in the goals against column. The goalkeeping position also seems to be a problem. How can that be? We have three England goalkeepers! Joe Hart has had possession of the gloves for the league fixtures and made some unbelievable stops. However, the view amongst many fans (including myself) is that while he is an admirable shot-stopper he does not command the box in the manner of Nick Pope. Tom Heaton can count himself unfortunate to have received no game time and seems likely to be on the verge of a move away from the club with the impending return of Pope.

What's the answer to it all? For sure I don't know, but worryingly it seems that Sean Dyche may not either. New recruits are urgently required to lift the descending gloom which is becoming obvious in the stands. Whether they will be forthcoming in the January transfer window however is by no means certain. One thing that is certain is that there will be no 'bargain buys' as clubs realise our desperation the prices will rise accordingly. Who will want to come? The prospect of a dour relegation battle with the likelihood of a reduced salary if it fails is hardly an appealing prospect.

On that happy note it's time to look forward to the last game of 2018. Sunday will see us play host to West Ham United in another 'must-win' fixture. I make that almost 19 must-win fixtures from now till the end! At this point I would like to wish all my readers a very HAPPY New Year. Three points against the Hammers will make that a more likely proposition. UP THE CLARETS!

Game 20 - Sunday 30th December 14.15 – Burnley v West Ham United

In keeping with the mood following the Boxing Day disaster the day dawned cold, wet and miserable ahead of the final game of 2018. A mood of doom and despondency had descended upon most fans and the fan's website 'messageboards' were as usual in meltdown. Against this backdrop I headed for Turf Moor in non-too optimistic mood. My demeanour was not improved by my decision that in view of the excessive amounts of alcohol consumed over the festive period, I would declare today alcohol free.

Team news showed the now customary multiple changes, but a major surprise was the selection of Tom Heaton in goal ahead of Joe Hart. Tom is a real fans favourite at Turf Moor and was reported to be increasingly frustrated by his lack of match action, to the point where he was seeking a move away. Other changes included the recall of Phil Bardsley at right back in place of the suspended Matt Lowton. Also

126

coming back was Chris Wood as we reverted to a favoured 4-4-2 formation. Also missing out due to the formation change were Ben Gibson and Jeff Hendrick with Johann Berg Gudmundsson (JBG) and youngster Dwight McNeil taking the wide midfield berths.

If the 'messageboard's' mood had been downbeat the atmosphere inside the ground was certainly not. Arriving unusually early, i.e. before kick-off, due to the fact that I didn't have to prise my colleagues out of the pub, there was a noticeably positive vibe about the place. The recall of Tom Heaton was largely responsible, and as Sean Dyche, who had been coming in for some flak in certain quarters, strode across the pitch there was a roar of encouragement. Even the miserable weather made a valiant effort to brighten up.

Buoyed by this positivity the team started in similar vein and we were immediately pushing the Hammers back. A good early chance from a left-wing cross from McNeil saw Ashley Barnes fire wide of the post. At the other end Heaton got an early confidence booster as he saved a header from a right-wing corner comfortably, accompanied by a huge roar. However, as we attacked at will, mainly down our left flank through the impressive youngster McNeil, the first goal soon arrived. On 15 minutes a ball in from Ashley Westwood was superbly cushion headed by Barnes into the path of Wood who beat Lucasz Fabianski in the visitor's goal with a fierce right-footer.

That was just the start we needed, and it gave us the confidence to push on with the somewhat subdued Hammers hanging on grimly. They were breached again on 34 minutes as a great ball in from the right by Westwood found McNeil at the far post who managed to squeeze his shot in from a tight angle. The delighted youngster wheeled away to take the congratulations of his equally delighted teammates. He almost doubled his tally shortly afterwards as the hard-working Barnes set him up, but he unfortunately put the effort wide.

Off at half-time and for a change 2-0 up. To be fair it had been pretty easy, and I did expect a better second half showing from our visitors. The game could and should have been wrapped up in the early period of the second half. Firstly, Barnes again teed-up Wood who completely missed his kick right in front of goal. Following more good work by McNeil, Wood repaid the favour, but 'Basher's' effort is foiled by the keeper. Yet another chance goes begging as a fine ball from

Westwood puts Wood in the clear but with only Fabianski to beat he puts his shot wide.

Finally, the visitors start to make something of a game of it as the human battering ram that is Andy Carroll enters the fray from the substitute's bench. He makes an impression with a shot from outside the box which is saved by Heaton. Then as the game draws to a close he produces an even better effort. His powerful header is destined for the net before Heaton acrobatically gets a hand to it to turn it onto the crossbar. It was a magnificent reflex save from a header that definitely deserved better. That just about summed up the day for Tom, a real hero's return to action and the crowd loved it.

What a turnaround from the Everton game! This was one where a four or five goal margin would not have flattered us. And this against a team in fine form having previously won five of their last six fixtures. However, this was a magnificent team performance with some individuals definitely deserving special mention.

Tom Heaton, what more can I say? He is our talisman and although Joe Hart has performed admirably, he could not replace Tom in the fan's hearts. Also, key to this performance was the outstanding contribution of Phil Bardsley. Up against the Hammers danger man Felipe Anderson his uncompromising style and total commitment completely nullified the Brazilian. A word here for the creative, often-unsung hero Ashley Westwood who was involved in both goals. The guy never put a foot wrong all day. Finally, how could I not single out Dwight McNeil. What a joy to see a young player take his big chance with both hands or should that be feet? He was involved particularly in the first half with everything going forward, and what a joy to see a winger actually running with the ball and creating space for his colleagues. Well done Dwight! Let's hope there's a lot more to come.

Result – Burnley (Wood 15, McNeil 34) 2 – 0 West Ham United

Burnley Team

Heaton, Bardsley, Mee, Tarkowski, Taylor, Gudmundsson, Westwood, Cork, Wood (Vokes 90+1), Barnes, McNeil

Subs Not Used – Hart, Gibson, Long, Koiki, Hendrick, Vydra

West Ham United Team

Fabianski, Antonio, Diop, Ogbonna, Cresswell, Snodgrass (Diangana 45), Rice, Noble, Anderson, Arnautovic (Silva 73), Perez (45)

<u>Subs Not Used</u> – Adrian, Masuaku, Obiang, Coventry

Attendance – 20,933

Season To Date – Played 20, Won 4, Drawn 3, Lost 13, Goals For 19, Goals Against 41, Points 15

League Position after Game 20 – 18th

Figure 7 - Club Captain Tom Heaton. His restoration to the team had an immediate impact on morale and results

Game 21 - Wednesday 2nd January 19.45 – Huddersfield Town v Burnley

It's a new year and following the encouraging win against West Ham United, hope springs eternal. I think it's fair to say that for our hosts this is a 'must win' game, and if perhaps not so for us, it is at least a 'must not lose' one. The Terriers, following an added time goal and consequent defeat at lowly Fulham, currently sit bottom of the table four points adrift of their conquerors and five behind ourselves. An opportunity here then to put some significant distance between ourselves.

Sean Dyche unsurprisingly names an unchanged team, with a couple of adjustments to the substitutes bench. Waiting in the wings this time are Robbie Brady and Matt Lowton, Ali Koiki and Ben Gibson make way to accommodate them.

As I sit down to eat a late tea, I opt for Radio Lancashire coverage of the game, with Scott Read commentating and Andy Payton summarising. I am immediately struck by the poor sound quality coming through the DAB radio but put this down partially to the radio and largely to my increasingly poor hearing. However, it's not long before the radio team are apologising for the poor signal and the commentary disappears and reappears at regular intervals.

It's difficult to follow it this way but I have the back-up of the BBC Sports App running 'Live Text' on my phone. That's little consolation as on 33 minutes I learn that we trail to a rare thing, a Huddersfield Town goal at the John Smith's stadium. It's also a rare occurrence for the Terriers star striker as he nets his first goal of the season. A ball in from the left is deftly flighted to land between Ben Mee and Charlie Taylor and is met by a downward header from Steve Mounie which Tom Heaton gets a hand to but can't keep out.

A bit of a blow that as Mee had previously gone closest to scoring with a header from a free kick well saved by Jonas Lossl, who then foiled Chris Wood to thwart the Clarets. However, there's not long to wait for an equaliser as Wood strikes from close range on 40 minutes. The goal comes from some fine play by Dwight McNeil who turns his marker in the box before crossing low for Wood to apply the finish.

A significant piece of the action then ensues as the Town centre-back Christopher Schindler, already booked for a foul on the lively Wood, drags back McNeil as he surges past him. Referee Mike Dean has no alternative than to produce a second yellow card and the German's evening is over. Now what an advantage! We have over half the game to play and the opposition are reduced to 10 men. The sending off forces Huddersfield into a tactical change and their most creative player Alex Pritchard is sacrificed in the interest of increased defensive capability.

There are no more goals before the break and I'm sure there'll be plenty of tactical discussion in both dressing rooms as we look to secure an advantage and the hosts attempt to keep us out. Radio Lancashire are still beset by gremlins and decide to hand over coverage at the start of the second period to their colleagues from Radio Leeds. I'm expecting some pretty biased reporting on behalf of their Yorkshire compatriots but to be fair they turn out to be pretty impartial.

It looks like being a war of attrition this half as we try to find the breakthrough whilst our hosts resolutely defend and hope to sucker punch us. On 59 minutes Phil Bardsley, already on a booking, is injured in a challenge and replaced by Matt Lowton. Our friends from Radio Leeds seem mightily impressed with young McNeil suggesting that he is creating havoc and suggesting the full back needs more assistance. That's the cue for Sean Dyche to remove him from the action and replace him on 63 minutes with Brady. Why? Perhaps it's a wise precaution to not over stretch our precocious talent and also an opportunity to get some game time for the returning Brady.

At this point Radio Lancashire seem to have got their act together and its back to our own 'dynamic duo', Scott and Andy. On 74 minutes our patience is rewarded. A long ball down the right flank finds Johann Berg Gudmundsson who transfers it to Wood. The striker turns his man and flicks the ball inside to the advancing Ashley Westwood. 'Westy' spots Ashley Barnes lurking in space to his left and finds him with pin-point accuracy. It's just the invitation 'Basher' has been waiting for and he promptly tucks his shot into the corner of Lossl's net.

Just over 15 to go plus added time and there's almost another as Barnes goes close from another set up by Wood. The clock runs down as an increasingly desperate Huddersfield throw caution to the wind in search of a much-needed equaliser. Then as we enter time added on for stoppages, a moment of madness. Brady loses the ball and sets off in pursuit of his adversary bringing him down with a reckless two-footed challenge. Mike Dean again has no alternative and this time it's a straight red card and a three-match suspension for our man.

Fortunately, there's insufficient time for the loss of our man advantage to prove costly and we record a second Premier League win on the bounce. How valuable was that! We open up an eight-point gap over the Terriers and move out of the bottom three going 16th, two points clear of Southampton in 18th. Poor old Huddersfield record their eighth consecutive defeat, six of them by a single goal, and now face a seemingly hopeless battle for survival.

Result – Huddersfield Town (Mounie 33) 1 – 2 (Wood 40, Barnes 74) Burnley

Burnley Team

Heaton, Bardsley (Lowton 59), Mee, Tarkowski, Taylor, Gudmundsson, Westwood, Cork, Wood, Barnes (Hendrick 90+2), McNeil (Brady 63)

Subs Not Used – Hart, Long, Vokes, Vydra

Huddersfield Town Team

Lossl, Hadergjonaj (Lowe 71), Jorgensen, Schindler, Kongolo, Hogg, Billing, Kachunga, Pritchard (Durm 44, Depoitre 83), Mbenza, Mounie

Subs Not Used – Hamer, Bacuna, Diakhaby, Stankovic

Attendance – 23,715

Season To Date – Played 21, Won 5, Drawn 3, Lost 13, Goals For 21, Goals Against 42, Points 18

League Position after Game 21 – 16th

FA Cup 3rd Round – Saturday 5th January 12.30 – Burnley v Barnsley

Yet another early kick-off today as we enter the FA Cup competition with a home tie against Barnsley. It's bad enough having the game moved from a traditional 3.00 pm slot for television but when the match is not actually being shown on British TV it's even more galling. This fixture is being screened for overseas broadcasting, but I can't think for the life of me who would be that interested in watching this seemingly lacklustre tie.

Anyhow, once again the interests of the paying fans at the turnstiles play second fiddle to our Lords and Masters, the TV companies. It's therefore a shortened Saturday morning gym session and hastily eaten butties on Woolworth's car park before a short walk to Turf Moor. On my way to the ground I get the notification of the team news and boy is there a lot of it. Eight changes today from Wednesday's victory at Huddersfield.

The only players keeping their places are James Tarkowski, Charlie Taylor and Dwight McNeil. Perhaps keeping their places is a little misleading as all three actually change positions. Tarkowski moves to an unaccustomed right-back role. Taylor moves up to a wide left midfield berth, and McNeil switches flanks to the right. Without doubt changes were expected for what has now become a competition of very much secondary importance, but eight is going some.

It's good to see three players coming back from medium to long-term injuries returning to action. Goalkeeper Nick Pope comes back for his first game since dislocating his shoulder way back in July in the Europa Cup game at Aberdeen. Steven Defour returns in centre midfield after a number of games out, and completing the trio is left-back Stephen Ward returning from a long lay-off following knee surgery.

Also recalled in defence are Kevin Long and Ben Gibson. Jeff Hendrick takes the other centre midfield place and up front we go with the much underused Matej Vydra and Sam Vokes. That's a lot of new combinations but hopefully should be enough to see off League 1 opposition. Having said that I really should be more careful as our recent history in cup competitions against lower league sides is incredibly poor.

Once again, it's a fairly mild day and it's good to see our Yorkshire friends have brought what looks to be a full complement of supporters. We however don't seem so well blessed with fans and I'd hazard a guess that the ground is about half-full.

With so many changes both positional and in terms of personnel it's no surprise that in the early stages we look somewhat disjointed. Conversely our visitors look neat and tidy and are enjoying a lot of possession without really troubling Nick Pope. They are certainly not playing the route one football often associated with lower division teams and there's certainly none of the over physical approach that sometimes is encountered.

To be honest the game was hardly one that will linger long in the memory and in the first half incidents of note are few and far between. That is until Defour fed a ball into Vydra in the box who was knocked over by a defender and the referee awarded something as rare as gold in Burnley, a PENALTY! I have to say that my first reaction was that it was a rather soft decision. Vydra spotted the ball up and we all waited to see him despatch it into the net. Then we waited, and waited, and waited for the referee's whistle which seemed be taking an eternity. Eventually as the striker started his run up the referee stopped him in his tracks and indicated that the penalty had been overruled by the Video Assistant Referee (VAR). Seemingly the correct decision was offside against Vokes and/or Vydra so the long wait for a Burnley penalty continued.

Things almost got worse shortly after as following a cross from the left a Black shirted Barnsley figure got his head to the ball first and nodded past Pope. Fortunately, no need to wait on this occasion for a VAR decision as the assistant referee already had his flag raised for offside. Phew! Just before half time Kevin Long brought a fine save from the visiting keeper with a header from a corner, but the first half ended 0-0.

A great chance at the start of the second half as a Taylor cross found the head of McNeil, only yards from goal however he managed to put it wide when it looked easier to score. We did look a bit more business-like in the second period and the surging runs of McNeil were becoming a feature. However, approaching the end, a replay and a very short and late berth on 'Match of the Day' looked very much on the cards. A fine free kick from Alex Mowatt, narrowly wide of Pope's left-hand post, was the nearest the visitors came but that was the end of their threat.

Just as it looked like they had secured their precious replay, disaster struck. As the game entered stoppage time Vydra moving onto a through ball in the box was felled again. No hesitation from the referee again and this time no interference by VAR, a PENALTY! Poor Vydra robbed of an earlier spot kick was robbed for a second time as regular penalty taker Chris Wood, now on as a substitute claimed the ball. Thankfully for him he made no mistake from the spot and we were into the draw for Round 4.

Has the penalty hoodoo been finally laid to rest? I'll reserve judgement on that one till I see one given in a Premier League game. A third consecutive victory, three goals in three games for Wood, and a definitely not wanted 3rd round replay avoided. I suppose it all turned out right in the end. Wembley here we come.

Result – Burnley (Wood 90+2 pen) 1 – 0 Barnsley

Burnley Team

Pope, Tarkowski, Long, Gibson, Ward (Berg Gudmundsson 59), McNeil, Defour (Cork 78), Hendrick, Taylor, Vydra, Vokes (Wood 74)

Subs Not Used – Hart, Mee, Westwood, Barnes

Barnsley Team

Davies, Cavare, Pinnock, Lindsay, Williams, McGeehan, Hedges (Moore 63), Mowatt, Bahre (Dougall 83), Thiam (Moncur 77), Woodrow

Subs Not Used – Jackson, Adeboyejo, Brown, Greatorex

Attendance – 11,053

Game 22 - Saturday 12th January 15.00 – Burnley v Fulham

Yet another cold, wet and miserable January day in soggy Lancashire. In the last week we've had the full range of weather conditions from torrential rain, brilliant sunshine through to thick mist, but today it's a football day so it's back to strong winds and driving rain. The weather conditions are so severe that we are forced to abandon alfresco beer drinking and settle for the interior comforts of the Talbot Hotel.

This is once again a 'must not lose' fixture for us, and very much a 'must win' one for our visitors who trail us by four points, and currently sit second bottom of the Premier League. Now managed by 'The Tinkerman' Claudio Ranieri, Fulham having spent in the region of £100m in the summer transfer window would have hoped not to be in such a perilous position at this stage. However, with only three victories in the league and the worst defensive record they need points urgently to avoid a quick return to the Championship. They have a poor record at Turf Moor not having won here for 68 years and hopefully we are about to extend that dire statistic.

As expected, Sean Dyche reverts to a much more familiar line-up following last week's FA Cup run out for the fringe members of the squad. Back come Tom Heaton, Phil Bardsley, Ben Mee, Ashley Westwood, Jack Cork, Ashley Barnes and Chris Wood. James Tarkowski and Charlie Taylor return to their favoured positions, whilst Jeff Hendrick takes up an unusual for him, right-sided midfield berth in the absence of the injured Johann Berg Gudmundsson. On the crest of a mini wave with three consecutive victories, two in the league and one in the cup, Clarets fans hopes are high for this fixture.

Those hopes are soon dented as almost from the off Fulham claim the lead with a goal of stunning simplicity and outstanding beauty. A long punt downfield from the right-back position finds the German Andre Schurrle running beyond Taylor to the right of goal. As the ball drops over his shoulder, he brings it down with one touch and allows the ball to bounce before hitting a stunning looping effort over Heaton and in off the underside of the bar. My PNE supporting mate texts me to say, 'cracking goal', to which I reply, 'no stopping them'.

That's a real shock to the system and the buoyant visiting fans are in high glee, sensing perhaps somewhat prematurely, a first away win of the season. To our credit we quickly overcome the disappointment and set about attempting to repair the damage. Chris Wood goes close with a header that hits the post and the Clarets continue to press with young McNeil again looking a formidable weapon on his favoured left flank. On 20 minutes his cross from the left eludes Tarkowski who appears to be fouled going for the header. The ball drops to Jeff Hendrick to the right of goal who fires goalward and around knee height. Perfectly at knee height as it happens for as the ball passes keeper Sergio Rico it cannons off left-back Joe Bryan's knee and into the goal.

Thank heavens for that, the early damage repaired and back to square one with the Clarets very much in the ascendancy. There's not long to wait for more joy as on 23 minutes we complete the comeback and take the lead. Hendrick plays a ball into the box to Barnes and continues his run. Barnes returns it to him and as he is now almost at the by-line, he turns the defender and aims a cross back towards our Ashley. Unfortunately for 'Ash', but even more so for Fulham defender Dennis Odoi who in his attempt to prevent it doing so, plants a header into his own net. Unbelievable, a goal down in two minutes and now a goal up and all in the first 23 minutes.

That's two own goals for the visitors and with their defence looking every bit as shaky as their record would suggest, you wouldn't bet against more. McNeil continues to weave his magic on the left, in one move classically leaving his full-back bemused and 'on his arse'. There are no more goals and the players leave the pitch at the interval to a rousing cheer.

I suppose you could say it's a game of two halves, Burnley so dominant in the first half surrender possession and territory in the second. The visitors well aware of the significance of a defeat in this fixture, and with nothing to lose, decide to give it a real go. The Clarets are pushed deeper and only a couple of fine saves from Heaton, and a tremendous goal-line block by Tarkowski, preserve our slender margin. Up front we are unable to make the ball stick, and all too often hasty, hopeful clearances are coming straight back at us. However, we do seem to have recovered our defensive poise in the last few games. Although its uncomfortable watching we hold out for a fourth consecutive victory and another three extremely valuable points.

Result – Burnley (Hendrick 20 – goal originally credited as Bryan o.g, Odoi o.g.22) 2 – 1 (Schurrle 2) Fulham

Burnley Team

Heaton, Bardsley, Mee, Tarkowski, Taylor, Hendrick, Westwood, Cork, Wood (Vokes 87), Barnes, McNeil

Subs Not Used – Hart, Lowton, Long, Gibson, Defour, Vydra

Fulham Team

Rico, Odoi, Le Marchand, Ream, Christie, Chambers, Seri, Bryan (Cairney 61), Schurrle (Kebano 75), Mitrovic, R Sessegnon (Vietto 45)

Subs Not Used – Bettinelli, Ayite, S Sessegnon, Cisse

Attendance – 19,316

Season To Date – Played 22, Won 6, Drawn 3, Lost 13, Goals For 23, Goals Against 43, Points 21

League Position after Game 22 – 15th

What a vital win that was for us! The three points edged us a further place up the table and opened up sizeable gaps of ten and seven points over Huddersfield Town and Fulham respectively. Our nine points from the three successive victories leave us two points clear of Cardiff City and the improving Southampton, and just one behind Crystal Palace. After the Boxing Day debacle, we looked as good as doomed but our recent upturn in form has at least given us a fighting chance of survival. There's still a lot of points required for safety and no easy games in this division. Every point will have to be fought for but there is a much healthier and positive feel about the club as we enter 2019.

Friday the 18th January and it's now over halfway through the transfer window with no signs yet of any incoming players. Promising young full-back Ali Koiki has gone out on loan to Swindon Town to hopefully gain some first team experience. Jimmy Dunne having returned from his half season loan to Heart of Midlothian early due to injury is back on his travels again this time to high riding League 1 side Sunderland. There are no shortage of rumours regarding possible targets which as usual contain a mix of possible and highly unlikely candidates. So far, and in no particular order we have had:

Adnan Januzaj – Winger – Real Sociedad (Spain)

Joe Allen – Midfield – Stoke City

Jarrod Bowen -Striker/Winger – Hull City

Gary Medel – Midfield – Besiktas (Turkey)

Demetri Mitchell – Left-back/Winger – Manchester United

Scott McTominay – Midfield – Manchester United

Che Adams – Striker – Birmingham City

Jayden Bogle – Full back – Derby County

Yaya Toure – Midfield – unattached

In typical straight-bat fashion Sean Dyche is claiming there are unlikely to be any signings in this window. No doubt we are looking at players, but the fees normally bandied about in January are far in excess of what we would consider reasonable. Still there's almost two weeks left and with most of the action coming in the final few days we may yet unearth the gem that helps preserve our Premier League status.

Following last week's victory over Fulham the media made a great play of the fact that we had won the game without having a shot on target. Today that statistic has been blown out of the water as our opening goal originally credited as a Joe Bryan own goal has been rightly credited to Jeff Hendrick. There is no doubt from television pictures that the shot would have hit the net without the intervention of the hapless Bryan. Well done Jeff you deserved that for a very impressive performance on the day.

Just a few words here off the main topic. As you may or may not be aware my daughter Stephanie is due to be married to her partner Tom on June 15th this year. Plans are currently being made for Tom's 'stag-do' and as Tom is an outdoor type of guy this will inevitably involve 'activities'.

It's going to be a small select bunch on the 'do' comprising, Tom, Tom's Dad Stu, Tom's brother James, Tom's friends Matt and Dan, my old mate Steve and myself. It looks as though we are heading for a weekend in the Lakes. Now bearing in mind that three of the party including myself are of pensionable age (Stu might quibble about that), and therefore perhaps a little more fragile than once was, I was a little horrified at one of the suggested 'treats'.

The younger contingent charged with the task of suggesting the fun came up with the idea of 'Canyoning'. To the uninitiated, of which I am one, this seems to involve taking leaps of faith from great heights into rivers, and ghyll scrambling. As a sufferer with Raynaud's syndrome (google it) the prospect of plunging into ice cold rivers at the end of March doesn't exactly fill me with glee! Thankfully I think the majority have managed to persuade Dan that this is probably not the ideal pastime for this group, and we have settled on more sedate adventures such as Go Ape and Karting. More details on how that goes to follow. Off road buggy racing was suggested and I did point out that I had recently (in October) had my own experience of off-roading which I have no desire to repeat!

Game 23 - Saturday 19th January 15.00 – Watford v Burnley

It doesn't come as a surprise to anyone that when the team news filters through Sean Dyche has named an unchanged starting XI. With three wins in the last three Premier League games the old adage, 'if it ain't broke, don't fix it' couldn't be more apt.

Watford go into the game in good form lying seventh in the table having lost only once in their last seven fixtures. Brimming with confidence they are at us from the off and we endure a torrid opening 10 minutes. A great save by Tom Heaton thwarts Gerard Deulofeu as he's put clear by Troy Deeney. The Hornets then go close again on five minutes and we are holding on by the skin of our teeth at this stage.

However, by the 15-minute mark we have taken the sting out of the Hornets (see what I did there?) and are starting to get a grip of the game. The defence has recovered its poise, the midfield is working hard, and the two strikers are starting to stretch the Watford rearguard. On 30 minutes there's a good chance gone begging as Ashley Barnes heads straight at Watford keeper Ben Foster.

We are playing much better now and once again Dwight McNeil, showing a maturity way beyond his years, is proving a real menace. On 39 minutes a misplaced header by Adrian Mariappa falls to Barnes who misses the target from close range. Radio Lancashire summariser Andy Payton shows commendable loyalty to the strikers' brotherhood by claiming that Ashley was slightly off balance when hitting the shot.

'Payts' expresses the view that he hopes the missed chances don't prove costly. So, do I! By half time we are now well on top and the only thing lacking is a goal. Though there is a sharp reminder of the opposition's threat on the stroke of the interval as Heaton is called in to action again to thwart Deeney.

Sometimes the half time break can disrupt the team's flow but thankfully not so on this occasion and we resume as we left off. Unfortunately, that means more missed chances! Jeff Hendrick has an effort blocked before feeding in Phil Bardsley whose ball into the six-yard box just eludes Barnes. McNeil fires over the top from close range, whilst at the other end there's not much threat this half from Watford.

As the game draws to a close I, and the radio commentary team, are torn between wanting to snatch a winner but at the same time not wanting to slip-up and come home pointless from a game that should have been won. As the board goes up to signal four minutes added time, it's definitely a case of must not concede now.

However, the Clarets are not of that mind and are still looking for that elusive winner. With time almost up McNeil fires in a shot that is parried by Foster, but the ball comes out to Chris Wood who duly despatches it into the net. A brief moment of celebration is cruelly ended as the assistant referee flags for an offside against Wood. Once again, we are on the wrong side of an incorrect decision as TV replays clearly show Wood onside as McNeil releases his shot. When are we going to get our slice of luck? If as they say the decisions even themselves out over the course of a season, then we have a large positive store on which to draw!

Another very good performance tinged with a little disappointment that we didn't take all three points. Still that's a mini run of four games unbeaten (five if we count the FA Cup) and 10 points garnered from a possible 12. Who could have seen that coming on Boxing Day?

Newcastle beat Cardiff 3-0 in a relegation dogfight whilst Southampton see off Everton 2-0 at St Marys. Crystal Palace are narrowly beaten at Liverpool 4-3, but defeats for Huddersfield and Fulham in the Sunday fixtures maintain a healthy gap between us and them. Cardiff City now trail us by three points and the gap to Fulham and Huddersfield is now eight and eleven respectively. Although we drop one position, we are level on points with Southampton and Crystal Palace and one ahead of the Geordies.

Result – Watford 0 – 0 Burnley

Burnley Team

Heaton, Bardsley, Mee, Tarkowski, Taylor, Hendrick, Westwood, Cork, Wood, Barnes, McNeil

Subs Not Used – Hart, Lowton, Long, Gibson, Defour, Vydra, Vokes

Watford Team

Foster, Femenia (Britos77), Kabasele, Mariappa, Holebas, Cleverley, Capoue, Sema (Success 56), Pereyra, Deeney, Deulofeu

Subs Not Used – Gomes, Masina, Gray, Quina, Wilmot

Attendance – 19,510

Season To Date – Played 23, Won 6, Drawn 4, Lost 13, Goals For 23, Goals Against 43, Points 22

League Position after Game 23 – 16th

It's now Friday 25th January and not unsurprisingly we are still to see any new faces arriving at Turf Moor. We were warned by the club that the January window would be difficult (aren't they all!) so we wait with bated breath as the window starts to creak slowly closed. Less than a week to go now and few if any credible links to suitable recruits. It looks like we are going to put faith once again in the squad we have and hope there are no serious injury problems.

However, there was one piece of good news this week as rising young start Dwight McNeil put pen to paper signing an improved and extended contract. His new deal will now take him through till the end of the 2022/23 season with an option of a further year. This is very much a timely intervention by the club in protecting what looks likely to become a major asset. In the sort of form that he is currently displaying in this his debut season (nay half season) he will no doubt soon be receiving the attention of wealthy predators.

This weekend sees a break from league action as we return to the FA Cup with the daunting prospect of an away trip to Manchester City. This will be followed quickly by another major test with another trip to Manchester coming on the following Tuesday. This will be a more important outing as we attempt to take something from a resurgent Manchester United in Premier League action. Since the departure of Jose Mourinho, and the temporary appointment of Ole Gunnar Solskjaer, the Reds have been in unstoppable form.

These next two fixtures I guess you could say represent 'free hits' for the Clarets. We are highly unfancied to get anything from either encounter and therefore have little to lose. It's likely that the FA Cup tie at City will see multiple changes and a line up more akin to that seen in the previous round at home to Barnsley. There will be no desire to risk injury to players ahead of the far more important league fixture coming close on its heels. By the same token Manchester City still going in pursuit of four competitions are likely to view this game as slightly less important and will rest players. Still, with a squad as big and rich in quality as theirs it's debatable whether that will mean a weaker XI on the field or not.

Let's hope we can give a good account of ourselves, and if we are not to be victorious, at least come away with our heads held high.

FA Cup 4th Round – Saturday 26th January 15.00 – Manchester City v Burnley

Well for sure this is definitely not a review I am going to dwell on. I suppose you could say I feared the worst when the line-ups were announced. As predicted Sean Dyche treating the FA Cup competition as of one minor importance, and this particular tie as highly 'unwinnable', selected a team that to be fair didn't have a cat in hell's chance!

Seven changes for the Clarets confirmed everybody's suspicions that the emphasis was firmly on Tuesday's fixture at Manchester United. In goal came Nick Pope, then in the absence of a recognised right-back we went with two left-backs, three centre halves, four across the middle and a diminutive lone striker in Matej Vydra! City also showed some changes resting the front three from their last outing, replacing but hardly weakening them with Riyad Mahrez, Gabriel Jesus and Bernardo Silva. In case things looked like getting a little tricky for them they reserved seats on the bench for Raheem Sterling, Leroy Sane, Sergio Aguero and the promising youngster Phil Foden.

On paper it looked like a mismatch, on the pitch it didn't take long to look exactly the same. Pope saved early with his feet from Silva, and then with his hands from Danilo. However, the almost inevitable arrived on 23 minutes as Jesus took advantage of a ball threaded through by Danilo. Arriving on the left side of the penalty area he collected it, turned inside two defenders with ease, and fired home right-footed from close range.

I think it's fair to say that for the rest of the first half we were completely outplayed, yet somehow, we reached the sanctuary of the dressing room just the one goal down. With possession statistics 77/23 in favour of the home team, and shots at 9/1, it didn't look promising, but we were still hanging in there.

At the interval Jack Cork replaced the returning from suspension Robbie Brady, who now becomes injured again! Then shortly after the restart we see perhaps the defining moment of the game. Vydra, who for almost the entire first period had been a stranger to the rest of his team as he ploughed a lone furrow up front, was presented with the golden opportunity. Dispossessing the dawdling Danilo, he motored towards the City goal, one-on-one with the keeper Ederson. This was the moment, the one chance that can change the game, he can't miss. Oh yes, he can! Last year's top scorer in the Championship, lethal in front of goal, can this time only put his shot into the side netting.

You just knew at that moment all hope was gone. Within five minutes of that miss the all too familiar collapse was about to begin. On 52 minutes Silva's shot despite taking a deflection beat Pope too easily for number two. Another nine minutes before Kevin De Bruyne's powerful shot gave Nick no chance and the rout was on.

With only 61 minutes on the clock I'm willing the game to end to avoid humiliation. The City slickers are toying with us and you just know there are more goals coming. My mate John W can't take much more of it and to divert his attention from the mauling decides to de-spider his conservatory lights. It doesn't make a ha'porth of difference, wave after wave of attacks keep coming and so do the goals.

On 73 minutes its number four as Kevin Long turns a hard cross from De Bruyne past his own keeper, but worse is to come for him on 85. Shepherding the ball from Aguero, recently introduced as a substitute, he waits for Pope to come and collect. Unfortunately, Nick is transfixed like a snake's prey, and stays rooted to his line. As Aguero bustles past young Kevin he has no option but to drag him back and concede a penalty. Aguero needs no second invitation and promptly rifles home.

Thank God it's all over. A 5-0 drubbing, a footballing lesson and once again the end of our Wembley dream. I don't know about a dream; in recent years the cup competitions have become something more of a nightmare! The only consolation is that we have at least been thumped by most probably the best team in the land.

Put it to bed, forget about it and move on, its only Manchester United at Old Trafford next!

Result – Manchester City (Jesus 23, Silva 52, De Bruyne 61, Long 73 o.g, Aguero 85 pen) 5 – 0 Burnley

Burnley Team

Pope, Taylor, Tarkowski, Long, Gibson, Ward, McNeil, Defour (Westwood 77), Hendrick, Brady (Cork 45), Vydra (Wood 62)

Subs Not Used – Hart, Mee, Vokes, Barnes

Manchester City Team

Ederson, Walker, Stones, Otamendi, Danilo, De Bruyne (Foden 75), Fernandinho (D Silva 66), Gundogan, B Silva, Jesus (Aguero 75), Mahrez

Attendance – 50,121

Game 24 - Tuesday 29th January 20.00 – Manchester United v Burnley

All my years of supporting Burnley FC, and these are now totalling almost 60, have still not conditioned me to the momentous changes of mood and wellbeing that a football game can impart. This without doubt was one of those occasions when a true fan feels the whole gamut of emotions in little over 90 minutes.

Following Saturday's depressing if not unexpected failure at the Etihad this fixture had all the makings of yet another disaster. Not since 1962 have the Clarets tasted victory at Old Trafford or 'The Theatre of Dreams' as they like to call it. What odds on redressing that tonight? Pretty remote I would imagine. The rejuvenated Reds, on the crest of a wave after replacing the odious Jose Mourinho, with the baby-faced assassin Ole Gunnar Solskjaer, were on the back of an eight-game winning run. The Clarets despite a much improved five game unbeaten run still sat just outside the relegation slots.

Once again on paper United's expensively assembled squad including massive buys, Romelu Lukaku, Paul Pogba and Alexis Sanchez looked formidable opponents. However, Burnley back to their more familiar Premier League line-up were in no mood to roll over and die. In front of a crowd of 74,529 a small but extremely vociferous Burnley contingent were about to witness an epic Clarets battle.

Unsurprisingly our confident hosts were quickly onto the front foot and looking for an early goal. There was a good opportunity for Marcus Rashford put through by Juan Mata but the young striker made a real hash of his effort putting it wide. Mata himself went close as Tom Heaton pulled off a magnificent save to tip his effort on to a post, but the assistant referee had already flagged him offside.

From this point the game evened out with United enjoying the lion's share of possession but the Burnley defence, superbly marshalled by Heaton, proving to be a formidable barrier. Up front Ashley Barnes and Chris Wood were giving the United centre-backs Victor Lindelof and Phil Jones a thorough examination from which they were looking decidedly uncomfortable.

In at half-time all square and that was a much better position than I had feared at the outset. More heartening though was the manner of the performance. We had taken the sting out of the opposition and were certainly not overawed by the occasion.

Then a magical start to the second period as on 51 minutes we take the lead. A poor ball out of defence put the young United midfielder Andreas Pereira under pressure. Jack Cork was on him in a flash and dispossessing him headed for goal. As Barnes peeled off to his left 'Corky' released the ball into his path. Without further invitation 'Basher' smashed an unstoppable rising drive past the helpless David De Gea.

Fantastic! For the second year in succession ahead at Old Trafford. With the hosts huffing and puffing and the Clarets standing resolute time edged slowly on and I started to believe we might get something here. On 81 minutes that belief grew even stronger as incredibly we went 2-0 up. Ashley Westwood's pin-point cross found Chris Wood and his glancing header gave De Gea no chance. Like last season we now had a two-goal cushion, but this time we only had 10 minutes plus stoppage time to hold on.

When you've been a Claret as long as I have you know not to count your chickens before they hatch. How many times have we had victory snatched from within our grasp? Surely not this time! Yet on 87 minutes a reckless hand on substitute Jesse Lingard's shoulder gave him the opportunity to go down in the penalty area. Referee Jon Moss could barely wait to point to the spot. Pogba duly despatched the spot kick and all of a sudden, the game had changed.

From coasting we were now hanging on. Five minutes of stoppage time were added, largely down to excessive time wasting by ourselves, and the heat was on. Something had to give, and it did. In the second minute of added time Heaton produced another miraculous save to keep out a Sanchez header but was powerless to stop the follow up from Lindelof.

I guess I just sort of knew it was going to happen although I thought that maybe just this once God might smile on us. For us a very creditable draw that felt like a defeat. For Manchester United a draw that felt like a victory. Sometimes it can be a very cruel game.

On the plus side the unbeaten run extends to five in the league and he last two have earned draws from difficult away fixtures at Watford and Manchester United. Confidence is once again high, and we are looking more and more like the Burnley we have come to know.

Result – Manchester United (Pogba 87 pen, Lindelof 90+2) 2 – 2 (Barnes 51, Wood 81) Burnley

Burnley Team

Heaton, Bardsley, Mee, Tarkowski, Taylor, Hendrick, Westwood, Cork, Wood, Barnes, McNeil (Gudmundsson 78)

Subs Not Used – Hart, Ward, Gibson, Benson, Vydra, Vokes

Manchester United Team

De Gea, Young, Jones, Lindelof, Shaw, Pereira (Lingard 63), Pogba, Matic, Mata, Lukaku (Sanchez 67), Rashford

Subs Not Used – Romero, Smalling, Fred, Dalot, Herrera

Attendance – 74,529

Season To Date – Played 24, Won 6, Drawn 5, Lost 13, Goals For 25, Goals Against 45, Points 23

League Position after Game 24 – 17th

Finally, after what seems to have been an interminably long month, the last day of January arrives and with it the closure of the transfer window. Now if you cast your mind back a few months I'm sure you will recall my thoughts on the summer transfer window were less than positive. I said at the time that our failure to capitalise on our most opportune time ever to strengthen the squad, was in my opinion, a severe misjudgement.

Subsequent events have I believe gone some way to proving my point. Failure to make the Europa Cup group stage and a poor start to the Premier League season find us where we are today, seventeenth in the table and embroiled in a relegation battle. True, results of late have been much more encouraging and we have at least given ourselves a fighting chance of survival. Sean Dyche himself commented that the summer transfer window activity had left us two or three players short of what he would have liked.

Clearly the January window was always going to be difficult. Selling clubs are reluctant to part with their prize assets ahead of what may be for them a tilt at promotion or a fight against the dreaded drop. Consequently, if we thought prices in the summer were ridiculous just imagine what they are now. Furthermore, we are not currently the attraction that we were back at the end of last season. There's no European competition to entice players, and worse still an imminent possibility of a relegation with dire financial consequences to their contracts.

However, I did feel that with the stretched nature of our already thin squad, and the problems caused by injuries both of late (Aaron Lennon), and of a prolonged nature (Steven Defour, Robbie Brady, Stephen Ward), that January would see us bite the bullet in order to strengthen for a determined push up the table. How disappointing then that after much speculation and links to various individuals, on the final day of the window we emerge as net sellers in the market.

Incredibly, we head for the remainder of the campaign arguably weaker than we entered it! Leaving Turf Moor after a lengthy and successful spell is striker Sam Vokes. Frustrated by his lack of match action Sam is lured away to Championship side Stoke City for a not inconsiderable sum of money, reputedly in the region of £9m. Coming the other way as a makeweight in the deal is England veteran Peter Crouch, on a short-term contract till the end of the season.

Now I'm sure I, and most fair-minded Clarets fans, have nothing against 'Crouchy', but the signing of a 38-year-old striker on a three/four-month contract seems like a distinct lack of ambition! Of course, now he is a Claret I will give him my total and unreserved support. However, I can't get my head round allowing a proven asset like Sam go, to be replaced by a player who let's face it, is past his best.

The word on the streets is that Sam wished to leave but we were reluctant to allow it without a replacement striker in situ. The target replacement is strongly rumoured to have been Birmingham City's Che Adams. However, it proved impossible to persuade the selling club, under a transfer embargo for Financial Fair Play (FFP) breach of regulations, to part with the player. Failing to land the target therefore meant that the signing of Crouch filled the vacant spot left by Sam's departure.

Now that's all well and good but it begs the question, what the hell are the recruitment team supposed to be doing? Surely their job is to identify realistic targets which presumably includes assessing the likely price and availability of the player. It should have been fairly obvious that Birmingham City, possibly facing a 15-point deduction for FFP misdemeanours, were highly unlikely to be willing sellers. Where were the alternatives and why was the pursuit left till the final days of the window?

It's obvious that the squad is extremely short of cover in centre midfield, and also with the current injury situation, of wingers. What moves were made to address that? There may well have been enquiries, but to the man on the terrace all we can see is once again an abject failure to bolster the squad.

So, for whatever reasons a poor summer of transfer activity has been eclipsed by an even worse winter one. To the fans it looks like we are engaged in a highly risky business of going with what we have got. Heaven help us if we get serious long-term injuries in the critical areas. If ultimately all ends in disaster, which relegation would certainly be, then the powers that be will certainly have something to answer for.

Rant over, time to get heads back in gear and look forward to tomorrow's upcoming yet again 'must not lose' encounter, this time with Southampton at the Turf. With the two sides locked on the same number of points I'm bracing myself for a no-holds barred contest. Perhaps we'll see a late winner from Peter Crouch to seal the victory!

Ironically the striker was almost a Claret back in 2001! With a deal agreed the player decided against at the last minute, reputedly due to the Burnley riots at the time. Oh well, better late than never!

Game 25 - Saturday 2nd February 15.00 – Burnley v Southampton

As expected, an unchanged team for the Clarets following on from Tuesday's magnificent performance at Old Trafford. Also, as expected a place on the bench for our towering new acquisition Peter Crouch.

I guess you could say this was a day that revolved around penalty decisions, and that's a rarity for Burnley who don't get Premier League penalties.

On a sunny but cold day there's a lively start from our visitors, who since the appointment of their new manager are enjoying something of a revival in their fortunes. Enjoying plenty of early possession and with strikers Nathan Redmond and ex Claret Danny Ings looking lively they are certainly posing a threat. In fact, they should probably have led as Ings latched on to a long ball to find himself one-on-one with keeper Tom Heaton. Fortunately for us Danny did the decent thing and only managed to hit Tom's shoulder with his shot which bounced to safety. Unfortunately for Ings his afternoon was over shortly after as he succumbed to yet another injury and had to be substituted.

By now the Clarets had established a toe hold in the game and were themselves looking dangerous. Chris Wood blazed a right-footer wide of the target after doing the hard bit to set up the opportunity. Ashley Barnes headed another chance straight at Alex McCarthy in the Saints goal before a moment of real controversy.

As Barnes latched onto a through ball from Phil Bardsley in the penalty area, McCarthy having lost the race to the ball downed our man with his sprawling challenge. It looked a 'dead cert' penalty, although as we all know Burnley don't get penalties. Incredibly the referee Anthony Taylor, interpreted the situation as a dive and promptly booked the now irate striker. How bloody ridiculous! In midweek Jesse Lingard won a penalty for Jeff Hendrick's hand on his shoulder, this time Barnes is 'wiped out' by the challenge and NOTHING! Ashley is in real danger of turning the yellow card into a red as he berates the assistant referee who must have clearly seen the incident. However, after a few moments he manages to suppress his anger and focus on the job in hand.

At this stage, approaching half time, referee Taylor has totally incurred the wrath of the home support with a series of incorrect decisions in favour of the visitors. He also manages to book Bardsley for admittedly a rather rash challenge, whilst earlier having let off a 'Saint' for a much more malicious assault on Charlie Taylor.

Off at the break all square but with the home crowd justifiably seething at the injustice of it all.

A slow start to the second period sees the Clarets finding it difficult to get into their stride. The Saints buoyed perhaps by their good fortune over the penalty decision are well in command. It's no surprise when on 55 minutes the impressive Nathan Redmond fires them ahead. Taking a pass from Jan Bednarek in his stride, he advances through the middle before striking unerringly from around 20 yards into Heaton's right-hand corner of the net. That's just what we didn't need but it had been coming.

That's the cue for changes, Johann Berg Gudmundsson is introduced to the fray replacing an ineffective Hendrick. That is followed on 76 minutes by Crouch's Turf Moor debut. The Clarets are now making chances which mostly fall to Barnes. From the first he hits the keeper at close range and then is decidedly unfortunate on the next occasion as his powerful shot hits the angle of post and crossbar.

The introduction of the giant Crouch has certainly unsettled the visitors and crosses are raining into the box at every opportunity. Ungainly he may look but his very awkwardness is rattling the defence. As we enter four minutes stoppage time it looks like it's going to be 'one of those days'.

Then incredibly as yet another ball is pumped high into the box Crouch's contact sends the ball in the direction of Jack Stephens. For some inexplicable reason the defender promptly handles the ball. Even referee Taylor can't miss that one and this time we duly get our just reward, a PENALTY!

Amazingly it's 67 Premier League games since our last spot-kick, and now the big question, who will take it! Regular penalty taker Chris Wood is off the pitch sacrificed for the introduction of Crouch. There's only one man for this job, Ashley Barnes make our day! Cool as a cucumber, and with almost the last kick of the game, Ashley ripples the net and a vital point is won.

Hopefully the penalty hoodoo is broken. Ironically, Sam Vokes making his debut for Stoke City, wins and then misses a penalty. It's a funny old game!

Defeats for Huddersfield 5-0 at Chelsea, and Fulham 2-0 at Crystal Palace strengthen our position in the relegation battle. Newcastle lose narrowly at Tottenham Hotspur to leave them on the same points as both ourselves and Southampton. The big disappointment though comes in the televised tea-time fixture as Bournemouth, conquerors of Chelsea in midweek by four goals, capitulate at Cardiff City leaving the Welshmen now just two points adrift of us. Still it's another point gained towards safety and the unbeaten Premier League run now stretches to six games.

Result – Burnley (Barnes 90+4 pen) 1 – 1 (Redmond 55) Southampton

Burnley Team

Heaton, Bardsley, Mee, Tarkowski, Taylor, Hendrick (Gudmundsson 58), Westwood, Cork, Wood (Crouch 76), Barnes, McNeil (Brady 81)

Subs Not Used – Hart, Ward, Gibson, Vydra

Southampton Team

McCarthy, Bednarek, Stephens, Vestergaard, Targett, Ward-Prowse, Slattery, Romeu, Armstrong (Valery 77), Redmond (Austin 87), Ings (Long 27)

Subs Not Used – Gunn, Elyounoussi, Sims, Jones

Attendance – 19,787

Season To Date – Played 25, Won 6, Drawn 6, Lost 13, Goals For 26, Goals Against 46, Points 24

League Position after Game 25 – 17th

I'm beginning to feel a little guilty now that I have been somewhat negligent in keeping my readers who like to follow the walking programme, up to date. I think this is a reflection of the fact that things have been of late pretty hectic on the football front.

Walking has as you can imagine has been in some varied weather conditions since the turn of the year. This has not deterred Tuesday's

Lancashire Dotcom walkers and since the turn of the year we have had two walks with 34 participants. Imagine that lot of arthritic knees attempting to cross slippery and dilapidated stiles! It's no wonder some walks feel like they are going to finish in the dark.

Still, we have been spoilt of late with a good run of pub lunches on Tuesdays. Memorable among these have been the New Waggoners (Burnley), the Chetham Arms (Chapeltown), the Crown Hotel (Colne) and the Wheatsheaf at Woodplumpton. All have provided excellent fayre after some pretty cold and wet outings. However, best value for money award must go to the Crown at Colne who put on a splendid 2 course lunch for an amazing £6.40!

Last week was notable for the wettest and coldest walks of the year. On Tuesday the Dotcomer's enjoyed (?) a sodden trudge around the environs of Woodplumpton. A good soaking was endured by all but quickly forgotten after lunch around a roaring fire at the Wheatsheaf and a pint of Marston's 61 Deep. The beer incidentally being named after the depth of the well in Burton from which the water is drawn for the brewing process.

This was followed by Gwen Walton's snow and ice spectacular on Thursday. Nine brave souls and 'Button the wonder dog' set out to tackle Thieveley Pike and Heald Moor before returning via Black Scout to the sanctuary of the Ram Inn at Cliviger. On this occasion the 'wonder dog' failed to live up to his name and had to be returned home early in the proceedings after suffering 'ice balls' on his pads. I must confess I almost succumbed to the same complaint but nowhere near my feet!

The trek across Heald Moor was made all the more interesting by the fact that the snow had completely obscured the path and most landmarks. Added to that was the descending freezing fog which necessitated keeping the group tight to avoid losing anybody. Heald Moor is a wet place at the best of times, so an added pleasure was finding oneself plunging through thin ice covered by snow to sink knee deep into freezing bog. What joy! After almost eight miles of that, one or two hardy souls were looking a little grey around the gills. Wait till Gwen suggests her next outing, a poor turnout is almost guaranteed.

Also put to bed by the weekend were the details of my son-in-law to be's stag weekend. After much deliberation and anguish over rapidly rising hotel fees, the final destination turns out to be Lancaster. Saturday will see a day of outdoor activities and the options agreed are quad biking, clay pigeon shooting, archery and axe throwing! I am particularly looking forward to the latter as I feel it may give me the opportunity to develop a new career. After a little practice I am sure I will soon master the technique. My plan is then to purchase one of those revolving wheels and hurl tomahawks at my wife Julie as she circles in her lycra leotard. I'll let you know how it goes.

After the initial shock of the Peter Crouch signing the good folk of Burnley seem to be warming to our amiable giant. Prior to the move there was a suggestion on the 'Up the Clarets' messageboard that the deal would not go ahead. The inference was that he had failed his medical due to banging his head on the Culvert which is a well-known canal aqueduct in the town.

Thoughtful as ever after the deal had been concluded, some kind-hearted Burnley folk erected a sign on the aforementioned bridge reading;

"WELCOME CROUCHIE. MIND YOUR HEAD LAD!"

The picture even managed a mention on 'Match of the Day 2' and prompted a response from the man himself;

"Everyone is so friendly in Burnley. So thoughtful"

By Monday 4th February, and on the back of an approximately 15-minute substitute appearance, he had joined the Clarets 'Hall of Fame' by having a sausage named after himself, 'Crouchie's Red Hot Robot'. Watch this space I think this guy may have the stuff that legends are made of.

Tuesday's Dotcom walk was a watery circuit from Rivington. After some confusion regarding car parking, we made a slightly belated start for a tour of Upper Rivington, Anglezarke, High Bullough and Yarrow reservoirs. Heavy rain was forecast for early afternoon, so leader Bob Clare had hoped for a prompt start. Thwarted in this aim by the car park issue but assisted by good terrain and flattish going, 30 Dotcomers enjoyed a great walk only getting caught out by the rain for the last 10 minutes.

Thursday's Burnley Contingent walk is a newly researched ramble courtesy of the 'Wandering Weirs'. This time we are heading from Oldfield Lane near Stanbury in Bronte country. It's a 7.5-mile circular taking in Haworth and finishing in the Grouse Inn, a Timothy Taylor's house.

The walk starts in heavy rain and cool temperatures, in fact pretty normal for early February in Northern England. By the half-way point it's still raining so lunch is taken sheltering under the bandstand in the park at Haworth. Miraculously as we finish our feast the rain halts and the bulk of the second part of the trek is in a mix of sunshine, cloud and intermittent showers. All in all, a good day out and a splendid walk once again by the Weirs.

The after walk debrief at the Grouse gave me the opportunity to visit this pub for the first time. It's quite a sizeable place enjoying a good reputation for food. It's quite off the beaten track but for a Thursday lunch was pretty busy, which is usually a sign of good quality. Beer of the day for Mike McD and myself was Timothy Taylor's Golden Best, a good session bitter from the Keighley Brewery. Just one negative here about the Grouse or should that be a grouse about the Grouse. Three pints of Timothy Taylor's Landlord set the unsuspecting Michael Coates back a whopping £12.30! Come on lads £4.10 a pint! It's not London or even the Ribble Valley you know. It's not as though the beer had a long way to travel, Keighley is practically on the doorstep. Still, it didn't seem to deter Michael and his team, they celebrated by having another.

Game 26 - Saturday 9th February 17.30 – Brighton & Hove Albion v Burnley

A teatime kick off for this one as the game is screened live by BT Sport. A difficult one for me to follow as I'm up in the wilds of North Yorkshire paying a visit to my daughter's wedding venue ahead of the event scheduled for June. Arkengarthdale is a beautiful location, but as is often the case with this sort of place, not best served by modern technology. Accordingly, mobile phone signals are at best hit and miss, and Wi-Fi at the Charles Bathurst Inn similarly variable. I am informed that the best Wi-Fi reception is in the bar so that's where I'm going to station myself.

Saturday dawns and it's a fairly uneventful trip to the first port of call Barnard Castle. I opt for a route by-passing Skipton then through the beautifully named Blubberhouses on to the Ripon by-pass. From there it's an easy, if somewhat breezy, run up the A1M to Scotch Corner then the A66 to Barnard Castle.

After a walking tour of the town whilst my wife and daughter sample the beauty treatment at The Hub, by way of a pre-wedding trial, it's off to the Charles Bathurst (CB) Inn. Arriving around 4.15 there is a meeting with the proprietors to discuss wedding day arrangements before checking in. By 5.30 we are unpacked and I'm itching to sample the beery delights in the bar for a pre-dinner drink. I'm already aware that Fulham have gone down 0-3 at home to Manchester United casting them 10 points adrift of us, surely too many to make up now. Unfortunately, WhatsApp messages from my colleagues are informing me that Cardiff City have snatched a late winner at Southampton, a result that plunges us into the bottom three.

The technology at the CB doesn't disappoint and with no phone signal and a spasmodic Wi-Fi reception it's going to be interesting. However, to cheer me up I do note that Chris Wood has given us a 21st minute lead ahead of my trip to a rather noisy and boisterous bar. There's just time for an excellent, if pricy pint, of Black Sheep Brewery's Baa Baa, before heading back to the room with the lead still intact.

I'm expecting a bit of a tortuous second half but before I hit the bath I notice 'Woody' has done it again! Two up, can we do it? I take my phone and glasses in the bathroom to keep in touch but it's pointless as there is zero signal in there. Once out there's even better news as I learn of a penalty to the Clarets. As we head back to the bar for dinner and a few scoops Ashley Barnes duly despatches it and with only about 15 minutes to go we must be home and dry. Not so fast, within a couple of minutes and before I've made it to the beer, having had to detour around a boozy 'stag do' at the bar, our hosts have pulled one back. Luckily that's the end of the scoring and I settle back for a great night with my family in a fantastic Inn. The food is excellent and just tops off for me what has been a marvellous day.

Back home again by Sunday evening and an opportunity to put a bit more meat on the bones of that score line. It transpires that this extremely vital victory is down largely to some magnificent goalkeeping from Tom Heaton., and some lethal finishing by the Clarets. There's also been some major assistance from 'Lady Luck', who I'm sure all of the Claret persuasion will agree, has been somewhat overdue in putting in an appearance!

There were early chances for the Seagulls notably from Solly March and Pascal Gross but both thwarted by brilliant saves from Heaton. Then an incredible escape at the other end as Shane Duffy deflects Dwight McNeil's cross onto his own crossbar the rebound falling to Ashley Barnes who heads it back onto the bar. There's no such good fortune for our south coast friends on 26 minutes as Barnes dinks a ball over the top, Lewis Dunk loses his footing and leaves Chris Wood bearing down on goal. His firmly hit shot rockets past the advancing Mat Ryan and into the roof of the net.

The second half pressure is eased by a second Burnley goal as McNeil picks up a pass around the halfway line. Running at the defence he gets a lucky break on the ball and is suddenly in the clear. To his left is Wood and as he reaches the box, McNeil feeds him in to fire a curler low into the far corner.

The desperate hosts now have no alternative but to throw caution to the wind and attack. Now comes a big slice of luck. As a ball into the penalty area is clearly to all but the referee taken under control by Jeff Hendrick's arm. Waving away the penalty appeals the official allows the Clarets to break quickly out. Barnes is quick to see the possibilities and as Wood puts him clear over the halfway line he races in on goal. Attempting to take the ball round keeper Ryan he is sent sprawling and the referee has no option but to award a penalty kick and yellow card the keeper. Incredible! No penalties for over 65 Premier League games then two in consecutive matches. Barnes is in no mood to miss his second opportunity in a week and despatches it low in the corner.

With just 16 minutes to go 3-0 up is an unassailable lead, and despite a goal back on 76 minutes it can be no more than a consolation. This extremely valuable, nay vital win catapults the Clarets up to 15th in the table level on points now with Brighton and Crystal Palace. The scrap to avoid the third relegation spot is now really hotting up with just three points separating no less than six clubs. It's nail biting time but with the Clarets now unbeaten in seven league games and in a rich vein of form, things are looking up.

Result – Brighton & Hove Albion (Duffy 76) 1 – 3 (Wood 26, 61, Barnes 74 pen)) Burnley

Burnley Team

Heaton, Bardsley, Mee, Tarkowski, Taylor, Hendrick, Westwood, Cork, Wood, Barnes, McNeil

Subs Not Used – Hart, Lowton, Ward, Gibson, Long, Vydra, Crouch

Brighton & Hove Albion Team

Ryan, Montaya, Duffy, Dunk, Bong, Gross (Bissouma 66), Stephens, Propper, March (Knockaert 48), Murray, Locadia (Jahanbakhsh 66)

<u>Subs Not Used</u> – Button, Burn, Kayal, Bernardo

Attendance – 29,323

Season To Date – Played 26, Won 7, Drawn 6, Lost 13, Goals For 29, Goals Against 47, Points 27

League Position after Game 26 – 15th

Saturday 16th February is a blank weekend in the Clarets fixture list due to our exit from the FA Cup. For me it means a stress-free weekend where I can collect my thoughts and channel my energies into a positive outlook for the remaining games. For the squad it means a nice mid-season break to Portugal for 'warm weather' training. It's a bit of an odd one that, why go warm weather raining when you have to return to the near sub-zero temperatures of a northern winter? I think it's what we would have described at work as a bit of a 'jolly'.

No rest for us walkers though. Tuesday 12th saw the last Dotcom walk of the half-term making an outing from an old favourite pub of ours, the Edisford Bridge, Clitheroe. Led by our old friend Nigel, we had a short walk which he described as a 'city break'! This involved short stretches of the Ribble Way and long stretches of a town stroll through Clitheroe. No less than 36 hardy souls turned out for this one, a Dotcom record, and we are now becoming a truly unstoppable force. No competition to pass through stiles from other walking groups. When they hear the sound of 72 pounding pensioners boots, they get out of the way smartish.

It wasn't the most challenging of walks, but Nigel enjoyed reliving his schoolmaster days regaling us with interesting facts about the town. It also afforded the opportunity for Dave Preedy to visit his ancestors grave in a local church yard, and also the church where he was married. Excellent fayre at the Edisford Bridge pub who handled the requirements of 30+ hungry walkers admirably.

This short easy outing was followed on Thursday by a more demanding circuit for the Burnley Contingent courtesy of the Wandering Weirs. This time it was a trip over the border to Yorkshire and a highly enjoyable hike in very spring like weather from Kildwick. John W took great delight in showing and describing various piles of stones along the route. They clearly meant something to him, but to me they were just a pile of stones. This observation earned me the dubious distinction of being branded a Philistine. Similarly, unimpressive to me at least, was the Jubilee Tower close to the end of the trek. This is possibly because by this time I had the scent of a calming pint of ale from the White Lion at Kildwick in my nostrils. Unfortunately, on arrival the hostelry was closed. Undaunted we pressed on to the Dog and Gun at Sutton-in-Craven. A lovely pub to end a lovely day. Disappointingly the beer of the day was Timothy Taylor's Golden Best, which sadly did not come up to the high standard set last week at the Grouse Inn.

No Dotcom walk on Tuesday 19th due to half-term holidays so a chance to accompany Ed & Gwen Walton, our tormentors-in-chief, for a recce of a proposed future Dotcom circular from Winewall, Nr Colne to Wycoller. Suffice it to say the route may prove a little precipitous and hazardous for a party of 36 mixed ability walkers. I estimate that we may well lose 50% of the walkers on the day! Further disappointment at the end with a closed pub, the Trawden Arms, so a hasty reshuffle to an old stalwart the Emmott Arms at Laneshawbridge. Our friends here never disappoint, and a splendid pint of Pennine Brewery Real Blonde hit the spot for me.

This walk was quickly followed by another Weir wander on Thursday from Slaidburn. The weather forecast for the day had been very good but on approaching the venue light rain started to fall. Undeterred weather-proof clothing was donned, and an early start made. Plenty of mud and boggy fields on this one as we headed out to Pain Hill, Parrock Head, Burn House and Beatrix. However, improving weather conditions made the going more pleasant and after the turn at Beatrix and lunch near Gamble Hole Farm the pace quickened. Downhill all the way now to Newton then back along the River Hodder to Slaidburn in T-shirts and glorious sunshine, in February! Post walk debrief was at the Hark to Bounty at Slaidburn and the beer of choice today was Lancaster Blonde.

So, after all that foot slogging, we are back to the serious business, Premier League survival. This week's resumption of hostilities is once again looking likely to be a formidable task. Our opponents are old foes Tottenham Hotspur who despite a number of recent injuries currently sit third in the league just five points behind the leaders. Last season in this fixture we were given something of a footballing lesson and treated to a Harry Kane masterclass. I'm hoping and praying we are not on the end of the same again. Kane has been out sometime with injury but is now declared fit again and likely to feature at some point in the game. Fortunately, the odious Dele Alli will miss the fixture through injury. I can't say I'll miss him and his cheating tactics one little bit.

Come on you Clarets a big effort called for here. Let's extend that unbeaten Premier League run to eight.

Game 27 - Saturday 23rd February 12.30 – Burnley v Tottenham Hotspur

Two Friday evening fixtures in the Premier League gave the Clarets a massive boost going into this crucial game. Fulham despite taking an early lead at West Ham United slumped to yet another defeat, leaving them still 10 points behind us. However, and probably more importantly, Cardiff City sitting one place above the drop zone and only two points adrift of ourselves, completely imploded at home to Watford going down to a catastrophic 5-1 defeat.

That meant that whatever happened in our fixture, barring a heavy defeat, our position wouldn't be too severely compromised this weekend. With Southampton occupying the final relegation spot facing a difficult away game at Arsenal on Sunday, the chances are if we could get something from our game things would be looking even healthier still.

On a brilliant sunny day in Lancashire all seemed set fair for a battle royal with our old and respected foes. An early start for me as I walked to the ground ahead of a 12.30 kick off for live TV coverage. Unbelievably for late February its T-shirt weather in Burnley and the setting is captured perfectly by The Mail on Sunday match reporter, Rob Draper.

"A stunning Lancashire midday sun shone brightly on the rows of terraced houses and rolling hills that form the backdrop to the evocative Turf Moor".

How could we fail to be inspired on such an occasion? Well the fact is we certainly weren't! After our great run of seven games undefeated it was no surprise to learn that we named an unchanged starting XI. Recovery from injury of Robbie Brady and Johann Berg Gudmundsson meant we were also able to field a pretty impressive looking substitutes bench, for once packed with options.

Spurs sprung somewhat of a surprise selecting England captain Harry Kane, prematurely recovered from injury, in an imposing starting line-up. Within five points of leaders Manchester City and Liverpool they clearly saw this as a good opportunity for a win to close the gap at the top.

The first half went pretty much as I had anticipated if not even a little better than I dared to dream. Spurs with an easy on the eye 'silky' style were enjoying the bulk of possession. However, this was being countered by Burnley's steely determination and a well organised pressing game that afforded our illustrious visitors few opportunities. Indeed, in a half of little goalmouth action probably the closest to a goal came from Ashley Barnes who after taking a pass from Jeff Hendrick fired just over from a difficult angle.

Level at half time the general consensus among the fans was that anything gleaned from this game would be a bonus. Just 45 minutes to keep the wolf from the door and pocket a valuable point.

Apparently though no such negative thoughts from a determined Burnley team. Ashley Barnes and Chris Wood were once again proving a handful for defenders and with every member of the team 'putting in a shift' they clearly had other ideas. A brilliant save from Tom Heaton denies an incredible long-range effort from Kane before things really start to heat up.

On 57 minutes a moment of controversy followed by a 'golden goal'. A goal-line tussle for the ball between Jan Vertonghen and Jeff Hendrick ends with the ball ricocheting between the two players and over the line. Referee Mike Dean awards a corner. Dwight McNeil delivers the kick invitingly and it's met by Wood climbing highest to glance a header into the corner of the net.

Delirium erupts, the home crowd can hardly believe we have the lead and the Spurs management team are furious at what they see as an injustice over the corner decision.

Stunned by the setback the visitors are driven forwards but the rock like defence is standing firm. That is until the second moment of extreme controversy. As the ball rolls out for a Spurs throw around the halfway line it is recycled by the fourth official to Tottenham full back Danny Rose. Spotting Kane lurking on the left side of the Burnley penalty area he advances rapidly several yards down the line before throwing the ball into the striker's path. Caught unawares by the speed of it we are exposed, and the England man shows commendable control and balance to fire across Tom Heaton and into the corner of the net.

Now it's our turn to be furious on two counts. Firstly, the official should not be handling the ball and giving it to the player, he should maintain a position of non-involvement. Secondly, Rose should have been instructed to retake the throw from the position where the ball went out not several yards further down the pitch.

This should be the spark that ignites the visitors flame but the Clarets react magnificently to the setback. Instead of retreating into a defensive shell and trying to protect a valuable point we up the pressure and go looking for a winner. A timely double substitution on 80 minutes as legs start to tire proves a masterstroke. On come Brady and Gudmundsson (JBG) for McNeil and Hendrick.

Immediately JBG in particular begins to look a threat. On 83 minutes a sublime piece of skill from the Icelander takes him clear of the defence. His low ball into the penalty area is scuffed rather than driven but eludes the defenders and Wood, but not Barnes who steers it home from close range. For a second time a wave of incredulity and unreserved joy envelops Turf Moor.

Seven minutes of normal, and four of added time are eaten up comfortably and we have an immense victory! What a performance! What a day! What joy to be a Claret! A magnificent team performance from back to front, every man a star performer on the day. There'll be some celebrating in Burnley tonight and I'll be joining in on that.

Result – Burnley (Wood 57, Barnes 83) 2 – 1 (Kane 65) Tottenham Hotspur

Burnley Team

Heaton, Bardsley, Mee, Tarkowski, Taylor, Hendrick (Brady 80), Westwood, Cork, Wood, Barnes, McNeil (Gudmundsson 80)

Subs Not Used – Hart, Lowton, Gibson, Vydra, Crouch

Tottenham Hotspur Team

Lloris, Aurier, Foyth (Lamela 76), Alderweireld, Vertonghen, Rose, Sissoko, Winks (Llorente 62), Eriksen, Son Heung-min (Moura 88), Kane,

Attendance – 21,338

Season To Date – Played 27, Won 8, Drawn 6, Lost 13, Goals For 31, Goals Against 48, Points 30

League Position after Game 27 – 14th

What an incredible turn round of our season. On Boxing Day after the humiliating home defeat to Everton, we had completed 19 Premier League fixtures that had yielded a meagre 12 points. In all honesty, we were doomed! The following eight games have seen us take 18 points from a possible 24, recording five wins and three draws. Twin strikers Ashley Barnes and Chris Wood have both managed to net in the last four games and are at the moment only being outscored in 2019 by Sergio Aguero at Manchester City.

What a huge victory that was against Spurs, probably the highlight of the season so far. What a tremendous confidence booster that must be in a week that pits us against fellow relegation strugglers Newcastle United and Crystal Palace. The players must be walking on air at the moment and long may it continue. The Saturday evening game saw Crystal Palace obliterate Leicester City in front of their own fans. The 4-1 defeat left us now just two points behind the Foxes and it was a result that cost their beleaguered manager Claude Puel his job.

Unsurprisingly Southampton lost the Sunday afternoon game at the Emirates and stay trapped in the bottom three now six points adrift of us. A big week coming up starting on Tuesday night at Newcastle United. Will the run continue? After Saturday's performance there's no reason why it shouldn't.

Game 28 - Tuesday 26th February 20.00 – Newcastle United v Burnley

Sad to report that if there was no reason why the unbeaten run couldn't continue, tonight we managed to find one. A totally lacklustre performance got us exactly what we deserved, nothing. If Saturday had been ecstasy, then this was the complete reverse.

I must confess I had some reservations when the team news filtered through and Ashley Westwood had failed to make the squad. In the tremendous run through 2019 'Westy' has been an integral part of our success. He has been one of the most consistent performers and his all action style has been a key factor. Jeff Hendrick moved into central midfield with Johann Berg Gudmundsson taking up the wide right position in midfield.

My overriding impression of the first half was how low tempo the game was with the Clarets in particular looking as if Saturday's exertions had drained the tank. The Magpies in truth were not much better and considering both sides were in good form there was little goal threat from either team. Tom Heaton made one or two fairly routine saves before Fabian Schar scored a stunner on 24 minutes. Advancing on to a ball about 20 yards out he hit a venomous drive which beat Heaton's dive before going in off the left-hand post. Even Tom in his current imperious form had no chance with that.

Up front the deadly duo of Ashley Barnes and Chris Wood spent most of their time chasing hopeful punts upfield, with zero success. There was no cohesion to our play, no energy and precious little width. Dwight McNeil was for once anonymous and without his sparkle we looked devoid of attacking ideas. The tactic appeared to be to keep the game tight and hopefully profit from set-pieces. From a free kick a good opportunity fell to Wood who did everything right but found his close-range volley stopped by an impressive on the night Martin Dubravka.

Perhaps a decent shout for a penalty was dismissed as Matt Ritchie appeared to impede Gudmundsson as he closed on goal forcing him to fire wide. Then on 38 minutes there is a mountain to climb as poor defending and a failure to clear presents Sean Longstaff an opportunity in the box which he gratefully accepts. Would this be the stimulus needed to shake off the lethargy? Well, just before half time a golden opportunity to get back in the game. From another set piece Barnes's header across goal falls to James Tarkowski a few yards out. With the goal beckoning 'Tarka' volleys hopelessly over the top, and that just about sums up our display.

Two goals down at half time and a performance as dire as those of the first half season. Things could only get better. I suppose they did in that we didn't concede any further goals. Robbie Brady replaced McNeil at the interval though his impact could best be described as minimal. We did at least start to take the game to our hosts but with little guile our efforts foundered on a rock-solid defence.

Probably the most effective attacking contribution came from full back Charlie Taylor whose determination to try and get around the back of the defence was commendable. It's a pity the so-called wingers didn't have the same desire. As the game limped on and we persisted with fruitless long-ball tactics it was apparent that this was not going to be our night. Peter Crouch replaced Ashley Barnes to provide a larger target for our long range Exocets, but it made little difference. Near the end Matej Vydra got a rare few minutes and almost profited from one or two goalmouth scrambles.

However, in the end we fell well short of our recent high standards and can have no complaints about the defeat. All the more galling really as I felt Newcastle were not particularly all that good. A more dynamic approach from the off may well have yielded some reward here. Perhaps our tremendous efforts over the last couple of months finally caught up with us. Here's hoping we get the ship back on course for another severe test on Saturday at home to Crystal Palace.

Result – Newcastle United (Schar 24, Longstaff 38) 2 – 0 Burnley

Burnley Team

Heaton, Bardsley, Mee, Tarkowski, Taylor, Gudmundsson, Hendrick, Cork, Wood (Vydra 83), Barnes (Crouch 71), McNeil (Brady 45)

Subs Not Used – Hart, Lowton, Ward, Gibson,

Newcastle United Team

Dubravka, Manquillo, Schar, Lascelles, Lejeune, Ritchie, Perez (Joselu 87, Hayden, Longstaff (Diame 85), Almiron (Dummett 80), Rondon

Subs Not Used – Darlow, Yedlin, Ki Sung-yeung, Atsu

Attendance – 48,323

Season To Date – Played 28, Won 8, Drawn 6, Lost 14, Goals For 31, Goals Against 50, Points 30

League Position after Game 28 – 15th

Game 29 - Saturday 2ⁿᵈ March 15.00 – Burnley v Crystal Palace

Ahead of this game I predicted a tricky fixture, by the end of it my worst fears were confirmed. All went well ahead of the game the usual meeting point, the Talbot Hotel providing pre-match refreshments. However, a slight hiccup with the beer (not literally) has me now wondering whether it may have influenced the result. The norm would have been two pints of Moorhouses's Premier Bitter, but on this occasion a misunderstanding with the barmaid resulted in the second round coming as Reedley Hallows brewery's Pendleside. Now I know it's only a minor difference, indeed both beers are brewed in Burnley, but as Sean Dyche never tires of telling us, fine margins make all the difference!

A welcome return to the starting line-up for Ashley Westwood whose energy in midfield had been sorely missed in midweek. Johann Berg Gudmundsson (JBG) dropped back to the bench and Jeff Hendrick reverted to a wide right midfield role.

It's a bit of a contrast to last week's home fixture when the game was played in wall to wall sunshine. This time we are in much more traditional early March weather, cold and wet. Attacking the Cricket Field end we are quickly into our stride and starting the game at a noticeably higher tempo than was evident at Newcastle.

We are enjoying the bulk of the play and most of the territorial advantage, but Palace are looking full of menace on the counter. Nevertheless, it's a bit of a surprise when they take the lead from one such breakout. Cheikou Kouyate makes a swift break upfield before releasing the ominously dangerous Wilfried Zaha on the right flank. His low cross is missed by all as it traverses the goalmouth and is seemingly going safe. However, to the left of goal is Jeffrey Schlupp who returns it instantly across the box where it hits the back-tracking Phil Bardsley on the thigh and flies past a surprised Tom Heaton.

That's definitely not the start we wanted and with just 15 minutes gone we are now facing an uphill battle. Undaunted, we continue to push Palace back without making too many clear-cut chances. The attack lacks guile and the Palace defence are making light work of a diet of poorly directed crosses. Probably the best chance of the half falls to Chris Wood who after being set up by Ashley Barnes blasts straight at Wayne Hennessey in the Eagles goal.

Trailing 1-0 at half time but I'm not too despondent. We are clearly lacking a cutting edge but apart from the unfortunate own goal Heaton has been largely unemployed. Jeff Hendrick is sacrificed at the interval as JBG is introduced to add a little more creativity. A quick goal back at the start of the second half will make all the difference.

Unfortunately, a quick goal is forthcoming, but not for us. Aaron Wan-Bissaka is allowed too much space to run into on the right flank, his low cross is met by on loan Chelsea striker Michy Batshuayi who rifles home from around the penalty spot. If we had a hill to climb before it has now become a mountain. The visitors now have their tails up and are oozing confidence. It's all over as a contest on 76 minutes as the hugely impressive Zaha bamboozles both Charlie Taylor and Ben Mee before firing past Heaton. Oh, for a player of his pace and dribbling ability, he is without doubt a player with match -winning quality.

For us its more of the same battering ram approach. Wood is replaced by a larger target in Peter Crouch and his introduction does have an unsettling effect on the previously comfortable Palace defence. On 90 minutes there's a consolation goal as Barnes glances home a header from a Westwood cross. It's taken us till almost the last kick to conjure a decent cross and that has been largely responsible for our failure. There's just time for Crouch to force a good save from Hennessey but it's all too little too late.

It's been a game where we are on the right side of the statistics but the wrong side of the result. Once again this is down to a lack of guile and flexibility in approach. We are the most one-dimensional team in the Premier League and so predictable to the opposition. In contrast Crystal Palace had players, particularly Zaha, who could create and unsettle a defence with pace, trickery and two-footed ability. If we survive this season, we surely must look to fixing this aspect of our play.

So, a second consecutive defeat in a week to a team down in the relegation dogfight. To be fair it's difficult to see why the Eagles are so low in the table and I'm sure they will pull clear. Also, at the bottom Brighton & Hove Albion record a narrow victory over doomed Huddersfield Town to hoist themselves above us as we slip to 16th. Fortunately, Southampton go down to a late goal in a five-goal thriller at Manchester United and stay two points below the Clarets. Cardiff City lose 2-0 at Wolverhampton Wanderers and remain five points adrift of us.

Those two defeats have once again got the fans glancing anxiously at the teams below us as the bottomless chasm looms closer. There's no doubt that the home game with Cardiff City scheduled for 13th April is going to be vital in our survival quest. Things are likely to look even gloomier after the next round of fixtures as its difficult to see us picking up anything from an away visit to title chasing Liverpool. Time to cross fingers, toes and anything else crossable and pray for divine intervention. Perhaps God is a Claret?

Result – Burnley (Barnes 90) 1 – 3 (Bardsley og 15, Batshuayi 48, Zaha 76) Burnley

Burnley Team

Heaton, Bardsley, Mee, Tarkowski, Taylor, Hendrick, Westwood, Cork, Wood (Crouch 81), Barnes, McNeil (Brady 72)

Subs Not Used – Hart, Lowton, Gibson, Vydra

Crystal Palace Team

Hennessey, Wan-Bissaka, Tomkins, Dann, van Aanholt, Zaha (Townsend 79), Kouyate, Milivojevic, Meyer (McArthur 71), Batshuayi (Benteke 83), Schlupp

Subs Not Used – Ward, Kelly, Guaita, J Ayew

Attendance – 19,223

Season To Date – Played 29, Won 8, Drawn 6, Lost 15, Goals For 32, Goals Against 53, Points 30

League Position after Game 29 – 16th

Before the game at Newcastle on Tuesday 26th February I was beginning to feel quite relaxed and confident of our survival chances. On the back of an eight-game unbeaten run and with a couple of 'winnable' fixtures coming up all seemed set fair. By today March 10th that confidence has all but evaporated.

Two consecutive defeats have dented our hopes but that has been compounded by the sudden surge in form of our relegation rivals. Unbelievably ahead of our Sunday game at Liverpool, Saturday's results could not have gone worse for us.

In the early kick-off Crystal Palace succumbed to Brighton & Hove Albion which did some damage but not major. What followed during the course of the afternoon was nothing short of disastrous. Tottenham Hotspur apparently coasting to an away win at Southampton surrendered two late goals in the space of five minutes to snatch defeat from the jaws of victory.

Cardiff City comprehensively overwhelmed a pathetic West Ham United to take a crucial three points, and to top it off Newcastle United trailing 0-2 at home to Everton stormed back to take all three points. The upshot of that little lot being that we dropped to 17th place one above the drop zone and just two points clear of Cardiff City.

Today we play at Championship chasing Liverpool, and to be quite frank, a hammering looks on the cards. As I write I am preparing to tune into BT Sport to watch live coverage from Anfield. My immediate feeling 14 minutes ahead of kick-off is one of trepidation. If there is a God please show yourself today, preferably in claret and blue colours!

Game 30 – Sunday 10th March 12.00 – Liverpool v Burnley

It's a weird day for weather, in Burnley we have had snow, strong icy winds, hailstones and sunshine, and that's all before lunchtime. It's the same story in Liverpool as the teams take the field ahead of the twelve o'clock kick off. No changes in the Burnley line-up. We don't do changes! Liverpool with their eye on the prize play all three main strikers despite a big midweek game coming up against Bayern Munich.

Would you believe it? God has shown up wearing not only his claret and blue hat, scarf and gloves but he has also brought along his lucky charms. On six minutes unbelievably we have the lead! A corner from the left is a perfectly placed in-swinger from Ashley Westwood. The penalty area is crowded and as the ball comes over it is missed by everybody including the home custodian and drifts gently into the bottom corner of the goal. That's the cue for all of the red persuasion, including BT Sports match summariser Steve McManaman (Scouser and ex Liverpool player) to cry FOUL. The keeper in trying to cover his ineptitude in dealing with the cross is claiming he is impeded by James Tarkowski. Thankfully referee Andre Marriner is having none of it and we have a precious goal start.

That's something for us to defend now, unfortunately for another 84 minutes at least. I'm not getting carried away at this stage because as a

Burnley fan I've seen it all before. The game settles down with Liverpool as expected having the lion's share of possession but not looking particularly dangerous. No doubt the bizarre weather conditions are having an effect as one minute the ball holds up in the wind whilst next it's carried by it.

In time honoured fashion I have spoken too soon about not looking dangerous. In the 19th minute Mohammed Salah wriggles free to the right of goal, his low cross should be meat and drink for Tom Heaton, but he makes a hash of it just pushing it on to James Tarkowski's outstretched leg before falling right into the path of Roberto Firmino. He has the simple task of prodding home from about three yards, a goal that even I wouldn't miss.

Tails up now for the Pool and the pressure starts to build. God has retreated back to his heavens seemingly sensing a lost cause. On 29 minutes the inevitable occurs as Charlie Taylor makes an impeccable block in the penalty area to deny the Reds. Unfortunately, as God now has his back turned, the ball falls straight to Sadio Mane who curls number two past Heaton.

There's just 15 minutes left in the first period to try and repel the red tide and prevent further damage to the scoreline. We don't really look like posing much threat as we persist in the usual tactic of thumping it long to the outnumbered Ashley Barnes and Chris Wood, neither of whom have the physique or pace to make anything from it. More success looks likely down the left flank as once again Dwight McNeil and Charlie Taylor continue to impress.

Half time secured with just the one goal deficit and a chance to re-group and hopefully come out with a bit more attacking intent. For the first few minutes of the second period this is exactly the case, but our flurry soon blows out and its back to business as usual.

On 67 minutes its game over. A hopelessly placed goal kick from Heaton (wind affected?) falls right at the feet of Salah on the right flank. Needing no second invitation he motors straight towards goal pursued by Taylor. Once again, an immaculate tackle by the full back denies Salah but the ball rolls free to Firmino to fire home. How unlucky has Charlie Taylor been and where was God when we needed him?

A stream of substitutions follows as Liverpool attempt to save legs whilst increasing their goal difference. Mane makes one of the misses of the season contriving to put the ball over the top from almost on the goal line. A brief re-appearance by God? We introduce ex Liverpool player Peter Crouch who gets a good reception from the home crowd. Also, into the fray are Johann Berg Gudmundsson (JBG) and Matej Vydra. Our new men give us a short-term boost and as we enter added time a lifeline? Vydra causes some confusion in the box and the ball comes to JBG who makes no mistake. Two minutes left can we force an unlikely draw? The answer as it invariably is, is NO!

As we push men forward in pursuit of the equaliser we are caught by a quick counter. Heaton has the option of 'cleaning out' Mane as he reaches the penalty area but opts on this occasion not to. Mane rounds our Tom and strokes home number four in the final minute of the game.

It was I suppose a result that most people expected from the start. We fought doggedly but without much craft. However, on this occasion poor errors, mostly from the usually impeccable Heaton, have cost us dearly. The only thing to enthuse about on another bleak footballing day is the growing impact of our left sided players McNeil and Taylor. Both are growing in confidence and developing a good on field understanding.

Eight games to go now and really back in the mire. I wouldn't like at this stage to predict our eventual fate, but we must battle in every game for every scrap. It's going to be a real nail-biting end to the season and no place for faint hearts.

Result – Liverpool (Firmino 19,67, Mane 29, 90+3) 4 – 2 (Westwood 6, Gudmundsson 90+1) Burnley

Burnley Team

Heaton, Bardsley, Mee, Tarkowski, Taylor, Hendrick (Berg Gudmundsson 79), Westwood, Cork, Wood (Crouch 79), Barnes (Vydra 86), McNeil

Subs Not Used – Hart, Lowton, Gibson, Brady

Liverpool Team

Alisson, Alexander-Arnold (Sturridge 86), Matip, van Dijk, Robertson, Wijnaldum (Henderson 68), Fabinho, Lallana (Keita 77), Salah, Firmino, Mane

Subs Not Used – Mignolet, Lovren, Shaqiri, Origi

Attendance – 53,310

Season To Date – Played 30, Won 8, Drawn 6, Lost 16, Goals For 34, Goals Against 57, Points 30

League Position after Game 30 – 17th

Hands up, or perhaps I'd better rephrase that, any of you that have had a colonoscopy. As a result of an abnormal result on the standard bowel cancer screening tests three years ago I had to undergo this somewhat dubious pleasure. Fortunately, the examination revealed nothing more than benign bowel polyps which were removed during the course of the procedure.

However, as a consequence I am now on a routine three-year cycle of colonoscopy examination. Tomorrow Friday 15th March is the scheduled date for my next opportunity to display the internal features of my intestines to the lucky people of the Endoscopy Unit at Burnley General Hospital (BGH).

For those unfamiliar with the procedure, it is in a nutshell, an examination of the bowel wall. A thin tube called a colonoscope is inserted into the rectum (back passage) and guided around the large bowel. At the end of the colonoscope is a small camera with a light attached which allows the specialist to see the inside of the bowel on a TV screen! Now this whilst perhaps being slightly embarrassing and unpleasant, is nevertheless a most effective tool for diagnosis of potential bowel cancers.

For me by far the worst part of this procedure is the necessity to completely empty the bowel to facilitate the procedure. This involves partaking in a reduced fibre diet 48 hours before the procedure, followed by a complete lack of food almost some 24 hours prior. During this latter period a strong laxative is taken consisting of 3 or 4 sachets of a soluble powder, inappropriately named Klean-Prep.

I can assure you the effects of such powder are anything but clean! The advice after taking the laxative is to stay close to a toilet and avoid travelling or going to work. In my experience this is very sound advice!

Have you ever tried going from lunchtime till bedtime without being able to eat anything? It's not nice, everyone around you is gorging on food, the TV adverts all seem to feature food, and you can't so much as nibble on a crisp. Its purgatory.

It's now 7.00 pm on Thursday 14th and I've just consumed the third Klean-Prep sachet. The powder is having the desired effect and I am definitely not straying far from a toilet as advised. I'm now also starving to death and rapidly losing the will to live. Boy, will I be glad when this is all over. Roll on 8-45 am tomorrow when we can get the show (literally) on the road or should that be the screen.

I'm already promising myself one of Varley's Butty shop's biggest sarnies as soon as I am released from BGH. That's assuming I haven't passed away during the night from malnutrition. Nothing for it but to retire to bed early and hope for a good night's sleep.

Well dear readers its now Friday 15th March and I'm sure you'll all be relieved to know that I survived my ordeal with the demon endoscopist Mr Grimley, no not Mr Grimsdale (youngsters google Norman Wisdom). Despite getting off to a rather belated start, 45 minutes behind schedule, I was soon through the preliminaries such as signing the consent form to prove you willingly submitted yourself to the indignities about to befall you.

After a short pre-procedure wait it was into the, for want of a better word, theatre. There was Mr/Dr Grimley readying himself for action and warming up to his favoured choral music pieces. This despite a request from a previous victim for some Pink Floyd. He is of the opinion that his line of work is best suited to something relaxed and uplifting. With your legs akimbo and backside on display to several nurses, who are we to argue.

A thorough going over with the aforementioned flexible tube then ensued with plenty of opportunities to view the proceedings on an adjacent screen. It's all very interesting seeing your body parts from the inside for a change but I couldn't help wishing it was all over. In due course a full examination of the colon was deemed by the magician with the wand to be a success. Just one small aberration removed on the spot and finally I'm free to attempt to regain my dignity.

I'm not joking when I say that I sure was glad to get out of there as fast as I could. However, a word here for Mr Grimley and indeed the entire Bowel Cancer screening team at BGH. I would hereby just like to express my gratitude for the splendid professional care shown to myself by all members of the team that I encountered. The NHS may have its critics but from my experiences it is a health service second to none in the world. How lucky we are to have such magnificent care from cradle to grave. Thank you BGH I will be back again in three years' time and we can do it all over again! They even sent me home with pictures of my internal parts to show to family and friends!

Now, that's enough of the frivolity I hear you say, let's get back to the serious business. Tomorrow it's time for another do-or die battle in the fight to escape relegation. This time our opponents are Leicester City who currently sit comfortably mid-table in the Premier League. However, it will be anything but an easy ride against dangerous opponents currently enjoying something of a 'honeymoon' spell under new manager Brendan Rodgers. Hopefully, the Clarets will have put behind them last week's defeat at Liverpool and be in determined mood to end a three-game losing run. On the pitch we should be buoyed by the call-ups of Tom Heaton and James Tarkowski to the full England squad. Dwight McNeil also makes the England Under-20's party and no less than five Clarets make the initial Republic of Ireland gathering. These five are subsequently whittled down to two, Robbie Brady and Jeff Hendrick, ahead of their games against Gibraltar and Georgia.

One player omitted from the five is Stephen Ward, who after an injury hit season, decides to call time on his International career. Citing family reasons, he has decided that after a long and successful career with the Republic now is the time to go.

Game 31 – Saturday 16th March 15.00 – Burnley v Leicester City

Just when you think you've seen it all and things can't get any worse, the Clarets contrive to find another way to astound. Yes, on this occasion, we defy all odds to lose against a team reduced to 10 players for 86 minutes of the game. To put the tin hat on it, to a 90th minute goal attributable to nothing short of crass stupidity. If that reads like I'm a bit disgruntled, that's because I am!

On a foul day, which with hindsight should have served as a warning, it's off for pre-match drinks in complete waterproof clothing. The torrential rain has continued throughout the morning and is compounded by a swirling gusty wind and low temperature. You could say a typical March day in Burnley.

No trouble parking today everybody must be leaving it till the last minute before setting off and this is confirmed by a less than usually crowded Talbot Hotel. No problems getting served today and the afternoon is off to a good start as the much-despised Leeds United engineer a major cock-up in their bid for promotion from the Championship, losing at home to main rivals Sheffield United in the lunchtime televised game. It's surprising how many Blades fans there are in Burnley as a huge roar goes up as the ball hits the back of the Leeds net to give the visitors a vital win.

Pints consumed it's a pre-match soaking as we make our way through the now crowded streets to Turf Moor. There's one team change, Johann Berg Gudmundsson (JBG) being preferred to Jeff Hendrick in a line-up intended to give more attacking flair in a must win game.

It's a ploy that seems to have worked splendidly as within four minutes JBG bursts on to a Jack Cork through ball. As he homes in on goal Harry Maguire foolishly in my opinion takes him down. The foul is outside the penalty area, but he has denied JBG a goal scoring opportunity and the inevitable red card is promptly shown by referee Michael Oliver. Less than four minutes gone and a man advantage, that's a good start.

It forces a tactical change for the Foxes as a threatening attacker Demarai Gray is sacrificed to allow centre back Wes Morgan to enter the fray. That should be the signal for all-out attack by the Clarets but strangely it's not. Indeed, it's the 10 men of Leicester who are looking the more dangerous and creating some nervy moments in the Clarets defence.

On 33 minutes an example of the poor decision making that has crept into our play this season hands the visitors the lead. James Tarkowski upends the tricky James Maddison just outside the penalty area. It's the perfect position for a right footed free kick specialist and Maddison shows that's exactly what he is as he fires home past Tom Heaton's despairing dive.

Just what we didn't need and what was turning into a difficult afternoon suddenly got much harder. Thankfully, not for long. On a rare occasion where we attempt to play some football instead of 'hoofball', a nice interchange between Charlie Taylor and Dwight McNeil gives the youngster a shooting opportunity. One that our new young maestro is not about to pass up and he despatches a shot from the left of goal inside Kasper Schmeichel's left hand post.

Thank God for that, the damage restored in a matter of five minutes and an opportunity now to push on and win the game. However, for the rest of the half its back to square one. Strikers Ashley Barnes and the hopelessly out of touch Chris Wood are making no impact on the central defensive partnership of Johny Evans and Morgan and it's all just hit and hope. To say we have a man advantage, on watching this display you would never think so.

Half time 1-1, and in the words of the song I'm hoping 'things can only get better'.

Out for the second period and the downpour continues, the tricky strong wind that had been mostly against us in the first half is now at our backs and hopefully driving us forwarded. We are certainly seeing lots of the ball and the visitors have seemingly decided a point will have to do today.

We press relentlessly but with little penetration. The most likely looking opportunities are coming from the left-wing raiding of Taylor and McNeil but a packed defence are coping comfortably with the succession of crosses. As the game rolls on a tactical discussion between my pal John W and myself concludes that it's time for something different. The battering ram approach of Barnes and Wood is having zero effect and we both are of the opinion that the introduction of a bit more pace in the guise of Matej Vydra may prove a more fruitful option.

However, knowing Sean Dyche's predictability we both suspect that the first change will be the introduction of another 'battering ram', the gangly Peter Crouch. Of course, we are correct and on 70 minutes Wood departs to be straight swopped for 'Big Pete'. More hopeful punts into the penalty area ensue, as usual to no avail although there are one or two half-hearted penalty appeals. One appeal that should have been given however was a foul by Wilfred Ndidi on Taylor as he closed in on goal. A blatant spot kick to all in the crowd but not to referee Oliver who waved play on. If that was not a penalty, then surely it must have been a dive as Taylor sprawled in the box. No booking for our man so how exactly did the referee view that?

As time began to run out both John W and I got the uneasy feeling that there was a sucker punch coming. On 90 minutes it duly arrived. A rare foray forward by the Foxes seemed to have broken down as Robbie Brady on as a substitute for JBG got possession. At this late stage the simplest thing to do was to 'lump' it long, but no! Instead he plays a ball back into our own penalty area to Ben Mee, who makes a complete hash of controlling it. Ben recovers sufficiently to get the ball out for a corner. However, the resulting kick is only half cleared and a static Tarkowski allows Morgan to get up above him and head downwards and into the net.

What a complete and utter disaster! Unbelievably Vydra is then thrown on in the first of four minutes added time. Why? What the Hell is he supposed to do now? Incredibly he almost snatches a leveller but is thwarted by an outstretched leg by Schmeichel.

What a bloody shambles! A fourth consecutive defeat and the eighth home defeat of the season, and that to a team playing with a man down almost the whole game. We are in the deep mire now and it's hard to see with the fixtures that we have to come how we are going to extricate ourselves. We are not down yet but the abyss is now looming large!

Result – Burnley (McNeil 38) 1 – 2 (Maddison 33, Morgan 90) Leicester City

Burnley Team

Heaton, Bardsley, Mee, Tarkowski, Taylor, Berg Gudmundsson (Brady 79), Westwood, Cork, Wood (Crouch 70), Barnes, McNeil (Vydra 90+1)

Subs Not Used – Hart, Lowton, Gibson, Hendrick

Leicester City Team

Schmeichel, Pereira, Evans, Maguire, Chilwell, Tielemans, Ndidi, Gray (Morgan 6), Maddison (Fuchs 64), Barnes (Mendy 77), Vardy

Subs Not Used – Ward, Ghezzal, Iheanacho, Okazaki

Attendance – 20,719

Season To Date – Played 31, Won 8, Drawn 6, Lost 17, Goals For 35, Goals Against 59, Points 30

League Position after Game 31 – 17th

By Thursday 28th March after what seems an interminable age, we are almost ready to reconvene the survival battle. Since the last game, the home defeat by Leicester on 16th March, little has happened to lighten the mood of creeping depression amongst most fans. The reason for the lengthy gap in fixtures has once again been down to an International break for Euro 2020 qualifiers. In customary fashion England have duly despatched a pair of no-hopers, Czech Republic 5-0 at Wembley, and Montenegro 5-1 in the away fixture. Whilst it's fair to say the young English side look a potent attacking force it's difficult to gauge their potential against such weak opposition. The test will come when they meet sterner opponents such as France, Spain or Germany.

When I say we are almost ready to reconvene battle, I have on this occasion to exclude myself. As the Clarets take the field at Turf Moor on Saturday 30th I will be otherwise engaged in the Lancaster/Kendal area on my daughter's partner Tom's 'stag do'.

A full weekend of fun and frivolity is planned to include two nights stay in Lancaster, and a day at an outdoor activity centre on the Saturday. This will comprise of four activities, Quad Bike trekking, Clay Pigeon shooting, Archery and Axe throwing! As I have never in my life engaged in any of these challenges an interesting time lies ahead. Whilst we are only a small party of six including the groom-to-be, I am sure there will be a certain amount of flak coming my way from the other party goers. In the group are Tom's father and brother, Sunderland and Arsenal fans respectively, who will both be revelling in the Clarets current discomfort. However, worse still is Tom's ex university pal Dan who it pains me to say is a Blackburn Rovers fan. I am praying that Saturday will see us return to some sort of form which will enable us to take some points from the game and make for a much more enjoyable evening for this lone Claret.

I'm up early but maybe not so bright after a first night stag 'warm-up' at Lancaster. It's an early start to the activities so just time for a hearty breakfast to set us up for the challenges and a 9.15 departure for the Kendal area. The 'stag' has at this point no idea where he is going, or what he is doing, having been fed a diet of misinformation in the lead up. This involved telling him to bring shorts and a sleeping bag. Now I know the Premier Inn is not exactly the Ritz, but I think a sleeping bag a bit unnecessary. In fact, he had been informed that the day's activity would involve a walk across Morecambe Bay which seemed to fill him with some trepidation. However, as we rocked up at the Outdoor Activity Company's premises and he spotted a line of quad bikes his smile began to re-appear.

First action of the day was indeed the Quads, six novice riders took to their steeds and after a thorough briefing from the instructor it was time for a few laps round the practice track. Five intrepid riders set off minus you know who, who's machine steadfastly refused to start. Primed with a little choke we were soon underway as I attempted to catch up somewhat hesitantly with the others. Having spent one occasion already this season in an upside-down position in a vehicle I was in no hurry to repeat the exercise!

After a couple of circuits round the training field the boss gave the signal to go and suddenly, I'm in front. Not wanting to spoil the youngster's fun I decide to give the throttle some 'welly' and hare off at breakneck speed in pursuit of our mentor. As we head away from the activity centre on deeply rutted steep stony tracks, I'm conscious that whilst I know how to make the thing go, I'm not too sure how to make it stop! However, after a few minutes I'm getting the hang of it whilst hanging on for dear life. Out now into open country and into a field with an additional hazard, inquisitive cows!

On and on we go over precipitous drops and steep climbs with even a seesaw thrown in for good measure. I'm just about to congratulate myself on my speedy pursuit when all the young bucks, Dan, Matt, James and his brother Tom the 'Stag' all flash past. Quickly followed even by Tom's Dad Stu, affectionately known as 'Codger'. From first to last in a matter of seconds. However, I must say there was an element of cheating here as to a man they left the rutted uneven tracks and took to the much easier even grass. Stu's overtaking manoeuvre soon came to nought as he stopped on the crest of a hill to blow his nose, allowing me the opportunity to sneak past.

What an exhilarating hour that was. All agreed it had been a fantastic experience and I'm sure most will take the opportunity to repeat it 'ere long. Just time for a quick stop at the centre for tea, coffee and home-made cakes before the next session, Clay Pigeon shooting.

I had my reservations about the prospect of peppering Clay Pigeons full of holes, never to the best of my knowledge having ever handled a gun. Perhaps that's not strictly true as in my younger years I was a dab hand with a spud gun and fired many 'caps' at unsuspecting individuals. However, having been warned of the dangers of recoil, and fearing the prospect of a broken collar bone I was somewhat apprehensive.

As it turned out my caution was unnecessary, after superb mentoring by our instructor George I was ready to let fly at anything that moved. Discretion being the better part of valour I opted to shoot last and stood back to observe all my fellow 'staggers' racking up an impressive tally of hits. That is until it came to one of the hot favourites for the competition the 'Stag's' brother James. To my relief and his brother's delight James managed to draw a complete blank in the first round of shooting. As I stepped up to the plate, I couldn't help thinking that at least I couldn't do any worse than that. Indeed, I didn't, managing to wing a couple of the low flying featherless critters.

Unfortunately, as the competition progressed youth triumphed over age and even James having been equipped with a pair of goggles with a blacked-out lens on one eye managed to hit the targets with ease. Needless to say, my final position in the contest was last but as losers always say; "It's not winning that's important, it's the taking part".

Two activities down and two to go, but before that back to the activity centre for lunch. Excellent proper man food served here, no 'pictures on a plate', instead tureens of sausages and onion, mashed potatoes and carrots. Help yourself and pile the plates high then top it off with a helping of sticky toffee pudding. Superb!

After lunch the activities resumed with Axe throwing. Now I may have mentioned earlier that I saw this as an opportunity to learn a new skill and create a potential supplementary income source. My plan being that I would perfect my technique with the hour's tuition then apply for a spot on Britain's Got Talent. I would acquire one of those large rotating wheels and strap my wife, the lovely Julie, to the board and hurl the projectiles at her narrowly avoiding her limb removal and decapitation. As the audience whooped with delight as the axes hit the target my fame would grow and offers of TV appearances and perhaps a tour would follow.

Unfortunately, after an hour of hurling the damned things I think a re-think is probably in order. On most occasions I failed to achieve the correct amount of rotation to make the blade stick in the board. Not only that, my accuracy left something to be desired and I fear the 'Lovely Julie' may well have become heavily dependent on the NHS. Still I avoided a last place finish in this event, that dubious honour going to the Stag himself. Oh well, back to the drawing board.

Back then to the centre for another exhausting round of tea, coffee and cakes, before the final activity of the day, Archery. Now I've always fancied myself as a bit of a Robin Hood, or if not the man himself, one of his merry men. I think it stems from my childhood experience of Easter trips to Pendle Bottoms and the return with the obligatory bow and arrow set. Off course the arrows didn't have points but suckers in those days. Great fun was had firing them at neighbour's front doors until the inevitable misplaced shot sent them sailing over into some unrecoverable location. Fun over then till next year.

This time though it's more like the real thing as these beauties have armour piercing points. Well perhaps that's a bit of an exaggeration but they can certainly do some damage as Harold found out at the Battle of Hastings. Once again, some excellent tuition from our lady instructor Kelly led to a practice round where most shots missed the target. However, quickly getting the hang of it our accuracy soon improved to the point when most shots were finding the mark.

Sadly, despite what I felt was a pretty impressive performance for a novice, the competitiveness of 'the lads' proved too much. You could almost feel the aggression and smell the testosterone as they fought it out. A joint last place with Matt on this one but no disgrace in that.

What a fantastic day out we had courtesy of the Outdoor Activity Company, Old Hutton, Kendal. Anybody fancying a day of new challenges and good fun I suggest you give them a try you won't be disappointed. We'd had five hours out in the fresh air enjoying new experiences and good company. What more could you ask for? Which leads us to...

Game 32 – Saturday 30th March 15.00 – Burnley v Wolverhampton Wanderers

What more you could ask for was a desperately needed Clarets victory! After the soul-destroying late defeat at home to Leicester this seemed like a big ask, particularly against an in-form Wolves side enjoying an impressive return to the Premier League.

I'd got my phone tuned into the BBC Sports App with goal alerts set up, and in case of internet blackout areas in Cumbria, had asked fellow

Claret John W to text me score updates. Before I got back to the vehicle to transport me back to Lancaster an ominous sound from the phone. Fearing the worst, I peeped to see it was just the match kick-off notification.

However, before we had left the car park, another tone from the phone which could only be a goal, but for who? Bingo! BBC Sport informed me *"Goal, 2 mins, Burnley 1-0 Wolverhampton Wanderers, Coady o.g."*

What a fantastic start, just what the doctor ordered, only 88 minutes plus to hang on now! Next message through on the phone was a less than helpful WhatsApp from John W simply stating 'GOAL'. A poor attempt at humour I thought.

Back to Lancaster clutching the phone all the way not knowing whether I wanted to hear the ominous tone again. On the one hand it could signal another Clarets goal to help us breathe easier, alternatively a dreaded equaliser. Back at base its half time and thankfully we still lead. A quick look at the match stats confirm Wolves with the major share of possession but apparently little to further trouble either goalkeeper.

I glean from the reporting that the goal has come from a smartly taken free kick by Dwight McNeil and equally clever run by Chris Wood to gather possession. Wood's touch is good and takes him round goalkeeper Rui Patricio from where his shot from a tight angle hits the post before trundling in off the retreating Wolves captain Connor Coady.

A quick discussion as to whether we should have a quick freshen up and hit the bar or take a longer break and catch final score. I'm strongly in favour of the latter and that gets the vote. Time for a quick bath and change with the phone eerily silent. At 4.30 its time for Final Score and as the game enters the final stages the match commentator is implying that the visitors are pushing hard for the leveller.

Then the moment, back to Turf Moor where there's been another goal. Immediately I can tell by the roar that it has gone in our favour and the relief emanating from the ground is palpable. 77 minutes gone and surely too late now to lose the vital points, although this season you wouldn't bet against it.

Match pundits in the BBC studio agree that it's a fine goal from the youngster McNeil who it would appear was about to be substituted.

James Tarkowski wins a header from a clearance on the halfway line with the ball dropping to McNeil. His surging run towards goal is blocked by two defenders but as he enters the penalty area a gap opens between the pair. Without hesitation young Dwight arrows his shot low and into Patricio's left-hand corner of the goal. Not a bad day for him, an assist and a goal, and a substitution near the end to allow him to take the crowds standing ovation.

Needless to say, the phone quickly signals a second offering from John W of 'GOAL' but by now I'm past caring. What a splendid way to end a fantastic day, three vital points garnered and a gap between ourselves and Cardiff City now stretched to five points.

Tomorrow, the Bluebirds will attempt to claw back the deficit in their home game with Chelsea, but for us the day is complete. Now at 5.00 p.m. it's time to hit the bright lights of Lancaster and let the double celebrations begin.

Result – Burnley (Coady og 2, McNeil 77) 2 – 0 Wolverhampton Wanderers

Burnley Team

Heaton, Bardsley, Mee, Tarkowski, Taylor, Hendrick, Westwood, Cork, Wood, Barnes, McNeil (Berg Gudmundsson 87)

Subs Not Used – Hart, Lowton, Ward, Gibson, Brady, Vydra

Wolverhampton Wanderers Team

Patricio, Saiss, Coady, Boly, Traore (Costa 72), Dendoncker (Doherty 59), Neves, Moutinho, Otto, Cavaleiro (Jimenez 59), Jota

Subs Not Used – Ruddy, Gibbs-White, Vinagre, Kilman

Attendance – 20,990

Season To Date – Played 32, Won 9, Drawn 6, Lost 17, Goals For 37, Goals Against 59, Points 33

League Position after Game 32 – 17th

On Sunday 31st March Cardiff City are somewhat unfortunately beaten in controversial circumstances by Chelsea. What a shame! This preserves our five-point advantage having played one more fixture. The game in hand for Cardiff will be played on Wednesday 3rd April away at title chasing Manchester City. Hopefully City will make no mistake and clatter in a few goals to enhance our already handy goal difference advantage.

Results in March's last round of fixtures, whilst being very positive for the Clarets, also saw the first team relegated from the Premier League. With six games still to go Huddersfield Town's defeat gave them the dubious distinction of being numero uno to drop. On Tuesday 2nd April they were swiftly followed by Fulham's expensively assembled squad of misfits, leaving just one relegation berth to fill. Our vital home win over Wolverhampton Wanderers had heaped the pressure right back on Cardiff City but other teams were looking far from safe. Southampton, Brighton and Hove Albion and even Newcastle United were still to a greater or lesser extent in peril.

Indeed, Southampton's position strengthened the week before by victory at Brighton weakened once again following home defeat to Liverpool on Friday 5th April. That result left them on the same points as ourselves and gave us a boost going into our next match at Bournemouth the following day.

Game 33 – Saturday 6th April 15.00 – Bournemouth v Burnley

There's something about Burnley away games on sunny Grand National days. I well remember back in our first Premier League season in 2009/10 it took us till the big race day to register our first ever away victory in the big league. On that occasion it came at Hull City as we came from behind to comprehensively win the game.

Well Saturday 6th April 2019 was another of those glorious sunny days and once again we are on our travels, this time to the south coast to meet former boss Eddie Howe's Bournemouth. Once again, it's the big day at Aintree so all the omens are in place for a happy ending. Unfortunately, that initially doesn't look like being the case.

There's just the one team change from the previous week with Matt Lowton replacing the injured Phil Bardsley. Needless to say, it's once again a fixture which we simply must get something from. I opt for a seat on the bench, garden bench that is, to soak up the rays and endure another nerve wracking 90 minutes.

The weather might be great but the start to the game is anything but. In lovely sunshine the Clarets in their all white change strip are rocked on their heels as the hosts score from their first meaningful attack. Perhaps I'd better rephrase that as in fact its Ashley Barnes who gets his name on the scoresheet, unfortunately at the wrong end! Ryan Fraser's in-swinging free kick is nodded on by Jefferson Lerma and as Nathan Ake closes in to apply the killer touch, Ashley intervenes. Having to get something on the ball, he does, but his header instead of going wide of the goal nestles unhappily in the corner. What a blow! Four minutes gone and a goal down to a side with a very good home record.

Now's the time to show some spirit and fight if we've got it. For the next few minutes we are understandably knocked out of our stride. However, remaining calm we start to exert more of an attacking influence and in a deadly two-minute spell the game has been stood completely on its head.

On 18 minutes we are level with a goal highly reminiscent of the recent opener at Liverpool. Ashley Westwood's left-wing corner is misjudged by home Keeper Asmir Begovic. As he flaps at the ball it sails over him, straight to Chris Wood, who has the simple task of heading home from almost on the goal line. Phew! What a relief.

Two minutes later and things get better still. Once again Dwight McNeil, enjoying giving former England full back Nathaniel Clyne a 'roasting', puts a low cross into the box. Cherries centre back Chris Mepham can only half clear to Westwood who immediately returns it with interest firing unerringly past Begovic.

Suddenly the sun is shining a whole lot brighter in a Lancashire back garden and I bet there's a dark cloud descending on Cardiff. I'm expecting a backlash from Bournemouth now and an afternoon of last ditch defending. However, that doesn't occur and with Barnes and Wood proving a real handful for the Cherries centre backs we are looking dangerous. Half time 2-1 up and that's as good as I could have wished for, especially after the catastrophic start.

Just 45 minutes to hold out for an extremely invaluable three points. Surely time now for one of our renowned defensive masterclasses. However, on 56 minutes the pressure is eased even further. Charlie Taylor's run down the left has the home team claiming the ball has gone over the touchline and out of play for a throw. Charlie doesn't think so and carries on, his low cross is fumbled at the near post by Begovic and Wood picks up the pieces. In an instant he lays it back to Barnes who gleefully slots home his second of the day, thankfully this time at the right end. Fantastic a two-goal cushion and just over 34 minutes to play.

The goal has knocked the stuffing out of Bournemouth, and they are hardly seen as an attacking force. We are managing the game expertly and perhaps the best chance falls to Ben Mee who can't keep his header down and on target. What looked like being an extremely uncomfortable afternoon at the start turns out to be the complete opposite. We return to Lancashire with all the points and a magnificent boost to our survival chances. On a good day all round, Newcastle United lose at home to Crystal Palace whilst Brighton & Hove Albion are in cup semi-final action against Manchester City.

Our points haul climbs to 36 and we leapfrog Southampton, Brighton and Newcastle climbing to the giddy heights of 14th. To round it all off my horse, 'Walk in the Mill', finishes fourth in the Grand National. With a small punt each way and pre-race odds taken at 25/1 I've even made a few bob. Now that's what I call a good day!

Result – Bournemouth (Barnes 4 og) 1 – 3 (Wood 18, Westwood 20, Barnes 56) Burnley

Burnley Team

Heaton, Lowton, Mee, Tarkowski, Taylor, Hendrick (Berg Gudmundsson 82), Westwood, Cork, Wood, Barnes, McNeil

Subs Not Used – Hart, Ward, Long, Gibson, Brady, Vydra

Bournemouth Team

Begovic, Clyne (Rico 45), Mepham, Ake, Smith, Brooks, Gosling (Solanke 59), Lerma (Stanislas 71), Fraser, Wilson, King

Subs Not Used – Boruc, Mousset, Ibe Simpson

Attendance – 10,446

Season To Date – Played 33, Won 10, Drawn 6, Lost 17, Goals For 40, Goals Against 60, Points 36

League Position after Game 33 – 14th

The excellent but vital win at Bournemouth made for a much more relaxed week ahead of the home game with Cardiff City. What just a couple of weeks ago looked like a season decider, today has perhaps a little less edge to it. Our two recent victories, coupled with two defeats for Cardiff, have opened a healthier eight-point gap between the two sides, albeit our Welsh friends having a game in hand. Our much more favourable goal difference is also a big plus in our favour, although God forbid it should come to that. Not only that, other teams have also fallen back into the mix and that can only work to our advantage as they look to take points from each other.

The general concensus is that a victory on Saturday should, whilst not making it mathematically certain, practically ensure our Premier League survival. A draw would also be an acceptable result denying the Bluebirds any points gain on ourselves whilst eating up another fixture. In short then anything bar a defeat will do. However, in our topsy-turvy season who would dare to predict the outcome with any certainty. With Burnley's penchant for doing things the hard way, anything can happen. A big crowd looks likely and a real no holds barred battle is on the cards. Hopefully our recent victories will have the home crowd in buoyant mood ready to carry the Clarets to safety. We'll soon see!

Game 34 – Saturday 13th April 15.00 – Burnley v Cardiff City

Hallelujah! After the Boxing Day debacle at home to Everton and a first half season tally of a mere 12 points, all hope of survival seemed just about gone. Today after a further 15 matches we have effectively, if not yet mathematically, achieved sufficient points to ensure a further Premier League adventure. What an incredible turn round 12 points from the first 19 fixtures then 27 from the next 15.

Once again, it's a dry sunny day in Burnley but there's a stiff bitterly cold wind blowing enough to require several layers of clothing. As predicted, there's a bumper crowd with a large contingent of travelling fans from Cardiff. Arriving at the ground just in time for kick-off, the lure of the pub proving hard to resist, I find the ground awash with claret and blue mini flags. Yes, every supporter in the James Hargreaves, Jimmy McIlroy and Bob Lord stands has been presented with a souvenir flag, whilst those in the home section of the Cricket Field stand have free scarves. It's a gesture by the club, following the same one apparently provided at the Wolves game, to make the ground a sea of claret and blue and lift the crowd for a vitally important encounter.

I've seen on the website messageboard some criticism of this approach saying that it is all a bit naff and doesn't really work with Burnley fans. Even the font of all knowledge, 'Up the Clarets' messageboard editor Tony Scholes, feels that way and puts it down to a lack of understanding of the fans by some people in the club. For my part I think it's a nice attempt to promote a positive atmosphere. Whilst it may be true that not many fans actually waved the flags during the game, I noticed as I made my way home at the end of the game almost everybody was carrying their souvenir home with them.

Figure 8 - My wife Julie feeling the emotion hoists the flag.

So, to the action. Firstly, and not surprisingly, Sean Dyche has named an unchanged starting XI. For sure it's important in this game, if not in them all, to get off to a good start. We definitely don't want to be chasing it against opponents with their tails up. To be fair a good start is what we get and almost an early lead as a Chris Wood header comes back off a post. I remark to my pal John W that I hope we are not going to live to regret that, to which he tells me to cut out that sort of talk.

We are having the better of the early exchanges though the Bluebirds are as they must, giving it a go. The visitors defence doesn't look too solid to me and the centre back pairing look like an accident waiting to happen. On 31 minutes a decent start suddenly gets a whole lot better. A fine in-swinging corner by the immaculate Dwight McNeil is met at close range by the head of the equally impressive Chris Wood and the Clarets have a crucial lead.

In fairness the first half is pretty much dominated by the Clarets and by half time we should have put the game to bed. On two very similar occasions Ashley Westwood is put clean through on goal from good set-up play, but on both occasions fails to beat the keeper. Once again, I wonder if we will come to rue those missed chances, but the break arrives with us nicely ahead. The most bizarre action of the half sees Ashley Barnes yellow carded for kissing an opponent on the nose! On the charge Ashley is brought down by full back Joe Bennett who subsequently tramples all over him. As Barnes remonstrates with him the defender sticks his head in his face at which point Ash plants a kiss on him. I can't say I've seen that before in a game and it's surely the strangest booking Barnes will ever acquire.

Obviously, there's got to be a reaction from the visitors, or their season looks almost doomed. The start of the second half certainly brings one and just a few minutes in another moment of extreme controversy. As the Bluebirds press a shot hits Ben Mee on the arm, there are mild appeals for a penalty, but nothing is given. The ball is recycled back into the area and Mee rises to head clear. As he does so his downward header hits his arm. Immediately the assistant referee (AR) (linesman to we traditionalists) flags a penalty. Referee Mike Dean sees the signal and points to the spot. That's the cue for a mass Burnley protest at which point Dean goes over to consult the assistant. To the relief of all Clarets he then overturns his decision and signals a 'bounce' to restart the game. What a let off!

It transpires that Mike Dean has not clearly seen the incident and goes of the AR's indication. However, the AR on the opposite touchline with a clear view of the incident informs the referee that the ball has been headed by Mee before accidentally hitting his arm. On the strength of this information the penalty decision is correctly overturned.

The visitors clearly aggrieved, continue to push and a glorious opportunity goes to waste as Junior Hoilett fires over from a pull back by Kenneth Zohore. Its backs to the wall stuff by the Clarets now and very nervy viewing. However, as we hit the 70-minute mark Cardiff's enthusiasm and effort is definitely starting to wane and we start to re-establish some sort of a grip. It's much better from us now, but there are still a couple of penalty shouts against as Aron Gunnarsson tumbles in the box under a Charlie Taylor challenge and a shot appears to hit James Tarkowski's hand. Thankfully neither are given although on another day both could possibly have been.

The fourth official signals four minutes added time, although I must admit I expected more like seven or eight following the penalty incident. Surely, we've done it now. The answer to that is a resounding YES as in the first minute we score again! McNeil picks up the ball in midfield and his tired legs set off towards the Cardiff goal. His control and dribbling are imperious as he leaves Gunnarsson trailing in his wake. Most of the crowd expect him to head for the corner flag and eat up some precious time. Not this youngster he beats the full back for good measure before firing in a low cross. Bruno Ecuele Manga who had not enjoyed the happiest of afternoons attempts to cut out the cross but merely deflects it on to goalkeeper Neil Etheridge. The ball loops up and behind the custodian landing on the head of the eagerly awaiting Wood to give him surely one of the easiest goals he will ever score.

Job done! What a relief. That was nerve wracking at times and so what if we enjoyed a bit of good fortune with decisions going our way. How many times this season have we been on the wrong end of some of those? Eleven points clear now of Cardiff City who have only a possible 15 to play for. It's not mathematically done and dusted but it sure is almost. Time to take a deep breath, smile and relax at last.

Result – Burnley (Wood 31, 90+1) 2 – 0 Cardiff City

Burnley Team

Heaton, Lowton, Mee, Tarkowski, Taylor, Hendrick, Westwood, Cork, Wood, Barnes, McNeil

Subs Not Used – Hart, Ward, Long, Gibson, Brady, Vydra, Berg Gudmundsson

Cardiff City Team

Etheridge, Peltier, Morrison, Ecuele Manga, Bennett, J Murphy, Gunnarsson, Arter (Reid 81), Camarasa, Hoilett (Mendez-Laing 73), Zohore (Niasse 78)

Subs Not Used – B Murphy, Ralls, Cunningham, Bacuna

Attendance – 21,480

Season To Date – Played 34, Won 11, Drawn 6, Lost 17, Goals For 42, Goals Against 60, Points 39

League Position after Game 34 – 14th

Game 35 for us comes as the final fixture of the Easter weekend, owing to Chelsea's continued involvement in the Europa Cup and this match being selected by Sky for live TV coverage.

Events of the previous week and this weekend mean that whilst we are still not mathematically home and dry going into this fixture our situation, barring a major catastrophe, looks safe. Cardiff remain eight points adrift of us despite a midweek win at fellow strugglers Brighton & Hove Albion. Indeed, the Seagulls are enjoying a miserable run of form which has plunged them right into the relegation dogfight and they remain five points behind us. Still not clear of trouble are Southampton who remain uncomfortably just one ahead of Brighton and four from Cardiff.

A point tonight, which may seem unlikely at high flying Chelsea, should confirm our Premier League status by virtue of a largely superior goal difference over the lowly Bluebirds. Come on Clarets let's get it over the line! This is the first of three consecutive Burnley games to be screened live by Sky so I'm hoping we can put on a decent show to whet the appetites of the avid viewers. A repeat of last season's opening day fixture which we amazingly won 3-2 would do nicely! Tonight's game will then be followed by Sunday's home fixture with title chasing Manchester City, before rounding off the sequence next Friday at in form Everton. A tough ask these three but where there's a will there's a way.

Game 35 – Monday 22nd April 20.00 – Chelsea v Burnley

Once again, an unchanged line-up for the Clarets and why wouldn't it be after three successive victories in which we have scored seven goals and conceded only once. Our hosts parade the usual string of household names led by Eden Hazard and there's no doubt that if we are to get anything here, we need to be well and truly at our best.

Well if the TV viewers needed something to whet their appetites this game was certainly it. We had a rash of superb goals, sublime attacking, resolute and sometimes spectacular defending and to cap it all controversy. I'm a TV viewer myself for this one as I manage to pick up a pretty decent stream albeit subject to some early buffering.

Our hosts are quickly into their stride and have a determined look about themselves as they push for one of the coveted Champions League places. With Eden Hazard and Callum Hudson-Odoi taking the wide berths and Gonzalo Higuain leading the line we have our hands full in the early minutes. Hazard is causing mayhem down the left side and almost gives the Blues the lead but is thwarted by a magnificent overhead kick on the goal line by Ben Mee.

However, they are rocked on their heels in the eighth minute as a Dwight McNeil corner is only partially cleared to the edge of the penalty area. Standing there completely unmarked is Jeff Hendrick who needs no second invitation to send a dipping and arcing shot into the corner of the net. What a superb strike and we have an unexpected lead.

That's the cue for Chelsea to step up the attacking fervour and it's no real surprise as in the 12th minute they level the score. Once again Hazard twists and turns the Clarets defence inside out before teeing up N'Golo Kante for a fine finish. We are under the cosh now, perhaps we shouldn't have antagonised them by scoring. On 14 minutes the game has turned full circle as Chelsea take the lead. This time it's an unstoppable Higuain shot which goes straight through Tom Heaton before cannoning in off the underside of the bar.

At this point it's beginning to look a little bleak and I fear a cricket score is on the cards. Yet undaunted we battle on in typical Burnley fashion. No heads down and panic just regain the shape and keep plugging away. Our efforts are rewarded on 24 minutes once again from a set piece. In a clearly rehearsed training ground move Mee cleverly gets around the back of the defence unmarked to head Ashley Westwood's free kick back across the penalty area. Highest to reach it is Chris Wood whose headed flick takes it clear of the defence and perfect for Ashley Barnes to volley home from close range.

What a start to the game four goals in the first 24 minutes, and with the hosts attacking prowess but questionable defending, the prospect of more to come. Its riveting stuff and you can't take your eyes off it for a minute. The Chelsea faithful, annoyed by what they perceive as time wasting by Heaton, manage to get our man yellow carded by the 31st minute. A bit of a tightrope now for Tom.

The early flurry of goals seems to have taken some of the sting from the game and it settles into an attack versus defence battle. Chelsea's main threat seems to be coming from the wings, but our defensive shape is holding firm. The next piece of significant action comes as half time approaches. As Hudson-Odoi takes a ball down out of the air with his right foot, he suddenly crumples to the floor with nobody within touching distance.

Unfortunately for him, but more fortunately for us, that's the end of his evening as after trying manfully to continue he is forced to limp off. It later transpires that this will be the end of the young England winger's season as he has suffered a ruptured achilles tendon.

Half time arrives with no further damage and we leave the field still with our precious point intact.

The second period continues with the compelling contest of Chelsea's attack trying to breach our solid defensive formation. From Heaton, through the team to Wood and Barnes up front, every man is giving his all. Special mention here though for Ben Mee who hasn't missed a header or challenge all game in what has been a truly outstanding performance.

Chelsea whilst maintaining their constant forward momentum have however become over-elaborate in their build up and are rarely threatening Heaton's goal. Efforts on target are almost always coming from distance and proving easier to deal with. At the other end the unselfish running of Wood and Barnes is keeping the less than dependable Chelsea defenders on their toes.

As our host's frustration mounts tempers both on and off the field are beginning to flare. Chelsea manager Maurizio Sarri, looking for all the world like some sort of Neopolitan gangster, is doing his best to harass and influence referee Kevin Friend. At the same time, he is encroaching the Burnley technical area, where Sean Dyche remains an oasis of calm. Unsurprisingly, referee Friend soon tires of him and despatches him to the stand. On the field the odious David Luiz and Ashley Barnes are proving not too be too keen on each other as tempers approach boiling point.

However, time rolls slowly on and the nearer we get towards the end the more determined we are to defend our well-earned point. Five added minutes are signalled, much to the disappointment of the Chelsea staff and some players who feel the game should continue till they win. These are safely negotiated, and a terrific team effort has gained us the point which must surely guarantee us a fourth consecutive Premier League season.

Result – Chelsea (Kante 12, Higuain 14) 2 – 2 (Hendrick 8, Barnes 24) Burnley

Burnley Team

Heaton, Lowton, Mee, Tarkowski, Taylor, Hendrick, Westwood, Cork, Wood, Barnes, McNeil

Subs Not Used – Hart, Ward, Long, Gibson, Brady, Vydra, Berg Gudmundsson

Chelsea Team

Arrizabalaga, Azpilicueta, Christiansen, Luiz, Emerson, Kante (Kovacic 45), Jorginho, Loftus-Cheek, Hudson-Odoi (Pedro 41), Higuain (Giroud 77), Hazard

Subs Not Used – Caballero, Zapacosta, Cahill, Barkley

Attendance – 40,642

Season To Date – Played 35, Won 11, Drawn 7, Lost 17, Goals For 44, Goals Against 62, Points 40

League Position after Game 35 – 15th

As usual it didn't take long before the post-match whingeing started to emanate from the so-called 'elite' club. The aforementioned Luiz was quickly on the scene to decry Burnley's performance as 'anti football'. He seemed particularly upset by the fact that Burnley players late in the game received treatment for cramp.

"Losing time all the time especially when you have the ball. Their players went to the floor and stopped the game.

"They were playing 11 inside the box. It's difficult to score against a team like that.

"It's difficult to play against a team who have two chances and score two goals and didn't want to play the game."

What planet is this guy on? Just what did he expect us to do in a game where one point virtually guaranteed our Premier League survival and a guaranteed income of over £100m next season? Does he not understand that defending is just as important a part of the game as attacking? His anger should be directed at his colleagues and himself for their inability to break down a well organised defence. These so called 'super teams' seem to be of the impression that teams of our stature are really only there to make up the numbers. We should turn up solely for the purpose of allowing them to demonstrate their superior skills, and then meekly roll over and die. Well sorry pal but that is not the Burnley way!

Sean Dyche's measured response defending his team's resilience was.

"We are allowed to win or get a point at these big clubs.

"I'd be interested to see the physical stats. If someone goes down with cramp, I've seen their players go down with cramp before.

"We're not blessed with the most technical players – they cost a lot of money.

"We have a resilience. You are allowed to defend it out – it's part of the game."

Meanwhile Chelsea boss Maurizio Sarri was charged by the FA after the game. He faces a a charge of misconduct after being sent to the stands at the end of the game.

Sarri refused to talk to the media after the game sending out assistant Gianfranco Zola to face the cameras. In his interview he claimed that Burnley staff had "offended" Sarri.

"I think there will be a follow-up on that. Maurizio felt very unhappy.

"We understand that it's a football game. You say words because of the adrenaline, but he wasn't particularly happy."

Well of course he wasn't, his expensively assembled team of under achievers had been held to a draw on their own pitch by 'little old Burnley!" A result that cast doubts over their qualification for next season's Champions League. Failure to do so will probably cost the Italian his mega paid job. No wonder he wasn't 'particularly' happy.

Sean Dyche, in his usual relaxed manner, commenting on the disturbances between the players and staff at the end of the game, and in the tunnel said.

"I don't know what happened at the end because I went over to applaud our fans and when I came back there was something going on. Call it handbags, man-bags, bum-bags; some kind of bags. I've been around the game to have seen a lot worse, but I was more concerned about clapping our fans because they have travelled a long way down here on a Bank Holiday and the lads have given them something to shout about."

It'll be interesting to see what happens with Sarri's misconduct charge and Zola's threat that there will be a "follow-up". Allegedly, somebody on the Burnley bench called Sarri a 's*** Italian'. Well if that is the case, I think he got away very lightly. I can think of much more appropriate terms than that!

By Friday the 26th all was once again sweetness and light between the two clubs. Maurizio Sarri was fined £8000 by the FA a sum probably equal to about five minutes wages for him. The members of staff of both clubs had apparently kissed and made up and the whole affair was committed to the history books. It's probably the last we will see of Sarri anyway, so we wish him 'bon voyage' back to from whence he came.

Saturday's defeat for Cardiff City at Fulham ended any remote possibility of our relegation, leaving it a straight fight between Brighton & Hove Albion and themselves. With only two fixtures remaining and a four-point gap between them it looks very much like our Welsh friends will be returning also from whence they came.

That meant the upcoming fixture with Manchester City was for us really just a matter of pride, whereas for City they are still involved in the titanic struggle with Liverpool for the title. Could we put a dent in their challenge? Read on and find out.

Game 36 – Sunday 28th April 14.05 – Burnley v Manchester City

Once again Sean Dyche names an unchanged side but there's a place on the bench for a very much unknown youngster Anthony Glennon. He takes Robbie Brady's place in the dugout who is presumably injured.

City field a formidable line-up with all the big guns up front, Raheem Sterling, Sergio Aguero and Leroy Sane, starting. It's got all the makings of a long afternoon for the Clarets and for sure we won't be seeing a lot of the ball.

On a pleasant Spring day and in front of a capacity crowd Aguero gets the game underway. I'm expecting the visitors to be at us from the off in an attempt to grab an early lead and make things a little easier for themselves. Certainly, they are enjoying plenty of possession but there's little threat in the early stages. We are getting plenty of bodies behind the ball and Ashley Barnes and Chris Wood are doing their best to stretch the Blue Mooners rearguard.

Whilst we are creating little in front of goal there is a good shout for a penalty for handball which of course as it is Burnley is promptly ignored. There's even an opportunity for Wood after being put through on goal but his control lets him down.

We are staying in the game through our splendid defensive organisation and Tom Heaton in goal is largely untroubled. Raheem Sterling, who of late has become somewhat of a 'darling' of the media, is attempting to influence the referee at every decision, and generally becoming a proverbial 'pain in the arse'. For such an important game for the visitors the first half is being played at a much lower tempo than anticipated, which is playing right into our hands.

Half time arrives with neither side troubling the scorer and I have to say I'm pretty relaxed and pleased with the way the first 45 minutes have gone. However, I'm also aware that with the quality in their team they will not need many opportunities before they inevitably take one.

The second half sees a much more invigorated start from the Blues. Clearly fired up from the half time team talk they are straight at our throats. Chance after chance is now being created, but a combination of dogged defending and brilliant goalkeeping is keeping them at bay. There's a big shout for a penalty as Barnes apparently handles a goal bound shot, but amazingly we get away with one from a largely inept referee.

It's inevitable that under such intense pressure something is going to crack, and that break comes in the 63rd minute. From a goalmouth melee Aguero fires a close range shot goalwards, Heaton is beaten but Matt Lowton hooks the ball clear from under the crossbar. Unfortunately, the goal line technology comes to the aid of City and referee Paul Tierney promptly awards a goal. That's the cue for a mighty sigh of relief from the visitors and their fans.

I'm expecting them to push on now and go for the kill but that's not how it pans out. A tiring Chris Wood is replaced by Matej Vydra and shortly afterwards Jeff Hendrick gives way to Johann Berg Gudmundsson. The Clarets now start to take the game more to City as they attempt to sit back and catch us on the break.

We batter away at the door, admittedly without much subtlety but sufficiently threateningly to force them into a more defensive strategy. Indeed, by the end of the game they are resorting to time - wasting tactics and cynical fouls to maintain their advantage. I wonder if anyone will accuse them of 'anti-football'.

After four minutes added time the game is up and City have their precious three points that returns them to the top of the Premier League. For the Clarets it has been a tremendous battling performance and one which they can feel justifiably proud of. There's no doubt that Pep Guardiola's side know they have been in a game and we have taken them all the way.

Once again, a great effort by Burnley and further proof if it was needed that we are once again back to our difficult to beat best.

Result – Burnley 0 – 1 (Aguero 63) Manchester City

Burnley Team

Heaton, Lowton, Mee, Tarkowski, Taylor, Hendrick (Gudmundsson 76), Westwood, Cork, Wood (Vydra 72), Barnes, McNeil

Manchester City Team

Ederson, Walker, Kompany, Laporte, Zinchenko, Bernardo Siva, D Silva, Gundogan, Sterling (Otamendi 90+2), Aguero (Stones 83), Sane (Gabriel Jesus 64)

Attendance – 21,605

Season To Date – Played 36, Won 11, Drawn 7, Lost 18, Goals For 44, Goals Against 63, Points 40

League Position after Game 36 – 15th

Just two games to go now, and the first of these takes us to Goodison Park, Everton. It could be said that our Boxing Day defeat at home to the Toffees marked the turning point of our season. Following that loss we had completed half our fixtures with a pitiful return of 12 points. We were as good as doomed. However, since that game we have turned our form around completely and now sit safe in the knowledge that we will once again be enjoying Premier League football next season.

Hopefully this game, once more screened live by Sky TV, will show how far we have come since that black day in December.

Game 37 – Friday 3rd May 20.00 – Everton v Burnley

If this game was meant to act as a mark of our progression from the dire first half season then I guess the report would say, substantial progress made but still a way to go.

Two team changes for this one as with survival guaranteed Sean Dyche took the opportunity to rest players. Both wide midfielders Jeff Hendrick and Dwight McNeil dropped to the bench and were replaced by Johann Berg Gudmundsson (JBG) and Robbie Brady.

On a wet and miserable night on Merseyside our hosts were quickly into gear. A high tempo start from the Toffees had us pinned deep into our own territory and chasing shadows. Everton, on an impressive run of form were in the early stages irrepressible, and a difficult night was ominously on the cards.

The first 15 minutes had us reeling after wave upon wave of attacks. Then ironically, just as it appeared we may have drawn their sting, on 17 minutes we fall behind to a rather unfortunate goal. As the Brazilian Richarlison, cutting in from the right flank, lets fly from outside the box. The shot appeared to be going wide of Tom Heaton's left-hand post before deflecting off Ben Mee's thigh and into the net.

Spurred on by the goal Everton resumed their assault on the Burnley goal, and before long things had gone from bad to worse. This time a raid down the Everton left saw a shot from distance by Lucas Digne palmed out by Heaton but only as far as Seamus Coleman who returned it with interest into the goal.

At this point a rout looked a likely scenario but fortunately our hosts lost some of their intensity and the game cooled a little. We seemed to have regressed into 2018 mode. We were conceding lots of shots and this largely stemmed from an inability to keep hold of the ball. Wayward passing was losing possession and creating self-inflicted pressure. Thankfully, half-time arrived with no further addition to the scoreline.

To be honest it had been a pretty dire first half performance and we had certainly helped to make Everton look good. The second period it has to be said showed some improvement allied to better ball retention. However, once again creativity was sadly lacking and the re-called wide men JBG and Brady were largely ineffectual.

Everton with their foot now off the gas were quite content to let us have more of the ball knowing that we were unlikely to hurt them. One real opportunity did come our way but once again we were robbed of a penalty by a horrific refereeing decision. Substitute Matej Vydra, on for Ashley Barnes, raced on to a long ball pursued by ex-Claret Michael Keane, as he entered the penalty area Keane sent him sprawling with a two-handed push in the back. As clear a penalty as you'll ever see and probably a red card offence. What did referee Chris Kavanagh award, yes you guessed a goal kick! Downright robbery!

That was the last we saw of an attacking threat and as the game drew to its close Everton once again started to reassert themselves and make chances.

A disappointing performance in many ways highlighting once again the need for more creativity in the squad. Our transfer dealings in the last two windows have been extremely poor and we have been fortunate to survive this time round. A much better effort must be made to secure a better-quality squad ahead of our next Premier League campaign or another extremely trying season lies ahead.

Result – Everton (Mee o.g. 17, Coleman 20) 2 – 0 Burnley

Burnley Team

Heaton, Lowton, Mee, Tarkowski, Taylor, Berg Gudmundsson (McNeil 69), Westwood, Cork, Wood, Barnes (Vydra 72), Brady (Hendrick 80)

Subs Not Used – Hart, Ward, Long, Gibson, Crouch

Everton Team

Pickford, Coleman, Keane, Zouma, Digne, Schneiderlin, Richarlison (Walcott 49), Sigurdsson (Jagielka 90+1), Gueye, Bernard (Lookman 73), Calvert-Lewin

Subs Not Used – Stekelenburg, Baines, Davies, Tosun

Attendance – 39,303

Season To Date – Played 37, Won 11, Drawn 7, Lost 19, Goals For 44, Goals Against 65, Points 40

League Position after Game 37 – 15th

As we approach the final game of a somewhat strange season things are cooling off a little on the footballing front. However, from a personal angle, things are certainly starting to hot up. In one week's time my wife and I plus two old friends will leave for a three-night stay in Edinburgh to celebrate a significant birthday for my wife. No expense spared on this one with first class rail travel booked both ways.

At the same time that we will be heading north of the border my prospective son-in-law will also be enjoying a milestone birthday. However, Tom has decided to enjoy his in a slightly different way. He will be attempting one of the most daunting fell running challenges in the UK.

His idea of fun will be attempting to run the Bob Graham Round, named after a Keswick guest house owner who in 1932 broke the Lakeland Fell record by traversing 42 fells in under 24 hours. His time was beaten in 1960 by a well-known local fell runner, Alan Heaton born in Haslingden in 1928. The new time set for the course of 42 peaks and 66 miles was 22 hours 18 minutes. Since then over 2000 individuals have completed the circuit with the current record time held by Kilian Jornet set in 2018 at an incredible 12 hours 52 minutes!

Entrants are usually accompanied by at least one support runner – a requirement for acceptance by the Bob Graham Club. These aides are there to carry some of the essentials such as sustenance and fluids, and to assist with navigation. To this end Tom has recruited a number of runners from his club, Durham Fell Runners. However, he will be accompanied over the last few miles by my daughter Stephanie, herself an enthusiastic road runner.

Here's hoping that the weather is kind to Tom. It's a tough challenge especially coming so close to the wedding. We are hoping that he successfully manages to avoid injury. Failure to do so will I fear incur rather more serious injury, inflicted by my wife Julie for spoiling the big day!

Following that we are just one month away from the event of the year, my daughter's wedding! What seemed to be a distant fixture on the calendar has suddenly, as is always the case, crept up on us. Hopefully all my daughter's meticulous planning will ensure all goes smoothly on the big day, but I'm sure there'll be a trauma or two before we get there. I think I'd better stop writing this diary and start concentrating on my 'Father of the Bride' speech.

Hot on the heels of the wedding, in fact just three weeks later, will be my wife and I's Mediterranean cruise. I think it's fair to say that after all the stress that the 'Mother of the Bride' will have endured, she'll be ready for it.

I couldn't let this week pass without mentioning what a massive and unbelievable one it has been for English football. On Monday night Manchester City finally overcame Leicester City with a truly stupendous goal from the unlikely Vincent Kompany. The result ensured that the most closely contested title race for years between Liverpool and City will go right to the last game to decide who will be Premier League Champions. What a fantastic tussle it has been as they have gone toe-to-toe over the - season and leap-frogged each other all the way. It will be a shame that both teams cannot win the trophy as both are equally deserving.

On Tuesday night a modern-day footballing miracle as Liverpool overturn a three-goal deficit to mighty Barcelona in the Champions League semi-final. At an emotionally charged Anfield the Reds demolish the Catalan giants with a 4-0 victory to take them through to the final. This incredibly achieved without two of their main strikers Mohammed Salah and Roberto Firmino.

If that wasn't enough, incredibly Tottenham Hotspur go on to repeat the feat on the following evening in Amsterdam. One nil down from the home leg Spurs seemed to have a difficult task away to the highly impressive Ajax. The difficult task then became an impossible one as they conceded two first half goals to trail 3-0 on aggregate at half-time. At that point you wouldn't have given them a prayer, but unbelievably a second half turn around and a Lucas Moura hat-trick, the deciding goal coming in the final minute of added time, saw them through.

So, Liverpool and Tottenham Hotspur will compete for the Champions League trophy in an all English final in Madrid on June 1st.

For those of you with long memories you will recall that way back in July 2018 we set out on the long road to Europa Cup glory. Unfortunately, our journey ended before it really got going. However, two other English clubs had battled their way through the Group stages and now sat on the verge of glory. Arsenal took a two-goal advantage into the second leg semi-final in Valencia, who by virtue of their away goal in the first leg, were still in the tie. What should have been a difficult night for the Gunners turned out anything but. A hat-trick from Pierre Emerick Aubameyang gave Arsenal a comfortable 4-2 victory on the night and a place in the final.

Not quite so comfortable for the other English side Chelsea. They had come away from the first leg in Germany with a handy 1-1 draw at Eintracht Frankfurt. However back at Stamford Bridge they found their opponents difficult to overcome and another 1-1 draw resulted. No more goals in extra-time so a penalty shoot-out to decide. Fancy that? A penalty shoot-out against the Germans? Well history will report that this one went to the English, or should that be the Spanish, Belgian, Brazilian and League of Nations, that currently make up the Chelsea team.

For the first time ever both major European club competitions will be contested solely by English teams. Arsenal and Chelsea will do battle for the trophy in Baku, Azerbaijan two days before the Champions League Final. It seems a hell of a long way to go for two teams who both hail from the same English city but that's the lunacy of football for you.

As we near the final countdown (I'm sounding like Frank Sinatra now) I am hoping that Thursday's euphoria for Arsenal has left them in a benevolent mood for their trip to Turf Moor this coming Sunday. Nine previous Premier League encounters between us have resulted in nine defeats for the Clarets. Many of these games have been lost to controversial decisions, offside goals, non-penalties, handballs, you name it we have suffered it. Whilst Sunday's result will be largely academic in terms of consequences it sure would be nice to end the season with a win and right some wrongs.

Ahead of this game the first news on player contracts ahead of the new season emerges. Phil Bardsley who has played a big part in our revival during the second half of the campaign will we learn be with us for another year. Apparently, he has made sufficient starts during last season (19) to trigger a one-year extension on his contract. Well-deserved Phil! His commitment and fight have been an important feature in our ultimate survival, more of the same next time round please.

Game 38 – Sunday 12th May 15.00 – Burnley v Arsenal

Finally, after what at times has felt like an interminable season we arrive at the final fixture. For some reason best known to themselves the Premier League have decreed that the last round of games will be played on a Sunday afternoon. Why?

For the Clarets there are only two changes to last week's line up, Wide midfielders Dwight McNeil and Jeff Hendrick replacing Johann Berg Gudmundsson and Robbie Brady. The Gunners meanwhile following Thursday's Europa Cup Semi Final exertions in Seville bench a number of players. Unfortunately, leading scorer Pierre Emerick Aubameyang is not one of them.

On a warm sunny afternoon with the Turf Moor pitch in immaculate condition referee Mike Dean gets the action underway. The start is marked by some aggressive tackling and harrying, particularly by ourselves, which seems odd considering there's nothing really at stake in this game.

Bizarrely the first name in the referee's yellow card collection goes to Clarets keeper Tom Heaton. As Arsenal break quickly Tom decides to intervene and chases out of his penalty area. Beaten to the ball he then handles it outside his area and is rightfully yellow carded. The resultant free kick is headed flush against the post from close range and we breathe a huge sigh of relief.

It's not all one-way traffic though and shortly after Chris Wood rattles the Arsenal post having been put through. With only 10 minutes gone I reckon the score could easily have been 2-2. There's no doubt that there is a real feisty feel about this one and I can only assume that there is some bad blood lingering between the sides. Ashley Barnes is his usual aggressive self and it's no surprise when he also finds himself cautioned.

Aubameyang following his hat-trick in Seville is looking a potent threat and his pace is a major concern. However, the game is pretty even, and we are also creating chances. In at half-time all square but we are definitely winning on the bookings count as I reckon, we have four already.

With goals being thrown around like confetti in most of the other fixtures, Leicester City v Chelsea and this game are the only ones bucking the trend. If I was a betting man, I wouldn't put money on that staying the course in this game. The first goal is going to be important and we start the second period in determined fashion to get it.

However as has so often happened in this season, we are quickly undone by basic errors. Jack Cork plays a sloppy pass in midfield to Ben Mee who fails to control it. Aubameyang is on him in a flash and takes the ball forward before slotting past Heaton. Trailing after 52 minutes, not the start to the half we were looking for.

Arsenal, sensing we are there for the taking, up the pressure and on 63 minutes double the lead. Once again, it's Aubameyang with a crashing unstoppable volley.

To our credit we are still plugging away and only being kept at bay by some resolute defending and top-class goalkeeping. However, there is nothing the keeper can do to deny Barnes on 65 minutes as he deftly glances substitute Johann Berg Gudmundsson's cross home.

In previous games we may well have still sat back and kept our rigid defensive shape, but not so on this occasion. Caution was cast to the wings as we set about finding a leveller. Peter Crouch was next to enter the fray in the hope his height and awkwardness would fashion an opening. As we piled players forward obviously gaps appeared at the back and how Aubameyang didn't go home with the match ball only he could know! A ball rolled across the six-yard box screamed to be driven home but he somehow contrived to put it wide. Unbelievable!

The game continued in the same vein, frantic attacking by us, cultured counter attacking at pace by our visitors but with no further addition to the scoring. The fourth official indicated four minutes added time and it seemed we would lose by the narrowest of margins. That is until the 94th minute when Arsenal substitute Eddie Nketiah got free to the left of goal and his cross cum shot came off Matt Lowton to trickle over the line. Cruel but not uncommon for us in this difficult season.

The campaign ends with another defeat but Southampton's inability to despatch relegated Huddersfield Town means we maintain 15th position. How many would have thought that possible on Boxing Day 2018? It's over now till August and then we can do it all over again!

Result – Burnley (Barnes 65) 1 – 3 (Aubameyang 52,63, Nketiah 90+4) Arsenal

Burnley Team

Heaton, Lowton, Mee, Tarkowski, Taylor, Hendrick (Brady 82), Westwood, Cork, Wood (Crouch 77), Barnes, McNeil (Gudmundsson 64)

Subs Not Used – Hart, Ward, Long, Gibson, Vydra

Arsenal Team

Leno, Lichtsteiner, Mustafi, Mavropanos (Koscielny 34), Monreal, Elneny, Guendouzi, Mkhitaryan, Willock (Nketiah 62), Aubameyang, Iwobi

Subs Not Used – Cech, Kolasinac, Xhaka, Maitland-Niles, Lacazette

Attendance – 21,461

Season To Date – Played 38, Won 11, Drawn 7, Lost 20, Goals For 45, Goals Against 68, Points 40

League Position after Game 38 – 15th

Hardly had the players had time to scrape the mud (or should that be blood?) off their boots came the news that one of our Premier League stalwarts' days with the Clarets were coming to an end. After five seasons of outstanding service Stephen Ward's contract will not be renewed. It's not really a big surprise as this season he has only made the starting XI on 10 occasions following a knee operation. The fine form of his deputy Charlie Taylor has secured the left back position for himself leaving the 33-year-old Ward to look for a new start.

It's a shame but an inevitable fact of life that players who have given excellent service eventually have to move on. The club have to make the decisions and manage the finances to ensure our future prosperity.

Speaking to the Burnley media Ward said.

"it's a sad time leaving but I suppose that comes many times in your career, you move on from different clubs.

"I can't speak highly enough of the club, the people, and the lads that have been here.

"I've thoroughly enjoyed every minute of it and it's great to see the lads have another great season this season and have another crack at the Premier League next year.

"I've come back from injury and felt really good, but the lads were flying at the time, so I've no complaints.

"I've great memories and to be a part of the last few years of success we've had here has probably been the best part of my career and something that will live with me forever.

"I will miss the place. It's been fantastic."

The player won 50 International caps for his country and made 113 appearances for the Clarets. Surely the most memorable being his fine goal scored in the historic 3-2 away victory at Premier League Champions, Chelsea. Many thanks 'Wardy' and all the best in your future career.

A quick update here to let all those interested know how Tom fared in his epic challenge, the Bob Graham Round. On the 18th May, whilst my wife and I were enjoying the sights and tastes of Edinburgh, Tom successfully slogged his way round the Lakeland peaks. His targeted time was 21 hours 12 minutes, but he managed, fuelled I'm sure by adrenaline and emotion, to cover the 66 miles in 20 hours 36 minutes. What a magnificent achievement. Accompanied all the way by support runners from Durham Fell Runners and joined for the last 5 miles into Keswick by my daughter Stephanie it was an emotional end to a fantastic day for the young man. I would have loved to have been there to see it.

However, the call of Scotland was strong, and we had a great weekend managing to fit in Edinburgh Castle, the Royal Yacht Britannia, Greyfriars Kirk, Arthur's Seat and the National Museum of Scotland. On top of that there were several restaurants and cafes and a liberal sprinkling of pubs. Just a word of warning here, don't expect Burnley bar prices in the pubs! I nearly had a heart attack at the price of a pint but that's capital cities for you. We've still plenty to see and hopefully another trip north of the border will be in the not too distant future.

Next up on the agenda is the 'biggie', my daughter Stephanie's wedding. June 15th will be the joyous occasion as we head for Arkengarthdale in North Yorkshire. Unfortunately, as the great day approaches so too do the demands for money. There's a whole host of people to pay, the photographer, florist, registrar, band and bus company to name but a view. Then of course there's the venue itself with the wedding breakfast, accommodation and the evening 'do'! It's no wonder I'm getting nervous and that's without the trauma of the Father of the Bride speech!

On Friday 24th May there's good news on the player contract front as goalkeeper Nick Pope commits to a new contract. This will tie him to the club until the summer of 2023 with an option for a further year. Being the youngest of our three current England goalkeepers it's important that he is happy to commit his future to the club. Unfortunately for Nick his shoulder injury sustained in his first game of last season ultimately led to a wasted campaign, his only starts coming in Cup fixtures. With his injury worries now behind him I'm sure he will be fighting hard to regain his first team place and hopefully resurrect his budding England career.

More good news surrounding the goalkeeping department is the selection of Tom Heaton for England's Nations League finals coming up in early June. Tom's form and inspirational presence were a major factor in our season's turnaround, and his selection for the English squad is thoroughly merited.

Of course, all this leaves a big question mark against Joe Hart's future with the club. We are certainly well blessed with keepers now and with Heaton and Pope set to battle for first team duty Joe is unlikely to want to stay as third choice. At this late stage of his career he desperately needs first team football and it will be no surprise if he moves during the summer transfer window.

SEASON REVIEW

What a funny old season that was. A start filled with excitement and anticipation as we enjoyed the glamour of European competition for the first time since the mid 1960's. However, by the end of the first month of the Premier League season, our adventure was over without making it through the qualifying rounds. From then on, we quickly became embroiled in what looked like ultimately becoming a serious relegation battle.

On Boxing Day, the season reached its lowest ebb as a 5-1 home defeat to Everton plunged us firmly in the mire. Half a season gone and only 12 points garnered, now sitting in 18th place and seemingly sunk. The considered wisdom being that 40 points would be the survival target, I and many others, questioned where were the required further 28 to come from?

Then an unforeseen and miraculous turnaround in form and fortunes. Starting with a victory over West Ham United at Turf Moor on 30th December, the Clarets embarked on a marvellous unbeaten run in the league of 8 games. Five of which were won with the other three drawn. Suddenly 18 points from just eight games had given us real survival hope.

Then once again a sticky patch, defeats at Newcastle United and Liverpool, and at home to Crystal Palace and a 10-man Leicester City, rocked the revival on its heels.

Once again, this topsy-turvy season had another twist as the Clarets then recorded three consecutive victories over Wolverhampton Wanderers, Bournemouth and vitally, Cardiff City. These were followed by an incredible battling 2-2 draw at Chelsea and magically the 40-point mark and safety were reached.

Just as well as the final three fixtures, albeit to high flying teams, were all lost. The following chart shows the league position throughout the season, and it's not very good viewing I'm afraid. Following a season where we were barely out of the top half, this time we failed to make it in there once!

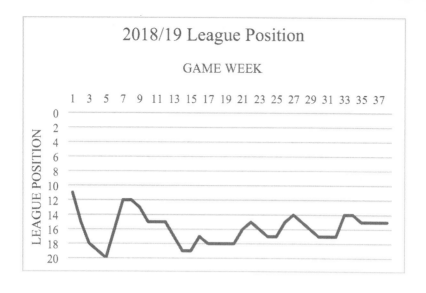

2018/19 League Position

GAME WEEK

What a weird set of results in the second half of the season! The first half had at least been consistent. Consistently poor that is! Then the final 19 games were characterised by winning sequences interspersed with losing sequences. Our points gathering against the 'elite' teams was meagre to say the least. A brilliant home win against Tottenham Hotspur and highly creditable draws at Old Trafford and Stamford Bridge being the only plusses. However, we did manage to pick up points from the teams that were most likely to be in the relegation battle and therefore managed to claw our way to safety.

I can't say it was a very comfortable, relaxing, or particularly pleasurable season for the fans. For sure it's not one I'd like to relive in a hurry, but I guess it's what comes with the territory if you're a Clarets fan. So, where did it all go wrong?

In my humble opinion, I think we missed a great opportunity to push on from last season and to my mind we took a significant step backwards that almost proved mighty costly.

The lack of investment in the summer transfer window, for whatever reason, left us way short of being competitive in four major competitions. There were just too many commitments for an overstretched squad that could and should have been beefed up ahead of the Europa Cup qualifiers. Some of it may have been down to an over belief in the ability of long-term injured players, Steven Defour and Robbie Brady, to return and make an immediate impact. As it turned out

Defour's contribution to the season was negligible, and Brady's at its kindest could be described as minimal.

Three new signings came in, two highly rated Championship outfield players, Ben Gibson and Matej Vydra, along with goalkeeper Joe Hart. Although without the unfortunate injury to Nick Pope, occurring in his very first competitive game of the season, Hart would not have been under consideration. However, with injury question marks against the other main goalkeepers, Tom Heaton and Anders Lindegaard, an experienced replacement was deemed essential. Despite Hart's brave efforts things didn't go well during his stay in the team and goals were being leaked at an alarming rate.

Gibson missed chunks of the season following two hernia operations and then was unable to displace Ben Mee. Vydra, previously the Championship top goal scorer, found time on the pitch very difficult to come by. One can only hope that the not insignificant outlay on these two players will yield better dividends in the forthcoming season.

So, an understrength squad set off on an a very demanding season. July saw no less than seven first team friendlies and the first Europa Cup tie away at Aberdeen. If that was the warm-up August bettered it with one friendly, five Europa League qualifiers and three Premier League games. It's no wonder the performances on the pitch often looked jaded and lacking energy. Coupled to that was the fact that almost out of necessity, we constantly changed the team. One line up, probably seen as second choice for the European games, and another consisting of more first team regulars in the Premier League. This couldn't have been helpful in maintaining any consistency and probably caused some resentment among players who had worked hard to earn the right to European competition and then found themselves side-lined.

What a poor first half to the season, characterised by performances that left Joe Hart regularly facing more than 20 shots at goal per game. After playing behind some of the most successful teams' defences both here and in Europe, the poor guy must have been shell-shocked! Fortunately, this aspect of our play improved considerably after the halfway mark and only the 'elite' teams hit us with so many attempts.

By Christmas and following the morale sapping defeat at home to Everton, things looked decidedly bleak. The majority of fans, myself included, felt relegation was well and truly on the cards. Why wouldn't they? Apart from the odd stand out performance, notably a somewhat flattering 4-0 home win over Bournemouth, we had witnessed a sequence of tired and depressing performances that were devoid of hope.

Then we got the completely unforeseen upturn, well by myself at least, as the New Year beckoned. Needing to arrest the slide immediately it was time to try something different. Fit again Tom Heaton, who had made no secret of his desire to be playing regular first team football and looking set for a move in the January window was recalled. At the same time highly rated but largely untried youngster Dwight McNeil was given his chance, more I suspect through injuries than by choice.

The pair made a spectacular and immediate impact. Heaton, a massive crowd favourite at Turf Moor lifted the crowd on his recall and you could almost sense the feeling of gloom lifting. Young McNeil clearly sensing the changed mood marked a stunning start to his fledgling career with a goal and an assist in a comprehensive home victory over West Ham United. How refreshing to see a Burnley wide man not stopping the play to pass sideways or backwards but instead taking on his defender and delivering a stream of crosses.

As the unbeaten run at the start of the year started to build confidence began to return in all aspects of our play. As McNeil began to supply more ammunition, strikers Chris Wood and Ashley Barnes again began to form the formidable partnership that had seen them score so many times the previous season. From being a team that looked certain losers after conceding the first goal we once again became the resilient Clarets, full of fight and controlled aggression.

The pushovers had begun to push back, and the eight-game unbeaten run provided the platform to enable the final push for survival. Sure, there were hiccoughs on the way, and the losing sequences once again temporarily raised the spectre of a real relegation battle. However, approaching the run-in a fine three match winning burst, and the continued mishaps of the teams below, ensured ultimately a relatively comfortable end to the season with a 15th place finish.

For those of you who like a few statistics to get your teeth into try these for size. These are the overall statistics for the 38 Premier League fixtures played during the course of the campaign, Burnley stats first:

Possession – 40.7%/59.3%

Shots at Goal – 359/652

Shots on Target – 115/210

Corners - 140/245

Fouls – 360/376

The games were watched by 1,084.370 people, an average of 28,536 per game.

Interesting, aren't they? With statistics like that it does make you wonder how we survive.

Let us hope that the lessons of a difficult season have been learnt. Instead of pushing on after our magnificent season in 2017/18 the club, certainly on the playing side, stalled and slipped backwards. A great opportunity I feel was missed, but thankfully it didn't on this occasion prove fateful. Next time we may not be so lucky. Without doubt survival at this level will always be a major ask for small clubs like ourselves. Every season larger and larger sums of cash are being spent, not only by the 'top six' but almost all other Premier League teams. Money of course, unless spent wisely, guarantees nothing, ask the fans of Fulham. Whilst our financial prudence is lauded the length and breadth of the country there has to be some loosening of the purse strings to give the manager the resources needed to keep the squad competitive. This coming summer transfer window will I am sure define our chances for our next campaign. Don't let's spend a season rueing the one's that got away!

Now dear friends some shocking, well for you that is, news. Whilst it turned out not to be the last Premier League season, it will be the last of my Premier League Diaries. Oh No! I hear you cry and believe me I share your pain. The truth is that after a never imagined from the outset five books, I think now is the time to call it a day. I think the format has become a little tired, and that could also be said of the author. I hope that those who have read some or all of the five volumes have found them informative and given them an occasional smile. Don't forget they are only one man's opinions, and every fan that attends will have their own. What a fantastic 10 years we have had since that fateful day, the 25th May 2009. Thank you, Sean Dyche and all concerned with the club. I've enjoyed every minute of it.

To be honest I never thought I'd say it, but I am losing some of my enthusiasm for football. The growing dominance of the super-rich clubs is in my opinion detrimental to the game. Not just in England but in all the major leagues around Europe the competitions are developing into at best a two-horse race. Indeed, in some they are not even that. What chance have clubs like ourselves got of winning trophies when in competition with clubs who have the budgets equivalent to that of small countries.

In England we had a thrilling race for the Premier League but solely between two clubs for the biggest part of the season. Manchester City were hotly pursued to the death by Liverpool, yet this pair were a staggering 25 points clear of Chelsea in third. In fact, Manchester City cleaned up all the domestic titles finishing with an emphatic one sided 6-0 victory over Watford in the FA Cup. Who would bet against a similar two horse race next time round? How can that be good for the game when the eventual winners are almost guaranteed before a ball is kicked.

In this climate what lies ahead for the Clarets? I fear at best we can only hope to continue to defy the odds and retain our Premier League status. Survival is our only realistic ambition. Eventually and inevitably at some point we will succumb to the deadly drop and our glorious flirtation with the big league will be over.

One thing is for sure, I may be becoming disillusioned with the game in general, but I will never lose my love of Burnley FC. For almost 60 years it has been an all-consuming passion, long may it continue. UTPREMIERC!

POSTSCRIPT

On Thursday 13th June the Premier league fixtures for the 2019/20 season were published. This was followed quickly on Saturday 15th by my daughter Stephanie's wedding to Tom. That's a new chapter starting for both Burnley FC and Stephanie and a fitting place to end this diary. It goes without saying that I wish both parties continuing success and happiness.

By the way, the first fixture is Southampton at Turf Moor on August 10th. See you there!

2018/2019 Season	Possession % For	Possession % Against	Shots BFC	Shots Against	Shots on Target For	Shots on Target Against	Corners For	Corners Against	Fouls Us	Fouls Opp.	Attendance
Southampton (A)	52	48	16	18	6	3	5	8	9	10	30,784
Watford (H)	58	42	8	9	3	6	5	2	8	19	18,822
Fulham (A)	36	64	12	25	2	12	4	6	8	11	23,438
Manchester United (H)	46	54	9	21	2	9	2	5	7	13	21,525
Wolves (A)	41	59	7	30	2	7	2	8	9	10	30,406
Bournemouth (H)	38	62	12	19	5	5	3	8	17	6	18,636
Cardiff (A)	46	54	3	19	2	5	2	10	15	11	30,411
Huddersfield (H)	32	68	6	19	3	2	1	10	9	11	20,533
Manchester City (A)	31	69	5	24	0	10	1	10	5	11	54,094
Chelsea (H)	30	70	7	24	1	8	4	4	14	10	21,430
West Ham United (A)	37	63	6	22	3	10	4	10	9	7	56,862
Leicester (A)	37	63	6	22	1	5	1	12	10	13	32,184
Newcastle (H)	57	43	14	17	4	3	5	5	6	11	20,628
Crystal Palace (A)	41	59	4	29	0	9	2	10	10	9	25,098
Liverpool (H)	26	74	10	18	6	12	5	9	10	3	21,741
Brighton (H)	37	63	14	14	4	1	2	7	11	11	18,497
Tottenham (A)	30	70	4	15	0	3	3	8	8	7	41,645
Arsenal (A)	40	60	7	11	2	6	3	1	14	10	59,493
Everton (H)	49	51	11	13	4	6	5	7	11	19	21,484
West Ham United (H)	43	57	17	11	5	4	5	5	15	11	20,933
Huddersfield (A)	57	43	16	9	8	2	2	5	9	11	23,715
Fulham (H)	42	58	11	12	0	4	2	6	5	9	19,316
Watford (A)	45	55	11	9	3	4	7	1	9	14	19,510
Manchester United (A)	26	74	6	28	4	9	3	11	9	10	74,529
Southampton (H)	54	46	15	10	6	4	4	2	10	9	19,787
Brighton (A)	32	68	9	16	5	6	3	9	7	8	29.323
Tottenham (H)	30	70	10	17	4	6	7	6	9	12	21,338
Newcastle (A)	46	54	12	13	2	3	7	4	8	8	48,323
Crystal Palace (H)	57	43	18	10	4	4	8	5	9	9	19,223
Liverpool (A)	31	69	3	23	2	5	3	7	7	4	53,310
Leicester (H)	62	38	13	9	2	4	9	3	9	10	20,719
Wolves (H)	37	63	6	8	1	1	1	5	12	10	20,990
Bournemouth (A)	40	60	10	10	3	2	6	3	16	12	10,446
Cardiff (H)	46	54	14	14	7	2	8	4	7	10	21,480
Chelsea (A)	24	76	6	22	3	9	1	10	4	9	40,642
Manchester City (H)	30	70	2	25	0	7	0	6	5	7	21,605
Everton (A)	40	60	5	20	1	6	1	8	9	8	39,303
Arsenal (H)	40	60	14	17	5	6	4	5	11	3	21,461
Season total	1546	2254	359	652	115	210	140	245	360	376	1,084,370
Average/Game	40.7	59.3	9.4	17.2	3.0	5.5	3.7	6.4	9.5	9.9	28536

Printed in Poland
by Amazon Fulfillment
Poland Sp. z o.o., Wrocław

52365967R00123